Building Connected Communities of Care

The Playbook For Streamlining Effective Coordination Between Medical And Community-Based Organizations

Best Regards

Keith

#SDoH Innovation

Building Connected Communities of Care

The Playbook For Streamlining Effective Coordination Between
Medical And Community-Based Organizations

Keith Kosel, PhD • Steve Miff, PhD

Parkland Center for Clinical Innovation

CRC Press
Taylor & Francis Group
Boca Raton   London   New York

CRC Press is an imprint of the
Taylor & Francis Group, an **informa** business

A PRODUCTIVITY PRESS BOOK

CRC Press
Taylor & Francis Group
6000 Broken Sound Parkway NW, Suite 300
Boca Raton, FL 33487-2742

Printed on acid-free paper

International Standard Book Number-13: 978-0-367-80006-2 (Paperback)
International Standard Book Number-13: 978-0-367-81923-1 (Hardback)

Library of Congress Cataloging-in-Publication Data

Names: Miff, Steve, author. | Kosel, Keith, author.
Title: Building connected communities of care: the playbook for streamlining effective coordination between medical and community-based organizations / Steve Miff and Keith Kosel.
Description: Boca Raton: Taylor & Francis, 2020. | Includes bibliographical references and index.
Identifiers: LCCN 2019049400 (print) | LCCN 2019049401 (ebook) | ISBN 9780367800062 (paperback; alk. paper) | ISBN 9780367819231 (hardback; alk. paper) | ISBN 9781003010838 (ebook)
Subjects: MESH: Community Health Services—organization & administration | Community Health Planning—organization & administration | Community Integration | Social Work
Classification: LCC RA966 (print) | LCC RA966 (ebook) | NLM WA 546.1 | DDC 362.12068—dc23
LC record available at https://lccn.loc.gov/2019049400
LC ebook record available at https://lccn.loc.gov/2019049401

Visit the Taylor & Francis Web site at
http://www.taylorandfrancis.com

and the CRC Press Web site at
http://www.crcpress.com

Contents

The Call to Action

The Upstream Guide

For the past several years, I thought someone should finally write the definitive guide on how to connect Health and Healthcare, i.e., a guide that would link providers to the vast network of community-based organizations who tackle the social determinants of health. We have all learned a lot in the past decade with regard to these social determinants and their critical importance in establishing health in any community. In a nutshell, it's not about providers: it's all about the community and the connections to the community. My wish has been granted with the publication of a fantastic new guidebook by the Parkland Center for Clinical Innovation (PCCI), *Building Connected Communities of Care.*

The authors Keith Kosel and Steve Miff are exactly the right persons to tackle this new area given their background in the provider arena coupled with ample public policy experience. They both cut their teeth with one of the largest, member-owned healthcare performance improvement organizations in America, Vizient, Inc. I had the distinct pleasure of working with both Kosel and Miff as they guided Vizient into new territory focused on improving operations by reducing waste and improving quality. They were early adopters of the notion that the only way to reduce cost was to reduce waste, and the principal way to reduce waste was to improve performance and reduce error. They were leaders more than a decade ago, and it's just a natural outgrowth of this sort of leadership that led them to tackle the linkage between provider groups and community-based organizations.

Building Connected Communities of Care has an easy to follow structure with essentially six tracks. The tracks cover all the key topics, including Governance, Legal and Policy, Technology Platform, Clinical Providers, Community Partners, and Program Sustainability. What I admire about each chapter are the key take-home messages based on cases and the ample supply of "how to information". Each chapter is a treasure trove of operationally relevant tools and techniques to make the connection with the community real.

I am smitten with two sections in particular. Notably the technology platform in Track 3 is free of jargon and gives readers a how-to, point-by-point guide on creating the data sharing platform, which we know is the backbone to making communities actually connected. Finally, the program sustainability Track 6 is an insightful guide for clarifying and grasping future challenges. It will help community-based organizations tackle issues that we cannot clearly see, but we know are just around the corner.

Kudos to Kosel and Miff for producing a playbook that is pragmatic and timely. It will no doubt serve as a bellwether as others attempt to clarify their relationship between health and healthcare. I would wager that there will be many copycats of their inaugural work in this area.

I only wish that this Playbook had been completed earlier, so we could have shared it with our community-based partners as we built the nation's first College of Population Health on the campus of Thomas Jefferson University in Philadelphia.

I imagine that this book will have a wide audience as it will appeal to providers and payers as they struggle to find ways to not only connect with one another, but with the communities that they both serve. Finally, funders would probably benefit from this book too as they are navigating the rough waters that swirl around the relationship between providers and payers.

Leaders in the relatively new field of population health understand that we must go upstream to figuratively shut the faucet instead of constantly mopping up the floor. I believe that PCCI has pointed us directly to the faucet and has given us the wherewithal to at least shut it half way. It will be the responsibility of providers, payers, and community-based organizations to finally close that faucet together. Kosel and Miff are outstanding guides on this journey.

– David Nash, MD
Founding Dean Emeritus
Jefferson College of Population Health

Foreword

A thriving community is built on the foundation of good jobs, strong relationships, enriching educational opportunities, quality healthcare and a safe environment. We believe that connected communities have the power to prevent social problems and repair brokenness. But this can only occur when we commit to bringing those who have been marginalized by past and current systems of exclusion into the center of our circle of care.

−Communities Foundation of Texas

Communities Foundation of Texas (CFT) is always looking for ways to support greater cooperation and coordination among local community-based organizations, particularly where the health and well-being of community residents might be enhanced through a holistic approach to care.

Through the partnership that has been built with the Parkland Health & Hospital System and the Parkland Center for Clinical Innovation (PCCI), we've invested in this approach, resulting in an Information Exchange Portal (IEP) that can be used by both healthcare providers and community organizations to share data and information. The Dallas IEP was among the first information exchanges in the nation to be built at scale tracking social determinants of health and linking healthcare providers with nonprofits serving vulnerable individuals. This has been, and will continue to be, a pioneering achievement with an enormous humanitarian purpose.

We strive for our investments in Dallas to positively impact the lives of our most vulnerable residents. PCCI's learnings are transferrable and now have the potential to positively impact other communities across the nation and around the world as well. We hope that this publication, *Building*

Connected Communities of Care: The Playbook for Streamlining Effective Coordination Between Medical and Community-Based Organizations, provides leaders with practical insights to create their own connected community, further spreading the positive impact of the legacy of the W.W. Caruth, Jr. Fund at CFT.

David J. Scullin
President & CEO
Communities Foundation of Texas

Preface

Several years ago, at Parkland Health & Hospital System (Parkland) in Dallas, a newly minted hospitalist tried in vain to keep a particular patient from cycling repeatedly onto his medicine service. The middle-aged male was admitted repeatedly for hypothyroidism, each time worse than before. Thyroid replacement medication is one of the cheapest on the market and it boggled everyone's mind as to why this kept happening. Finally, on the umpteenth admission, a social worker discovered that he was homeless, barely literate, and bedded at The Salvation Army shelter between hospital stays. The hospital care team contacted the shelter staff and established a cross-agency care plan to make sure he would not run out of medicines and to arrange for follow-up clinic appointments to maintain control over his condition. He was not readmitted after this.

As a nation, we are realizing the fundamental role that social determinants play in an individual's health and well-being. The literature is now replete with discussions on health-related social determinants and how—if left unaddressed—these determinants not only negatively impact an individual's health but also result in the suboptimal use of costly healthcare resources, such as an Emergency Department (ED).[1] While we are gaining greater knowledge of the importance of social needs (e.g., food, housing, transportation, and personal safety) to an individual's health and well-being, the healthcare sector has faced a number of barriers in successfully addressing these upstream factors as they relate to morbidity and mortality of vulnerable populations. Historically, healthcare providers (i.e., hospitals and clinical practices) have struggled to seamlessly and effectively work with those Community-Based Social Service Organizations, aka Community-Based Organizations (CBOs), that help many (especially vulnerable or underserved) community residents address these social needs. From differences in missions to an inability to effectively communicate and share needed information, healthcare providers and CBOs often operate in separate—yet parallel—worlds despite the acknowledgment that greater cooperation and collaboration would be beneficial to all involved.

Parkland is the largest safety net hospital in North Texas and one of the largest in the country, delivering over one million outpatient visits, 12,500 deliveries, and nearly 243,000 ED visits annually.[2] Like most other safety net hospitals across the country, Parkland's patients are a mix of Medicaid (31.8%), Medicare (16.6%), and uninsured (27.5%) individuals from the surrounding Dallas Fort Worth (DFW) area.[3] While these patients receive exceptional care, many of them are repeat visitors to Parkland's ED, some logging multiple visits per week. An assessment of many of these cases revealed a direct connection to the absence of one or more social needs, usually food or housing. This constant cycling of vulnerable, at-risk patients has also placed a heavy financial burden on Parkland.

These facts were not lost on the Communities Foundation of Texas (CFT), a large, forward-thinking philanthropic organization based in Dallas, Texas. Leaders from CFT reasoned that if healthcare providers, particularly Parkland, had the ability to work in a more cooperative and coordinated way with local CBOs, then the health and well-being of those at-risk community residents might be enhanced through a holistic approach to their care.

With this vision as a starting point, in 2012, the W.W. Caruth, Jr. Fund at CFT provided a generous grant to Parkland's affiliate, the Parkland Center for Clinical Innovation (PCCI), to develop an Information Exchange Portal (IEP) that could be used by both healthcare providers and CBOs to share data and information in the form of a referral and case management system. Two years later in 2014, PCCI unveiled its Dallas IEP, electronically connecting Parkland with several DFW CBOs. During the preceding 2 years, PCCI clinicians and data scientists used a PCCI-developed readiness assessment to assess the needs of the Dallas community and then leveraged that information to construct a series of use cases forming the backbone of the software technology providing the information exchange network's connectivity. The Dallas IEP was among the first information exchanges in the nation to be built at scale, linking healthcare providers with CBOs to serve vulnerable individuals. It has since grown and expanded, first through providing the information technology support behind a large demonstration program targeting health-related social determinants, and later by developing cross-sector linkages with other institutions in the community, such as correctional facilities, schools, and crisis/behavioral health centers. In 2017, as a result of the inclusion of additional CBOs and other diverse social service entities and providers, PCCI renamed the IEP *Connected Communities of Care* (*CCC*) to recognize its community-wide focus.

This Playbook represents a blueprint for the design and deployment of a *CCC* and highlights many of the challenges, successes, and lessons learned from this work over the past 6 years. Healthcare and social service leaders alike will find this book helpful as they contemplate implementing a *CCC* in their community. Loaded with practice pointers and several actual case studies, this Playbook will serve as a valuable resource for those interested in advancing community-based population health.

Contributors

Many superb colleagues contributed to this book—most importantly Elizabeth Powell, Dennis Tkach, and Paula Denney, who drafted and edited major sections throughout the book. A special thanks to all the book contributors, who are listed below.

PCCI Contributors	
Kim Aston	Donna Persaud, MD
Vikas Chowdhry	Elizabeth Powell, JD
Paula Denney, JD	Aida Somun
Rae Esters	Dennis Tkach, PhD
Tammy Pastor	Venkatraghavan Sundaram, PhD
Yolande Pengetnze, MD	Alex Townes
PCCI Editor	
Leslie Wainwright, PhD	

PCCI would also like to recognize Pieces Technologies, Inc., and express our appreciation for its founder and CEO, Ruben Amarasingham, MD. Ruben's vision led to the creation of PCCI and the software Pieces Iris® that powers the Dallas iteration of the *Connected Communities of Care*. The collegial relationship between the two companies has been invaluable as PCCI has moved forward with making the *CCC* a reality. The team at Pieces Technologies also reviewed portions of the Playbook to ensure that its description of Pieces Iris® accurately captured how this software supported the Technology Platform Track.

The authors individually and on behalf of everyone at PCCI especially wish to express our gratitude to the W.W. Caruth, Jr. Fund at the Communities Foundation of Texas. Their generosity supported the Parkland Foundation and PCCI as we built the Dallas *CCC* from the ground up. Their visionary giving helped transform ideas about how to connect medical and social services in order to benefit the most vulnerable in our community into reality. They have created a lasting legacy that demonstrates the value of philanthropic investment in early-stage innovative ideas. It is their vision that has provided the Dallas *CCC* model that we hope other philanthropists and communities will continue to emulate and advance.

We also want to acknowledge the tremendous and ongoing support received from the Parkland Health & Hospital System. Parkland and its leadership enthusiastically championed PCCI's efforts—from ideation to implementation—in creating the *CCC*. Parkland, as the safety net hospital for Dallas County serving mostly uninsured and Medicaid patients, was our first clinical partner and thus served as the laboratory to test and refine the concepts described in this *Playbook*.

Space constraints preclude us from mentioning all our clinical and community partners who have been part of this journey, but the list could fill its own book. We are grateful for all who leaned in as early adopters of the technology powering the *CCC* and provided PCCI with important feedback about how to "make it work" for volunteer-based community organizations.

About the Authors

**Dr. Keith Kosel** is a Vice President at Parkland Center for Clinical Innovation (PCCI), a leading, non-profit, data science, artificial intelligence and innovation organization affiliated with Parkland Health & Hospital System, one of the country's largest and most progressive safety-net hospitals. At PCCI, Keith is leveraging his passion for - and extensive experience in - patient safety, quality, and population health by focusing on understanding social determinants of health and the impact of community-based interventions in improving the health of vulnerable and underserved populations.

Keith earned a PhD in anatomy from the University of Iowa College of Medicine, an MHSA in medical care administration at the University of Michigan School of Public Health, and an MBA in finance from the University of Detroit. Keith taught for twenty-five years at the university and medical school level, most recently focusing on epidemiology and population health. He has authored thirty publications, including multiple book chapters, and co-authored a book on population health.

Before joining PCCI, Keith served in various leadership positions at Vizient, Inc., where he designed and led Vizient's national initiatives around population health, established company strategies and large-scale quality improvement programs for hospitals and clinicians related to healthcare reform (i.e., bundled payments, patient safety, and patient engagement), led the company's measurement and analytics group, and as Senior Vice President oversaw Vizient's national office focusing on public policy and legislative advocacy. Before coming to Vizient, Dr. Kosel was Director of

Clinical Programs at Blue Cross Blue Shield of Michigan where he built, implemented, and oversaw disease-management and care-management programs for BCBSM's three largest customers – Ford, General Motors, and Fiat Chrysler.

Keith lives in the Dallas area and is an avid college and pro football enthusiast. When he is not working, he can be found spending time with his diverse family of 8 horses, ranging from show-winning Arabians to Paint rescues.

Dr. Steve Miff is the President and CEO of Parkland Center for Clinical Innovation (PCCI), a leading, non-profit, data science, artificial intelligence and innovation organization affiliated with Parkland Health & Hospital System, one of the country's largest and most progressive safety-net hospitals. Spurred by his passion to use next-generation analytics and technology to help serve the most vulnerable and underserved residents, Steve and his team focus on leveraging technology, data science, and clinical expertise to obtain unique social-determinants-of-health data and incorporate those holistic, personal insights into point-of-care interventions. Steve was the recipient of The Community Council of Dallas' 2017 Social Innovator of the Year award and a finalist for the 2019 Dallas Business Journal most-admired healthcare CEO. Under his leadership, PCCI was named one of the 2019 Dallas Best Tech Startups by the Tech Tribune.

Steve earned his PhD and MS degrees in biomedical engineering and a BA in economics from Northwestern University. He has been an adjunct professor of biomedical engineering for more than five years and has authored more than 100 thought leadership, white papers, and peer-reviewed publications.

Before joining the nonprofit world, Steve served as the General Manager at Sg2, a national advanced analytics and consulting business serving over 1,200 leading healthcare systems, and as the Senior Vice President of clinical strategy, population health, and performance management at VHA (Vizient Inc.). He has also performed in various roles at the Rehabilitation Institute of Chicago, the National Institute of Standards and Technology, and St. Agnes Hospital System.

Steve has served on the Senior Board of Examiners for the Baldrige National Quality Program and on the Executive Quest for Quality Prize Board Committee for the American Hospital Association. He currently serves on multiple other boards, including DFWHCF, NurseGrid and the SMU Big Data Advisory Board.

Steve is a first generation American and he lives in Dallas with his wife of 23 years and their precocious seven-year old daughter. He is a data and technology geek, an avid sports enthusiast, world traveler, and a self-taught sous-chef and mixologist.

List of Commonly Used Abbreviations

AI	Artificial Intelligence
CBO	Community-Based Social Service Organization (*aka* Community-Based Organization)
CCC	*Connected Communities of Care*
CHF	Congestive Heart Failure
CPT	Current Procedural Terminology
DFW	Dallas Fort Worth
ED	Emergency Department
EHR	Electronic Health Record
HHS	U.S. Department of Health and Human Services
HIPAA	Health Insurance Portability and Accountability Act of 1996
HIV	Human Immunodeficiency Virus
HIMSS	Healthcare Information and Management Systems Society
HMIS	Homeless Management Information System
HUD	U.S. Department of Housing and Urban Development
IEP	Information Exchange Portal
IP	Intellectual Property
IT	Information Technology
ML	Machine Learning
MOU	Memorandum of Understanding
Parkland	Parkland Health & Hospital System
PCCI	Parkland Center for Clinical Innovation
PHI	Protected Health Information
RFP	Request for Proposal
ROI	Return on Investment
SDOH	Social Determinants of Health

SNAP	Supplemental Nutrition Assistance Program
SOP	Standard Operating Procedure
SROI	Social Return on Investment
QA	Quality Assurance
WIC	Women, Infants, and Children

Chapter 1

Playbook Overview

A *Connected Communities of Care* (*CCC*) is designed to accomplish the critical alignment of providers and Community-Based Social Service Organizations *aka* Community-Based Organizations (CBOs) to support the safety and well-being of vulnerable and underserved community residents. These individuals suffer disproportionally from poor health, job loss, a lack of stable housing, high utility costs, substance abuse, and homelessness. In addition to medical care, these individuals typically need access to CBOs that provide a distinct and complementary set of services, such as housing, food services, emergency utility assistance, and employment assistance. These services are just as vital as healthcare services to an individual's long-term health and well-being.

A *CCC* serves as a comprehensive foundation for this partnership between a community's clinical and social sectors. It typically leverages a cloud-based information exchange/case management software platform providing seamless connection, communication, and coordination between healthcare providers and a wide array of CBOs and other entities, such as criminal justice entities or educational systems. The software platform enables bidirectional communication, referrals, service, and program tracking and offers a continually updated inventory of clinicians and CBOs. Through a *CCC* platform, a community can establish—and leverage—a wide variety (both in size and in region) of community partnerships, serving any type of population, to ensure the right type of assistance, adequate program enrollment, limited program dropout, and successful program implementation.

Among the key drivers of success of a *Connected Community of Care* is a sustainable technology infrastructure that supports information sharing among the providers and other community partners. The Parkland Center for Clinical Innovation (PCCI) *CCC* is powered by Pieces Iris® software, licensed through Pieces Technologies, Inc. Similar to an Electronic Health Record (EHR), the software and associated applications capture, securely store, and appropriately provide access to vital information about individuals and service organization clients in a way that supports the unique, under-lying workflows. If all participating organizations on the *CCC* platform are using the software, then they all are connected through the secure, closed-loop referral system and are thus able to communicate and share informa-tion with each other. For organizations on a different platform, the software offers connectivity through industry-standard, data connectivity methods. PCCI's *CCC* not only connects CBOs via a secure, state-of-the-art, two-way messaging platform but also wraps around the technology a wealth of field-proven and leading clinical and CBO workflows to make services and coordination of community populations more effective and cost-efficient.

A *CCC* facilitates the secure exchange of critical case management infor-mation at various steps in the process, such as when an individual first seeks food assistance or requests emergency housing. It lays the groundwork for an innovative system of assistance and broader social service delivery and creates a longitudinal perspective of care via referral tracking and access to a broad array of services to improve individual well-being and community health. Ultimately, a *CCC* streamlines assistance efforts; reduces repeat crises and emergency funding requests; helps address disparities of care; and improves the health, safety, and well-being of the most vulnerable community residents.

Playbook Purpose

PCCI's *CCC* Playbook provides a tactical guide to enable organizations to succeed in designing, deploying, maintaining, and sustaining a *CCC* in a community. The approach to success is described in this Playbook through the following key elements:

- Detailed description of the six core Tracks orchestrating *CCC* design and implementation
- Key roles and responsibilities
- Requirements (and associated Milestones) to successfully complete each Track
- Strategies for success and overcoming challenges

- Case studies and practice pointers highlighting PCCI lessons learned
- Workflows/processes
- *CCC* measurements of success
- Key sample documents for successful *CCC* design and implementation

Guide to Playbook Terminology

This terminology guide defines the common words and phrases PCCI uses throughout this Playbook:

- "Track" is a primary pathway supporting a *CCC*'s design, implementation, and ongoing operations.
- "Requirement" is an essential element that should be completed within each Track. Although the Requirements are numbered sequentially, based on PCCI's experience, the actual timing of the work across Requirements may vary or occur in parallel with work in other Requirements or even work across other Tracks.
- "Milestone" is a waypost measuring the progress of the work conducted in a specific Requirement towards the ultimate goal. Although the Milestones are numbered sequentially based on the typical progress towards goal attainment, it is possible that certain Milestones may be completed in parallel with other Milestones within a Requirement or even across Requirements.
- "Practice Pointer" is a PCCI example strategy in overcoming challenges to successful *CCC* implementation.
- "Key Task" is an essential activity (in no specific sequential order) to be performed in achieving Milestones.

The Six Tracks for *CCC* Implementation

Figure 1.1 illustrates the *CCC* ecosystem made up of six core Tracks. Development activities and level of model sophistication/complexity flow from the center of the figure outward; each concentric circle represents a core component and development stage of the *CCC*.

Governance and Legal/Policy are at the core of the *CCC* as these are essential, foundational components of the work covered in every Track. While PCCI recommends that *CCC* leaders pursue the Tracks in the

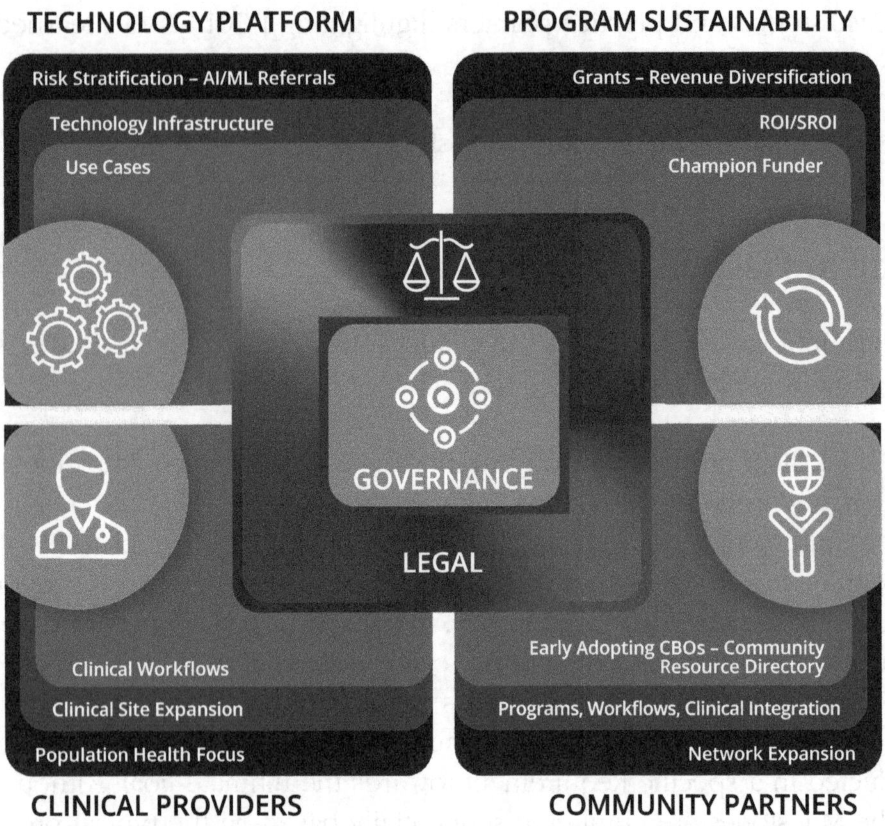

TECHNOLOGY PLATFORM

Risk Stratification – AI/ML Referrals

Technology Infrastructure

Use Cases

PROGRAM SUSTAINABILITY

Grants – Revenue Diversification

ROI/SROI

Champion Funder

GOVERNANCE

LEGAL

Clinical Workflows

Clinical Site Expansion

Population Health Focus

Early Adopting CBOs – Community Resource Directory

Programs, Workflows, Clinical Integration

Network Expansion

CLINICAL PROVIDERS

COMMUNITY PARTNERS

Figure 1.1   PCCI's CCC Model.

following general order, much of the work in various Tracks can (and should) be performed in parallel with work in other Tracks.

Key roles and responsibilities across all Tracks are described in the next section, "*CCC* Roles and Responsibilities". PCCI recommends that the *CCC* leaders assign a designated Track lead for each specific Track. The work in the six *CCC* Tracks will also require input from additional stakeholders specific to the implementation of that particular Track. The six Playbook Tracks are as follows:

1. **Governance Track.** A *CCC*'s governance structure relies on a collective decision-making model rather than on leadership by a specific individual or organization. This Playbook assumes that a few key community organizations have already formed an initial steering group to make the significant decision to undertake the *CCC* initiative. It is critical, at least initially, for an empowered, established group of decision makers to provide leadership through a "readiness assessment" process and during the initial *CCC* design stages. The "readiness assessment" comprises a set

of activities designed to collectively uncover a community's clinical and social needs and level of preparedness and commitment to hosting a *CCC*. See Chapter 2 The Readiness Assessment.

These key decision makers should initially include Anchors, Partners, Sponsors, or Funders (defined in the "*CCC* Roles and Responsibilities" section). As the *CCC* evolves, the governance entity can (and should) expand to include the perspectives of a wider group of community participants. Formal establishment of a governance entity (e.g., a Board) can take place at any point in the process but likely occurs in parallel with (or shortly after) readiness assessment completion or when required by a Funder.

2. ***Legal/Policy Track.*** Communities should identify considerations related to contracts, policies, and procedures to provide an overall *CCC* legal and policy framework for Governance and as part of the development of each Track. The construct of a legal framework requires a review of applicable federal, state, and local law, along with requirements imposed by Funders, Sponsors, and clinical and community Partners (defined in the "*CCC* Roles and Responsibilities" section). As these requirements and considerations are tightly integrated with the business requirements, PCCI has incorporated some of the Legal/Policy considerations within each respective Track. The *CCC*'s Legal/Policy Track lead and *CCC* legal counsel should review all relevant key documents in all Tracks to ensure compliance. To streamline *CCC* preparation and implementation, PCCI recommends that *CCC* legal counsel leverage Participants' existing legal structures, policies, processes, and agreements, where possible.

3. ***Technology Platform Track.*** The Governance Track provides a framework for strategic assessment of *CCC* technology needs, ranging from required features to market analysis. The Technology Platform Track builds off that strategy and explores in depth the nuances and critical activities necessary to ensure successful deployment of the *CCC*'s backbone—the data-sharing platform. The technology infrastructure creates an integrated electronic platform to exchange clinical and social information securely between health organizations (i.e., hospitals, clinics) and CBOs (e.g., homeless shelters, food pantries) that are part of the *CCC* network. Construction of the platform should facilitate future data and external solution integration and provide an information exchange platform on which to customize additional case management functionalities to meet the *CCC* users' service coordination

requirements. Through data collection and reporting, the technology platform also enables network Participants and stakeholders to (1) understand the impact and effectiveness of various programs in fulfilling their mandates and (2) leverage the insights from the data to build effective strategies.

4. ***Clinical Providers Track.*** Although clinical *CCC* workflows vary across selected clinical sites, the workflows need to converge on the *CCC*'s common goals. The Clinical Provider Track lead should contemplate the key factors and related nuances in establishing the clinical *CCC* consortium, including but not limited to the following: executive sponsorship, clear definition of roles and responsibilities, handling of clinical information, the compliance framework, and integration of the new workflows resulting from this work. To ensure appropriate *CCC* alignment and function, providers should integrate the *CCC* requirements for handling healthcare data in compliance with their existing Health Insurance Portability and Accountability Act of 1996 ("HIPAA") policies and procedures.

5. ***Community Partners Track.*** Community workflows also require consideration of a unique set of circumstances, relationships, and nuances. Even more so than the clinical provider workflows, community workflows vary widely across CBOs but ultimately must align to support the global *CCC* goals. Leadership, staffing, and management models may vary from those of the clinical Partners, thus requiring dedicated, deep expertise from the Community Partners Track lead working to engage CBO Partners. For many CBO Partners, this program may require a significant change in existing workflows and in the scope of their influence in the community. To ensure CBO Partner readiness, the Community Partners Track lead should clearly define roles for CBO staff. Training activities should cover consent workflows, case management workflows, and technical interface and functionalities.

6. ***Program Sustainability Track.*** Stakeholder and Participant support and revenue generation are two of the most important factors contributing to *CCC* sustainability. The *CCC* can garner that support through defining and demonstrating its value in providing better services and outcomes and in creating a vehicle for research and innovation benefiting the entire community. Significant funding may be required to design, build, implement, and sustain your local *CCC*. Unlike hospital quality improvement programs that are expected to be deployed and to generate results within annual budgets, *CCC* deployments

require several years to reach scale and maturity in order to pro-
duce meaningful Return on Investment (ROI) and Social Return on
Investment (SROI) results.

CCC Roles and Responsibilities

The guidance in this Playbook is predicated on the assumption that a few
key community organizations have already formed an initial steering group
or an informal governance entity to make the significant decision to undertake the *CCC* initiative. These key decision makers will provide leadership
through the readiness assessment process and during the *CCC*'s design
and initial implementation stages. The key roles required during the readiness assessment, *CCC* design, and the initial implementation of all Playbook
Tracks are as follows.

An **Administrator** means the entity responsible for day-to-day *CCC*
management. This entity may be a Partner or a separately contracted third
party, but it is typically selected (with prescribed functions) by the Board.

An **Anchor** is a large, highly respected organization in the community
with broad reach and often financial resources to initiate large-scale community initiatives, such as a community readiness assessment and *CCC*.
Examples of an Anchor could include a large healthcare system or regional
hospital, large physician group, health plan, or social service organization,
such as the United Way and Salvation Army. An Anchor is a Partner and
could be a Sponsor or a Funder.

Board means a Board of Directors/Trustees who has responsibility for
CCC governance functions. The Board is typically formally established during
(or shortly after) the execution of the readiness assessment, as part of the legal
framework for *CCC* governance. For the design and initial implementation
stages of the *CCC*, the Board should generally only consist of Partners and
Funders. In later implementation stages as the *CCC* evolves, the Board may
choose to invite a select number of other participating organizations to join.

Clinical Advisory Group means clinical expert advisors representing multiple perspectives at healthcare organizations. The Clinical Advisory
Group's purpose is to provide important guidance on clinical matters for the
CCC. One of the first and most critical roles of the Clinical Advisory Group
will be to consider health and social data from the *CCC* readiness assessment and come to consensus regarding target clinical conditions that the
CCC should target in its initial implementation.

CBO means a public or private nonprofit organization that provides a variety of social service programs and services (e.g., food banks and housing assistance) to meet economic, social, or physical needs that may be contributing to poor health outcomes, particularly for a community's high need and vulnerable populations.

Funder means any person or entity that provides financial assistance to support the creation, operations, or sustainability of the *CCC*. A Funder could include philanthropic organizations as well as governmental or private sector entities. Funders may change over time depending on their level of commitment and the stage of *CCC* maturity. The governance entity (e.g., Board) should consider whether persons or entities that provide in-kind services for the *CCC* for free or at reduced prices should also be included as Funders.

An "**information exchange platform**" or "information exchange portal" is the framework that allows for mobilization of an individual's healthcare and social determinants of health (SDOH) information to be securely accessed and transmitted electronically, via an interdisciplinary care network, across healthcare providers and CBOs within a community or region. The goal of the information exchange platform is to streamline and facilitate coordination between healthcare providers and CBOs, and to provide improved care coordination that will advance the overall health and well-being of the community's residents.

A **Participant or participating organization** is an entity that, through a Memorandum of Understanding (MOU) (or other means approved by the Board), agrees to participate in the *CCC*. Participants can include clinical Partners, faith-based organizations, governmental entities, and CBOs. In the early stages of *CCC* governance, a Participant generally does not participate in governance decisions or serve on the Board unless the Participant is also a Partner. As the *CCC* expands, the Board may invite a limited number of Participants to join the Board.

A **Partner** is a well-established organization in the community (e.g., clinical provider or CBO) that provides, along with other Partner organizations, a commitment to lead the design and implementation of the *CCC*. Partners make up the initial governance unit for the *CCC* and are the primary decision makers for the design and launch of the *CCC* in a community. Partners can represent any of the entities identified as Participants. The term "Partner" denotes the important and cooperative relationships that exist between the various key organizations and that are necessary for a successful *CCC* implementation. The term "Partner," as used by PCCI in this Playbook, is not meant to imply that any of the *CCC* Partner entities are, in fact, "partners" in the legal sense of the word, absent a written partnership agreement that spells out all the rights and remedies of the entity and constituent partner.

A **Sponsor** may be either an entity that is responsible for initial creation of the *CCC* in the local community or an organization that contributes resources to the ongoing success of the *CCC* (e.g., local bank or auto dealership). The Sponsor is typically an Anchor or a Funder.

A **Workgroup** is a temporary or permanent committee that is generally made up of committed Partners/Participants and possibly community residents or patients so as to ensure the "voice of the community" is fully integrated into the initial deployment and ongoing evaluation of the initiative. A Workgroup is approved by the Board to work on any number of *CCC* topics (e.g., sustainability, best practice dissemination, funding). A Workgroup is designed to:

- Give Participants a voice in the *CCC* operations.
- Offer community residents the opportunity to participate in *CCC* governance.
- Provide feedback to the Board, Administrator, or Sponsor.
- Share best practices among Participants.
- Surface and resolve disputes informally.
- Create a vehicle for positive publicity and sharing of *CCC* successes.

Timeline to Implement a *CCC* Model

In general, the preparation, design, setup, and implementation of a fully functioning *CCC* (spanning the work of all six Tracks) occur over approximately 28 months as indicated in Figure 1.2. It is important to note that the timeline described represents a conservative estimate and also assumes

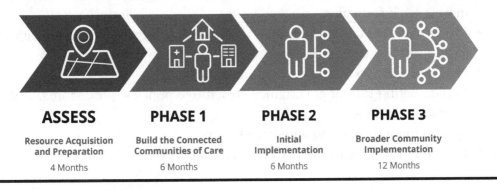

ASSESS	PHASE 1	PHASE 2	PHASE 3
Resource Acquisition and Preparation	Build the Connected Communities of Care	Initial Implementation	Broader Community Implementation
4 Months	6 Months	6 Months	12 Months

Figure 1.2   *CCC* Timeline.

primarily sequential work. Timelines can vary based on a number of factors, such as (1) general community readiness and engagement, (2) establishment of governance structures, (3) availability of funding, (4) ability to simultaneously complete Track frameworks, (5) Anchor and Partner organization preparedness, and (6) achievement of buy-in from leadership at potential Participant sites.

Resource Acquisition and Preparation Phase

During this phase, the Anchors or Sponsors will complete a readiness assessment and will typically procure funding sources to support the operational costs of building and maintaining the technical infrastructure, onboarding Partners, and operating the *CCC* during initial implementation.

Phase 1: Build the CCC Framework

During Phase 1, the key decision makers and designated Track leads should focus on the following:

- Finalizing legal requirements and agreements, especially for Participants and the technology vendor, which includes defining patient consent, data sharing, and role-based access to patient information by the Partners and Participants
- Creating, integrating, or modifying policies and procedures as required to address *CCC* specifics (e.g., HIPAA compliance, securing Institutional Review Board (IRB) approval if *CCC* is part of a research design for the clinical Partners)
- Designing workflows at Partner sites
- Initial development of the community referral directory that incorporates 2-1-1 information
- Identifying functional requirements and providing the technical platform to support those requirements
- Defining *CCC* goals and desired outcomes
- Implementing formal governance structures, policies, procedures, and operational plans
- Identifying and training authorized users
- Examining technical security and data integrity

Phase 2: Initial Implementation

Phase 2 represents the initial *CCC* implementation with the Anchor organizations and a minimum number of clinical and CBO Partners. This Phase encourages authorized users to incorporate the *CCC* workflows daily in their work through a phased rollout approach beginning with:

- Exchanging very basic information (e.g., demographic information or discharge summaries
- Documenting any troubleshooting needs or opportunities for system enhancement
- Providing feedback necessary to support further improvements. During this Phase, the initial *CCC* performance measures are collected and evaluated to determine the initial *CCC* impact on the clinical Partners, CBOs, and community residents. At the end of this Phase, the governance entity should possess in-depth knowledge about the implementation process in different types of organizational settings, which will enable more efficient scaling in Phase 3.

Phase 3: Broader Community Implementation

CCC expansion during Phase 3 may take the form of additional targeted clinical conditions, additional service lines at existing Partner sites or additional Participants. During this scaling-up process, the *CCC* leadership should achieve the following:

- A lean operational budget
- A sustainable *CCC* operation not as reliant on external funding
- A flexible governance structure adapted to *CCC* expansion
- A strong technical infrastructure supporting all prescribed functionalities, and positive outcomes that can be leveraged to drive further *CCC* investment and potential expansion into additional communities

Chapter 2

The Readiness Assessment

A critical *Connected Communities of Care* (*CCC*) prerequisite is the assessment of the community through implementation of a readiness assessment, which uncovers the clinical and social needs in the community along with provider and Community-Based Social Service Organization *aka* Community-Based Organization (CBO) readiness to support care coordination activities that will address the needs of all stakeholders. A readiness assessment utilizes quantitative and qualitative data to provide both the breadth and depth of the required understanding to design and implement a *CCC*.

Once the readiness assessment is completed, the insights gained will drive the selection of clinical programs, social services, and workflows to reach the global goals of the *CCC*. Therefore, a request for a readiness assessment presupposes that a Sponsor or a few key community organizations have already formed an initial steering group or early governance entity and made the decision to undertake the initiative. It is critical, at least initially, for there to be an established key group of decision makers to provide leadership through the readiness assessment process and during the initial *CCC* design stages. These key decision makers should include Anchors, Partners, Sponsors, or Funders. Formal establishment of a Board or other formal governance structure typically takes place in parallel with, or shortly after, the completion of the readiness assessment, as part of the *CCC* legal process. As the *CCC* is later implemented and evolves, the governance structure may expand to include the perspectives of a wider group of community participants.

While the Parkland Center for Clinical Innovation (PCCI) has developed its own readiness assessment tool (PCCI Readiness Assessment), other Sponsors or communities may use any similarly structured assessment that provides information across five key readiness assessment requirements:

1. Identify target clinical/behavioral health conditions.
2. Identify social needs that impact clinical outcomes or the general health of the population.
3. Describe the client/patient profile that would be targeted by a *CCC*.
4. Describe the organizations and potential users (staff) of a *CCC*.
5. Identify functionalities required and develop *CCC* use cases.

While PCCI believes that more current data provides the best guidance upon which to develop use cases, we recognize that other organizations may have previously completed a readiness assessment or Community Health Needs Assessment (CHNA) that provides the necessary community context to build a *CCC*. Our experience suggests that data collected more than 12–18 months in the past should not be used to construct use cases, as circumstances can (and do) quickly change.

Readiness Assessment Requirements

The PCCI Readiness Assessment uses a combination of primary and secondary data obtained through original research, surveys, interviews, and focus groups of key stakeholders to better understand a community's clinical and social needs and the readiness of that community to undertake the deployment, operation, and management of a *CCC* today and into the future. In addition to these sources of qualitative information, PCCI suggests that *CCC* planners consider gathering quantitative information at the neighborhood or "block level" where people live, work, play, etc., using one of the currently available Community Data Initiative (CDI) applications. In general, a readiness assessment strives to discover and report on five key components (requirements) that underlie the *CCC*.

patient → CBO
is it ever CBO to clinical
initially?

Requirement 1: Identify Target Clinical/Behavioral Health Conditions

The Clinical Advisory Group members will consider health and social data based on prevalence rates of chronic diseases in the health system and community at large as well as data from surveys and interviews with clinical and CBO leaders. Members of the initial governance entity and the Clinical Advisory Group will then come to a consensus regarding target clinical conditions that the platform should support in the initial *CCC* implementation phase. Generally, the focus is on chronic conditions, such as diabetes, heart disease, and arthritis, which impact the elderly and most vulnerable segments of the population and generate a large cost to the healthcare sector and society. In addition, these chronic conditions require added support from both healthcare providers and CBOs to support patients in the management of their current conditions and aid them with the adoption of alternative behaviors to place them on a path towards better health.

PRACTICE POINTER

Start Small and Then Scale

PCCI's experience suggests that choosing more than three target clinical conditions can impose a level of complexity that may hinder *CCC* implementation efforts. Starting small and scaling is the most effective approach in this transformational effort. The Clinical Advisory Group may want to initially identify ten clinical conditions and then prioritize the top three. The remaining conditions can be targeted in later implementation phases.

Requirement 2: Identify Social Needs That Impact Clinical Outcomes or the General Health of the Population

The initial governance entity will also identify (through surveys and interviews with clinical and CBO leaders and staff) the top social needs negatively impacting clinical outcomes. These include barriers, such as lack of transportation, lack of social support, lack of adequate housing, and lack of insight into health problems. These Social Determinants of Health (SDOH) have received much greater attention in recent years as many are believed to be direct contributors to unnecessary utilization of healthcare services, such as Emergency Department (ED) visits and healthcare costs.

The nature of social needs identified by clinicians and by CBOs can be both overlapping and divergent. Clinicians can provide insight into patients' health problems and may even have some information about social factors as a secondary focus. Conversely, CBOs interact with clients who may or may not have received health services; some of these clients may not even be aware of their health issues. For clinical providers and CBOs, addressing social factors and providing access to clinical services represent primary targets for interventions to improve the health of at-risk populations. There are subsets of the population that interact only with the social service sector, only with the healthcare sector, or with both. In addition, there is a subset of the population that needs to interact with both sectors but does not receive the care needed.

Requirement 3: Describe the Client/Patient Profile That Would Be Targeted by a CCC

The intent of this portion of a readiness assessment is to help develop a clearer picture of the type and number of community residents needing clinical or social assistance via a *CCC* (e.g., low income, multiple chronic conditions, lack of (or minimal) health insurance). Through surveys (including resident surveys taking place at provider clinics or CBOs), interviews, and focus groups, as well as an analysis of service utilization patterns, a readiness assessment provides approaches to segment and stratify at-risk populations or subpopulations. It facilitates a determination of the population that would benefit most from a *CCC*; namely, those that utilize or would benefit from services at both clinical and CBO partners. The population characteristics of interest may include:

- Demographics
- Insurance coverage
- Clinical conditions
- Barriers to access
- Unmet medical and/or social needs

Requirement 4: Describe the Organizations and Potential Users (Staff) of a CCC

The complement to Requirement 3, this requirement strives to better understand the organizations and staff that will be part of the *CCC* network, specifically: (1) the programs they offer, (2) their catchment areas, (3) client profiles, (4) technology infrastructure in place and staff competency with the technology, and (5) their financial position. CBOs are diverse and vary by size, services provided, technology capacity, and clinical populations served. There is also a wide range of potential users within organizations, including volunteers, case workers and community health workers. As a result, users will have different educational and training backgrounds and may have limited prior experience using and interpreting health information. By profiling (through CBO staff surveys and interviews) the CBOs active in the community to be served by the *CCC*, a readiness assessment aims to define the functional requirements, user-training needs, and governance structure that will achieve optimal *CCC* alignment. An understanding of the organizational settings also helps in the development of a strong value proposition that benefits each CBO and the populations they serve. In addition, a *CCC* would not only help CBOs access health information, it would increase knowledge of community resources and services offered at other CBOs, including services that the CBO's own clients are accessing.

Requirement 5: Identify Functionalities Required and Develop CCC Use Cases

This requirement focuses on highlighting the technical requirements needed by the users (e.g., the ability to track patients across care settings, identification of eligible services, capture of relevant medical history). It also encompasses the development of use-case interactions between healthcare providers and CBOs, addressing at least one of the identified functional requirements informing the *CCC* design.

The last two readiness assessment requirements focus on helping the governance entity to perform the following actions: (1) identify *CCC* Partners (for the initial implementation phase) and Participants (when the network later expands) and (2) assess the level of community support for a *CCC*. Both of these are critical determinations that can have a profound negative impact on the deployment and operation of a *CCC* if ignored or assessed erroneously.

The selected Partners may represent diversity in client population, service programs, organization size and settings, and technical capability and sophistication. All recommended and identified Partners serve a large population of clients who also receive healthcare, ostensibly through the identified clinical provider Partners.

Leveraging the readiness assessment to determine the level of community support is critical to the success of a *CCC*. It is well recognized that social factors, such as socioeconomic status, race and ethnicity, and lack of social support, can be barriers to healthy behavior, which consequently can severely complicate chronic illness management.[4,5] Social conditions not only provide a framework for understanding individual health risk factors but also determine access to critical health resources. Social and disease management needs often compete; therefore, prioritizing one set of needs can often lead to deterioration of the other, or both. While healthcare providers and CBOs share mutual goals of enhancing care delivery and improving the health and well-being of those community residents who suffer from chronic conditions and are indigent or underserved, the level of cross-sector cooperation and trust varies greatly from community to community as does the level of support from the surrounding community. Many CBOs are equipped to partially address unmet social needs. However, they are ill-equipped at best to address medical care coordination. The absence of collaboration between clinical providers and CBOs leaves many residents' needs either sub-optimally addressed or not addressed at all. Going forward, cross-sector collaboration is vital for the delivery of quality and cost-effective care. Ultimately, the information gained through the readiness assessment process will help augment greater understanding and cross-sector collaboration to improve health outcomes and to achieve financial savings.

Readiness Assessment Methodology

As potential users of a *CCC* platform, clinical and community stakeholders play a significant role in guiding its design. Those tasked with introducing *CCC* into a community must initiate a multipronged approach to ensure that their assessment captures perspectives from a representative, cross-section sample of clinical and community leaders, organizational frontline staff, and community residents, as described in the readiness assessment requirements. The readiness assessment's multipronged approach supports independent research (using existing secondary data sources) of social factors and the prevalence of health conditions across a target community. In addition to this background research, the readiness assessment incorporates surveys of the following: (1) CBO clients, (2) patients and families visiting outpatient clinics or other clinical provider sites, (3) frontline CBO staff, and (4) front-line clinical staff. Complementing the extensive survey process, the readiness assessment may incorporate semi-structured interviews with clinical and CBO leaders.

In addition to the surveys and interviews, PCCI recommends that communities consider conducting focus groups with clinical and community leadership, staff members, and patients as part of the readiness assessment methodology. These focus groups are essentially "deeper-dive" meetings that can supply a rich exchange on potential uses of the *CCC* as well as barriers and enablers to use of the platform. In addition, these focus groups provide an opportunity for collecting additional anecdotes and specific perceptions about how the *CCC* platform may play a role in coordinating transitions of care, reducing redundancies and inefficiencies, and improving clinical and social outcomes. These focus groups can also provide further opportunities to directly engage CBOs and clinical social work, case management, and community outreach staff in frank discussions about use cases that present opportunities for improved care coordination.

Milestone 1: Obtain Data through Research, Surveys, Interviews, and Focus Groups

In the readiness assessment process, the leaders should ideally collect qualitative data needed to meet readiness assessment requirements through the following: (1) surveys of clinical provider and CBO staff and patients/clients, (2) interviews with both provider and CBO leaders with experiential insight into community health problems, and (3) focus groups with both clinical and CBO staff and with patients/clients. The readiness assessment can (and should) also leverage existing datasets and information from other community assessments or data sources, such as the following:

- Administrative data from individual hospitals, health systems, and large healthcare providers
- Local medical society databases
- Local Community Data Initiatives
- Health departments (e.g., Medicaid/Medicare databases)
- National databases, such as:
  - CDC National Health Interview Survey (NHIS)
  - Healthcare Utilization Project (HCUP) datasets
  - Behavioral Risk Factor Surveillance System (BRFSS)

Hospital and community health leaders and local medical societies, health departments, and umbrella organizations for healthcare entities can help facilitate the gathering of the necessary data. The resulting comprehensive and data-supported description of community clinical gaps and outcomes is often an eye opener that builds community coalitions around problem-solving. For example, for the Dallas Information Exchange Portal (IEP), in addition to data obtained through surveys, interviews, and focus groups, the Dallas Fort Worth Hospital Council Foundation database provided a rich source of data on community-level clinical problems and outcomes.[6]

Milestone 2: Generate a List of Gaps for Prioritization

As part of the readiness assessment process and requirements, the Clinical Advisory Group will convene and review data and then create and prioritize a list of clinical issues and outcomes. A few actions to guide the prioritization of clinical problems and outcomes include:

- Evaluate the alignment of the *CCC* vision with identified needs and gaps.
- Consider local context, such as ongoing community initiatives.
- Factor in SDOH in shaping the issue or outcome.
- Project the community impact of solving the problem or improving the outcome.
- Seize opportunities for intervention (e.g., a new grant opportunity).
- Align with local, regional, or national health policy (both current and planned).

PRACTICE POINTER

Leverage Existing Local Programs

Carefully investigate existing local programs to identify those aligning with the *CCC* clinical goals and then leverage these as anchor programs to introduce the *CCC* in the community. For example, in Dallas, homelessness has represented a critical problem to diverse stakeholders, including political leaders, community housing providers, healthcare organizations, and community and faith leaders. The Dallas community's rallying efforts to solve homelessness presented an ideal opportunity to introduce the Dallas IEP as a convening framework for that initiative. The IEP technology did provide a platform and legal framework for data sharing and community resources access, referral, monitoring, and management, in order to reduce homelessness in Dallas. The *CCC* technology platform in a community could also potentially be modified to receive certification from the U.S. Department of Housing and Urban Development (HUD) as a Homeless Management Information System (HMIS) for housing organizations.

Milestone 3: Document Use Cases

The readiness assessment interviews and focus groups should foster a rich exchange of information on potential use cases to be addressed through the *CCC* model as well as barriers and enablers to using the technology. For these use cases, the Partners will discuss examples of how the *CCC* may play a role in coordinating transitions of care, reducing redundancies and inefficiencies, and improving clinical and social outcomes.

Case Study: Dallas Readiness Assessment

HOW PCCI USED ITS READINESS ASSESSMENT TOOL TO LAY THE GROUNDWORK FOR THE DALLAS IEP

In 2012, shortly after receiving funding from the Communities Foundation of Texas, PCCI developed its PCCI Readiness Assessment and began the process of identifying clinical, social, and technological needs in the Dallas market, along with a list of potential Partner and Participant organizations to form the initial IEP. The following describes some of the key PCCI findings across the five requirements resulting from that exercise.

TARGET CLINICAL/BEHAVIORAL HEALTH CONDITIONS

PCCI's Readiness Assessment recommended an initial target of up to 10 clinical/behavioral health conditions. The Clinical Advisory Group then pared that number down to three or four clinical/behavioral health conditions based on an analysis of the following:

- Prevalence rates of chronic diseases at Parkland and in the Dallas community at large
- Desired alignment with nationwide Health Information Exchange (HIE) efforts
- Data from surveys and semi-structured interviews with local clinical and CBO leaders
- Interventions that were available and deemed to be effective

Based on these factors, the Dallas Clinical Advisory Group unanimously decided that diabetes, Congestive Heart Failure (CHF), and Hypertension (HTN) would be the initial, prioritized conditions. In addition, the Clinical Advisory Group determined that behavioral health, pediatric asthma, and Chronic Obstructive Pulmonary Disease (COPD) should be targeted in later implementation phases.

TARGET SOCIAL NEEDS THAT IMPACT CLINICAL OUTCOMES

Within the Parkland community, the Stemmons Corridor, South Dallas, Southwest Dallas, and Southeast Dallas were all home to populations with the highest medical needs. These same areas had high incidences of the three targeted, chronic health conditions identified in the first readiness assessment requirement. These same areas also had a high proportion of adults with

Table 2.1 Dallas IEP List of Unmet Social Needs

Top Five Unmet Social Needs—Clinical Perspective	Top Five Unmet Social Needs—CBO Perspective
Inability to pay for care	Lack of social support
Unemployment	Inability to pay for care
Lack of transportation	Lack of insight into their health problems
Inability to keep track of referrals/appointments	Mental health challenges
Lack of adequate housing	Substance abuse

less than a high school diploma and the highest levels of poverty in Dallas. The areas of Southwest Dallas, Southeast Dallas, and South Dallas had correspondingly low per-capita incomes and high unemployment. Additionally, large numbers of households in all four areas were on the Supplemental Nutrition Assistance Program (SNAP/food stamps). Based on the in-depth interviews with clinical and CBO leaders, the top five unmet social needs are described in Table 2.1.

Population That Would Be Targeted by the IEP

Parkland's outpatient population is disproportionately indigent and vulnerable. The population characteristics of interest included (1) demographics, (2) insurance, (3) clinical conditions, (4) barriers to healthcare, (5) unmet medical needs, (6) unmet social needs, (7) Parkland service utilization patterns, and (8) possible information-sharing concerns.

To gather the necessary information, PCCI conducted surveys with clients at CBOs and with patients at Parkland clinics. The survey data showed the following:

- *Clinical Conditions.* HTN and diabetes were among the top chronic medical conditions reported by clients/patients.
- *Demographics.* Client/patient educations levels were low, and most surveyed clients and outpatients fell below the federal poverty level.
- *Insurance.* Most clients/patients had either Parkland Community Health Plan insurance or no insurance.
- *Healthcare Barriers.* The top three barriers to healthcare were (1) the inability to pay for care, (2) transportation problems, and (3) lack of health insurance.

- *Unmet Health Needs.* The top three unmet health needs were (1) dental care, (2) vision care, and (3) transportation for healthcare services.
- *Unmet Social Needs.* The top three unmet social needs were (1) transportation, (2) financial assistance for rent or utilities, and (3) assistance in applying for insurance.
- *Information Sharing.* Survey results indicated that nearly 90% of patients were comfortable sharing information about themselves and their care with healthcare providers and CBOs participating in the Dallas IEP.

ORGANIZATIONS AND POTENTIAL USERS OF THE CCC MODEL

By profiling the CBOs active in the Parkland area, the PCCI Readiness Assessment aimed to define the functional requirements, user-training needs, and governance model that would achieve optimal alignment. An understanding of the organizational settings also aided in developing a strong value proposition benefiting each CBO and their service populations. Based on the survey data, the CBOs were diverse and varied by size, services provided, technical capacity, and client populations served. There was also a wide range of potential users within organizations, including volunteers, case workers, community health workers, and directors. As a result, users had different education and training backgrounds, often with limited prior experience using—and interpreting—health information. The majority of CBOs provided case management, daily living skills training, job-seeking assistance, and substance abuse counseling. Most CBOs wished to exchange medical and social information to better serve their clients. Information deemed especially valuable included (1) scheduled appointments, (2) medication lists, (3) inpatient discharge instructions, and (4) insurance eligibility.

DEVELOP USE CASES FOR THE IEP

The development of a library of use cases illuminated how the use of an IEP could potentially result in a better clinical or social outcome for the patient. In addition to the series of interviews with leaders at Parkland and CBOs covering a range of different program types and client populations, PCCI also conducted "deep-dive" focus groups with leadership and frontline staff from 15 CBOs (52 attendees). These meetings fostered a rich exchange on at least 20 different scenarios in which an IEP could potentially be used, as well as barriers and enablers to using the platform. Most CBOs wanted the ability to track clients, identify services for which their clients qualified, and view (1) past and current referrals and resources provided, (2) demographic information, (3) relevant medical history, (4) standard documentation required by Parkland or social service agencies, and (5) client/patient insurance coverage.

The discussions with community and clinical leaders generating the list of "uses" resulted in five *CCC* use-case categories: (1) background information (e.g., demographic information, insurance coverage); (2) service eligibility (e.g., service eligibility identification); (3) service history (e.g., relevant medical history, current medications, past service enrollments); (4) service planning, coordination, and delivery (e.g., service request/referral at other agencies, client encounters at other agencies, medical equipment, or dietary needs); and (5) research and reporting (e.g., research study participation). Each use case incorporated the interactions between healthcare providers and CBOs and addressed one or more requested functional requirement.

Chapter 3

Governance Track

Introduction to the Governance Track

A strong *Connected Communities of Care* (*CCC*) governance structure is vital to successful *CCC* operations and longevity. Foregoing the work to establish a strong governance foundation up front often results in a solution that does not meet the needs of the stakeholders, a lack of participation in the model, or a lack of buy-in from key stakeholders, all of which result in the loss of dollars and time. A *CCC* governance framework partners two different sectors (clinical and community) in sharing responsibilities and accountabilities towards a united vision and mission. The governing body needs to lead and manage the *CCC* operations, engagement, and eventually, community ownership of this collaborative effort.

The *CCC* requires an elastic structure enabling flexibility in technical development, organizational oversight, community drivers, and future growth and development. The *CCC* governance entity and Governance Track create accountability mechanisms to ensure all Participants understand the vision and operational aspects relative to their respective roles. In addition, the governance entity will implement decision-making processes to overcome unexpected hurdles, address necessary changes, and maintain forward momentum. As the *CCC* grows, the set of stakeholders will also continue to grow to include the wider community of Community-Based Social Service Organizations *aka* Community-Based

Organizations (CBOs) and healthcare systems. It is necessary to define the collaborative relationships that will support the roles of *CCC* ownership and operation, sustain *CCC* development and growth after the initial implementation phases, and continue to create and derive value from the *CCC* for the entire community.

The *CCC* governance structure may vary based on community particulars (e.g., size, location) and Funder and legal requirements. For example, some communities may simply form an informal governance entity or steering group made up of Anchor organizations. Others may initially form this type of informal group and then later move to a more formal governance structure (e.g., Board). Still other communities may establish a formal governance structure before beginning any work on a *CCC*. But to be successful, a *CCC* requires establishment of some type of governance framework that accomplishes the Governance Track requirements, complies with Funder and legal requirements, and provides the foundation and ongoing oversight for the four operational Tracks: Technology Platform, Clinical Providers, Community Partners, and Program Sustainability.

Much of the governance work will occur in the Resource Acquisition and Preparation Phase and Phase 1 of the *CCC* Model timeline (see Chapter 1), although governance work continues through all stages of *CCC* evolution. As the *CCC* grows and expands, the governance plans, technology requirements, contracts, Funder requirements, legal requirements, and Participant requirements will continue to evolve.

Once your community has established a comprehensive governance structure and plan, you are positioned to create a person-centered ecosystem that fosters the exchange and use of information in multiple ways to immediately assist individuals and enhance the ability of community programs to coordinate care to improve individual outcomes.

Roles and Responsibilities

The *CCC* Roles and Responsibilities section of Chapter 1 covers the key roles for *CCC* governance as some of these roles will represent the community's key decision makers and the Governance Track lead. The Track lead will also work closely with the Legal/Policy Track lead and *CCC* legal counsel, who will likely participate heavily in governance activities given the integral aspects of legal and policy considerations in *CCC* governance.

Figure 3.1 CCC Governance Responsibilities.

A *CCC* governance model should accomplish the following (Figure 3.1):

- Articulate a consistent *CCC* vision.
- Demonstrate flexibility based on changes in *CCC* environment, size, and scope.
- Provide a mechanism for strategic planning and set strategic direction and priorities via both inspirational (e.g., mission statements) and pragmatic (e.g., budget) means.
- Define the approach to engage *CCC* Participants and other stakeholders (e.g., community leaders).
- Define the approach to engage the general community (i.e., those not directly participating in the *CCC*).
- Provide general oversight and evaluation of *CCC* operations.
- Establish decision-making processes to overcome unexpected hurdles and to maintain focus and momentum.
- Meet Funder/Sponsor requirements.
- Provide oversight of compliance with legal standards.
- Allocate resources fairly and in a way that maximizes *CCC* performance.
- Define the desired outcomes and measurement framework to track performance of *CCC* Participants and vendors.
- Create value propositions for various stakeholders.

- Establish processes to identify and pursue potential funding sources.
- Provide reports to Funders, stakeholders, and the community.
- Resolve disputes, while maintaining commitment to *CCC* progress.

Requirements for Successful *CCC* Governance

Although the type of governance structure and timing of governance requirements (and related actions) vary based on the community, the Anchors, Sponsors, and Governance Track lead should address each of the following eight requirements:

1. Secure *CCC* resources and initial commitments.
2. Choose your governance model.
3. Set up the formal governance structure.
4. Define an aligned, comprehensive *CCC* strategy.
5. Select clinical programs.
6. Formalize participation agreements and begin implementation of the governance plan.
7. Define a strategy and general requirements for *CCC* technology and data integration at Partner sites.
8. Define and perform Quality Assurance (QA) activities to ensure intervention integrity across the *CCC*.

Requirement 1: Secure CCC Resources and Initial Commitments

In any community, the Sponsor and Anchor clinical providers and CBOs collaborate to jointly define the need (and vision) for a *CCC*. At that point, these decision makers and *CCC* "champions" effectively form the initial *CCC* governance organization and begin the process of overseeing *CCC* funding, design, and implementation and engaging additional Partners. This initial *CCC* governance entity (e.g., Board) may be a precursor to the final desired (and chosen) governance entity. At this stage of the work, however, the governance entity's primary function is to engage high-level clinical leaders in the community (e.g., hospital and health system leaders, university medical centers, local healthcare provider groups and organizations, public health authorities, Federally Qualified Health Centers, community health centers, and charity care leaders).

Milestone 1: Create the CCC Value Proposition

Successful engagement of potential Partners requires a clearly defined need, vision, and goals for the *CCC*. As with any collaborative engagement, a compelling and concise value proposition drives engagement. The Governance Track lead should structure a value proposition that not only speaks to the operational and strategic goals of potential Partners but also highlights the impact on the community and the patient. The value proposition should align with the overall *CCC* goals and establish the patient as the common focus of effort. To the extent possible, leverage historic financial, performance, and outcomes data to clearly demonstrate the expected impact of the *CCC* on the potential partner's key strategic goals (e.g., anticipated reduction of Emergency Department (ED) visits by XX% within the first 12 months for a YY patient cohort).

Milestone 2: Select CCC Partners and Secure Early Commitments

Acquiring new Partners and Participants is an ongoing process throughout all stages of *CCC* design and implementation. The Anchors and Sponsor should obtain commitments from clinical and CBO Partners as early in the process as possible. Many Sponsors (and Funders) will require some type of Memorandum of Understanding (MOU) or letter of commitment from each potential Partner—even if not legally binding—before they commit their own resources/funding. See also Chapter 4 Legal/Policy Track Requirement 1.

The securing of funding, resources, and Partner engagement may require a prolonged period (6–12 months is not unreasonable). During this time, potential Partner organizations may experience restructuring, staff turnover, or other changes potentially impacting the detailed letter commitments (e.g., a clinical Partner site that originally commits to the effort later ceases operations). For this reason, Parkland Center for Clinical Innovation (PCCI) recommends that you structure letters of commitment in a general sense, emphasizing a commitment to participate and to achieve the *CCC* goals. You will later negotiate and document the commitment details in the actual Partner participation agreements and supporting documents.

Key Task: Select Clinical Partners and the Clinical Advisory Group

If community-level programs involving multiple clinical entities are currently ongoing, the Governance Track lead can leverage these existing relationships to engage clinical entities in the *CCC*. Indeed, clinical participants already involved in community-level initiatives are likely to be more responsive to (and early adopters of) the *CCC*. Once on board, these clinical Partners can help kick-start *CCC* activities and serve on the Clinical Advisory Group, while the remaining clinical Partners are onboarding. The Clinical Advisory Group's purpose is to provide important guidance on clinical matters for the *CCC*. When few (or no) community-level initiatives involving multiple clinical entities are ongoing, the convening process may take a bit longer. In this case, one approach is to engage local and community leaders who have existing relationships with clinical entities. For instance, local health departments, medical societies or organizations, or political and community leaders (such as a Mayor or County Judge) can often assist with initial clinical entity engagement.

Key Task: Select CBO Partners

The *CCC* goals and desired program outcomes usually drive Partner CBO selection. For example, some communities may pursue a broad impact (e.g., addressing multiple health-related social needs). For these communities, screening high patient volumes across all sectors of the population may be a key goal. This type of *CCC* model requires CBO Partners who provide a variety of services to address multiple health-related social needs. Other communities may choose to focus on very specific community subpopulations (e.g., food insecure residents), which will drive the selection of CBO Partners to those who are able to provide these related services to the targeted subpopulation. CBOs provide varied categories of services and programs to their clients. See Chapter 7 for a discussion of many of these various categories and programs. Some CBOs provide one specific service (e.g., food pantry services), while others provide overlapping services (e.g., utility assistance, nutrition counseling, and food pantry assistance). The *CCC* Governance Track lead should proactively review unique CBO requirements based on the categories of services provided. For example, some CBOs receiving program funding from states (e.g., nutrition programs) may require additional time to negotiate agreements given expanded legal requirements linked to those programs. Therefore, when selecting potential CBOs to participate, the *CCC* Governance Track lead should take the following actions:

- Identify CBOs serving the defined target populations.
- Perform a high-level (e.g., qualitative) analysis of the CBO level of need, services, programs offered, strategic direction, and engagement in similar initiatives.
- Analyze the data to determine which organizations would have the greatest impact and potential to yield desired outcomes (e.g., organizations with the greatest client volumes belonging to the targeted population).
- Identify these CBO critical stakeholders and leaders; program success largely depends on the level of CBO leadership buy-in.

Key Documents for Requirement 1

- MOU for Clinical Participation in a *CCC*
- Letter of Commitment (see Chapter 4 Legal/Policy Track Requirement 1)
- Clinical Advisory Group Guidelines
- *CCC* Value Proposition
- Considerations for Working with Umbrella Organizations
- List of Participant Clinical Sites and CBOs

Requirement 2: Choose Your Governance Model

A governance model assists the initial decision makers in organizing the best structure for governance of the *CCC*. The initial *CCC* governance structure created as part of Requirement 1 typically forms the basis for the final *CCC* governance structure. Any modifications to the governance structure should encompass: (1) funding (grant, contract, or mixed) requirements; (2) desired governance structure based on state law and Sponsor, Anchor, or Partner input; (3) funding parameters and stakeholder interests; (4) legal concerns raised by (or anticipated from) Partners and other stakeholders; (5) known legal requirements for each step of the workflows; and (6) measures of success. The following are three governance model examples.

Board Governance Model

In this model, the Sponsor or other *CCC* decision makers and Governance Track lead establish a Board, which is initially made up of clinical and CBO Partners, to oversee the community *CCC*. The primary advantages of the Board form of governance include the following:

- Deep stakeholder engagement and commitment, which often results in broader acceptance of decisions made (and investment in) the *CCC*'s long-term success
- Broadened ability to share responsibilities
- A wide variety of perspectives
- The benefits of group decision-making

The primary drawbacks of Board governance include the following:

- Potential for slower decision-making and gaining of consensus, which can result in loss of momentum
- Potential challenges in Board replacement (e.g., finding candidates)

Hybrid Governance Model

In this model, a Sponsor and other *CCC* decision makers formally establish a Board that then delegates administrative functions to (and provides oversight of) an Administrator. The primary advantage of this type of model is that it provides the best of both worlds, as an Administrator has the ability to act more quickly (and often more flexibly) than a Board, especially for day-to-day operational needs. The primary drawback of the hybrid governance model is that for a relatively small, local *CCC* or one where selection of an Administrator would create undue controversy, a hybrid model may not be necessary or prudent.

Administrator Governance Model

PCCI does not recommend this model for a community *CCC*. The reason for this is that as a single entity, an Administrator should be required to operate within well-defined guidelines for success and accountability. Ideally, those guidelines are determined by a Board (i.e., hybrid model) as a community should not leave governance decisions to a single entity for an initiative of the size and scope of a *CCC*. Other drawbacks include the lack of a variety of perspectives and range of participants. Despite the drawbacks, the overarching Funder contract could potentially govern the *CCC* to such a degree that an Administrator will need to have authority for governance functions. In that circumstance, the Administrator must ensure that its internal policies, processes, and structures are organized to provide an alternate vehicle for resolution of issues. The Administrator must also take special care to solicit and respect community input.

Milestone 1: Identify Governance Requirements

The Funder's requirements (e.g., grant) may provide baseline parameters for the formal governance of your *CCC*. For example, one Funder may require a strict Board model with full *CCC* representation, while others may prefer a hybrid model resulting in a smaller Board and an Administrator. However, despite some baseline requirements, most Funders will allow the Sponsor, Anchor, and Partners some flexibility in choosing certain aspects of the desired governance model.

Because the constellation of *CCC* Partners spans multiple sectors of healthcare (e.g., CBOs; governmental entities; and potentially other community organizations, such as schools, jails, or payers), the creation of a workable governance structure requires deep knowledge of the community and thoughtful input from the Sponsor, Partners, and (likely) other Participants. Moreover, as the local *CCC* grows, its Participants must be open to other governance possibilities that will best meet the needs of the expanded *CCC*. Hence, the chosen governance model should be strong, yet flexible enough to adapt to changes in the environment or in the governance structure in future phases of implementation.

In addition, each organization should reconcile their independent missions with those of the *CCC* to create a shared vision that all of the *CCC* Participants will initially accept, then come to "own" as the *CCC* progresses.

Practically, Participants will need to share responsibilities, accept varying roles, and remain accountable for their part of the *CCC* under the chosen governance model.

While this Playbook covers important considerations and provides recommendations, it does not dictate a particular governance model or resulting governance structure. In addition, this Playbook presumes that requirements and timing for selection of a formal Governance model will vary within and across a community. For example, some communities will utilize an informal governance structure through the readiness assessment process and later move to a more formal governance structure, particularly if required by a Funder. Other communities may establish a formal governance structure at the outset. The important point to keep in mind is that the *CCC* must have some type of established governance structure to ensure accomplishment of the governance requirements.

Key Task: Determine CCC Entity Status

The *CCC* Sponsor or Anchors or Governance Track lead (in conjunction with *CCC* legal counsel and Legal/Policy Track lead) should determine: (1) if the *CCC* should be a separate legal entity organized according to the laws of the state in which it operates and (2) any legal/tax/accounting reasons to choose one form of organization over another. See Chapter 4 Legal/Policy Track Requirement 1.

Key Task: Incorporate Sustainability Factors in Governance Model Selection

The Sponsor or Anchors should work with the *CCC*'s initial Funder, *CCC* legal counsel, and Legal/Policy, Governance, and Program Sustainability Track leads to select the form of governance that is most likely to create favorable conditions for additional fundraising to maintain the *CCC* well into the future. The governance entity can contribute to these efforts by identifying—or tasking others to identify—funding opportunities that align with the *CCC*'s mission. To facilitate this, *CCC* staff should develop impact measures (Return on Investment/Social Return on Investment [ROI/SROI]) and also create a forum for knowledge sharing (both successes and challenges/failures). See also Chapter 8 on Program Sustainability.

The Sponsor or Governance Track lead should also address the need for flexibility as a result of internal changes. For example, the Sponsor should establish a process for efficient Board member replacement if a Board member resigns. Similarly, the Sponsor should consider a mechanism for appointment of an interim Administrator if the initial Administrator is terminated or resigns. It is prudent to plan for other contingencies and maintain a modest emergency fund to ease the *CCC* through unexpected events or to cushion any budget shortfalls or funding gaps. This emergency fund should be budgeted into the scope of *CCC* sponsorship (e.g., 5% of the total award).

Finally, the governance model should also flex to permit change within the *CCC* itself, when warranted. For example, it may make sense to move from a Board model to a hybrid model as the *CCC* gains Participants or complexity. As another example, if a Funder initially requires a combined Sponsor/Administrator, new Funder requirements may provide for these roles to be split. Accordingly, the governance documents should permit easy amendment to accommodate change.

Key Task: Contemplate Local Factors in Model Selection

Individual, local factors may also weigh heavily on the choice for the optimal *CCC* governance model. Obviously, the identity, capabilities, and resources of the Administrator (if applicable) and the composition of (and interactions between) the Board members, as well as the community climate, will directly impact the effectiveness of the governance model chosen. The Sponsor and Governance Track lead should contemplate the health provider competitive landscape within the community, any political affiliations, and timing with respect to local legislative activities. The Sponsor and Governance Track lead should also consider the individual characteristics of potential Board and Administrator candidates within their unique community ecosystem.

Milestone 2: Analyze Funding Documents to Identify Governance Parameters and Ensure Compliance

Once the Governance requirements are identified, the next step is to analyze the funding documents, contracts, and policies/procedures to construct the necessary documents addressing the identified governance requirements and issues.

The funding documents (whether a government entity cooperative agreement, grant from a private philanthropic organization, or another arrangement), along with state law, are likely to provide the baseline *CCC* requirements. The Governance Track lead will review these requirements in conjunction with the Legal/Policy Track lead and *CCC* legal counsel, Partners, and Sponsor. This Playbook assumes that an initial Funder may set expectations about the *CCC's* purpose and establish some requirements (e.g., minimum number of patients served, minimum numbers of clinical providers to participate) but otherwise will give the Partners and Sponsor broad latitude to determine how to best meet the requirements without mandating particular legal forms.

Funding documents may contain both positive requirements (e.g., at least 100 patients per quarter must be referred from clinical providers to CBOs) and negative prohibitions (e.g., no funds may be spent for referral to affiliates of religious organizations that discriminate on the basis of sex or religion). The Governance Track lead (working with the Legal/Policy Track lead) may find it helpful to chart all of the requirements and prohibitions to ensure that they are all addressed in the governance documents.

Milestone 3: Obtain Partner Commitments Not Previously Obtained during the Readiness Assessment

Some Funders require, as a condition of an award (either explicitly or as a practical matter to be a successful bidder), that the Sponsor or initial decision makers have commitments from a number of clinical and CBO Partners. Many Sponsors and Funders will want to obtain these commitments (e.g., MOU)—even if not legally binding—before they commit their own resources. This may occur early in the initial planning stages or during the *CCC* readiness assessment process. But if it has not occurred at that time, PCCI recommends that you obtain these commitments before creating any formal governance structure because Participants may request, or even demand, to be involved in *CCC* governance.

Key Documents for Requirement 2

- Funder's Request for Proposal (RFP) providing *CCC* requirements, including technology/security specifications (may include technology certification requirements). Given the funder-specific nature of an RFP, we have not included an example in the key documents section of this book.

Requirement 3: Set Up the Formal Governance Structure

Once the *CCC* decision makers and Governance Track lead have selected the governance model, they will then set up the governance structure through the following actions.

Milestone 1: Draft and Finalize Governance Documents

The Governance Track lead will work with the Legal/Policy Track lead and *CCC* legal counsel, who will draft the appropriate governance documents. For example, these could consist of: (1) bylaws for a Board to serve as the *CCC*'s governing body or (2) internal policies, processes, and structures for the Administrator to provide the same governance functions that a Board would otherwise provide. The Governance Track lead will provide input to the *CCC* attorneys on factors such as: (1) staggered terms for Board members, succession planning, and functional cross-training within the Administrator; (2) provisions for replacement of departing Board members and transitions of Administrator employees and subcontractors; (3) a means to replace derelict Board members or poorly performing Administrator employees/subcontractors; and (4) winding-up provisions in the event the *CCC* is acquired, becomes administered by a different Sponsor, obtains different funding that sets far different parameters, or terminates at the end of a funding period.

The Board and any associated entities should meet often enough to maintain ties and handle business promptly but not so often as to overburden members. PCCI suggests revisiting the bylaws, elections/appointments, and the meeting schedule for the next year periodically or at least during the last meeting of each calendar year to ensure that any needed changes are promptly implemented.

In addition to the legal requirements to observe corporate formalities, as a matter of good practice, PCCI encourages all types of governance entities within the *CCC* to retain agendas and to keep detailed minutes so that Participants can readily identify decisions made, issues analyzed, and work completed. This helps minimize waste of Participants' time, which in turn may deepen their commitment.

CAVEAT: *While PCCI presumes Board governance in most instances, this Playbook does not provide legal advice on the appropriate corporate form (or lack thereof) that your community CCC should take nor does it provide advice about the tax consequences of particular forms of funding* *or governance. The governance entity should periodically review the CCC's progress with its legal counsel and tax advisor in order to determine if its corporate form should be modified or to make an affirmative decision that the current form is adequate.*

Key Task: Consider Conflicts of Interest

The Governance Track lead, working with the Legal/Policy Track lead and *CCC* legal counsel, should approve conflicts of interest policies, disclosure forms, and conflicts management plans for Board or Administrator employees and subcontractors to sign and follow. The conflicts of interest policy should address actual or perceived conflicts that not only apply to Board members and Administrator employees/subcontractors (if applicable) but that also extend to their family members and business partners. PCCI recommends that Board members and Administrator employees/subcontractors and their family members and business partners be prohibited from operating as a *CCC* vendor, absent disclosures of all relevant financial interests, and subsequent Board approval. Because it is likely that a Board member or Administrator may have at least apparent or perceived conflicts, it is important to require disclosure of those conflicts and to develop and adhere to a conflicts management plan that typically requires refraining from voting or trying to influence decisions that may affect the conflicted party or that party's family members or business interests. These conflicts of interest policies may extend to members of the Clinical Advisory Group or Workgroups, as applicable.

Key Task: Define Criteria for Board Selection and Service

Assuming some type of Board governance is selected, the Governance Track lead should determine Board service criteria that may include the following:

- Representation of the major Participants, such as the Sponsor, Funder, and Partners
- Later representation of non-stakeholders (may not be desirable but should be considered as a way to provide new perspectives and to obtain future funding)
- Representation of Administrator (if Hybrid governance model is selected)
- Representation of the patients and community residents (e.g., patient advocate)

- Inclusion of historically underrepresented constituents
- Capabilities and resources desired from Board members
- Consideration of each candidate's potential contributions to *CCC* operations
- Ability of the candidates to work together and to make timely decisions

The Board is most effective when it includes the top-level clinical leaders who represent key clinical *CCC* stakeholder Partners and who are decision makers within their respective organizations. This is important because at times, the Board will require Partners to make difficult decisions or changes. The clinical leaders will further leverage their organizational teams (including mid-level clinical leaders) to define and implement the clinical aspects of the *CCC*'s evaluation and supervisory framework.

PCCI strongly recommends that the Sponsor or other initial decision makers limit the Board size to five to seven Partners or (if larger) that the Sponsor give a very small executive committee (three to five Partners) authority to make necessary decisions related to operational oversight and performance measurement. This action would eliminate some of the drawbacks to the Board model previously described. While a larger Board may foster inclusion, it can quickly become unworkable as a means to efficiently govern the *CCC*. The Sponsor should consider other means to ensure that all stakeholders are included, such as: "term limited" and relatively brief (3- to 4-year) Board terms, advisory and consultative groups, appointment of non-Board members to Board-based Workgroups or subcommittees, and other methods of inclusion that have worked in the community.

PRACTICE POINTER

Create a CCC *Board Charter*

While not legally required, PCCI recommends that the governance entity (e.g., Board) consider developing a document that sets forth the reasons for undertaking the *CCC*. This document should include the *CCC*'s high-level goals, vision, and any other principles that all Participants should be mindful of whenever governance issues arise. This inspirational document can take the form of a Charter, a Statement of Principles, a *CCC* Constitution, or some similarly titled document that provides a quick reference. All Participants should become deeply familiar with this "know your why" statement because knowing and understanding it will be helpful in maintaining focus and in maintaining (and seeking) funding to sustain and extend the *CCC*.

Key Task: Consider Intellectual Property and Insurance Needs

Early in the process, the Governance Track lead (working with legal counsel) should determine if Intellectual Property (IP) protections are needed for patentable or copyrightable or trademarked materials arising from the *CCC* operations. The Governance Track lead should also consider what types of insurance are appropriate for the *CCC*, Sponsor, vendors, and Partners. The Governance Track lead should regularly ensure that the *CCC* and its constituent entities have appropriate coverage and that circumstances have not changed to the degree that additional insurance requirements should be imposed on vendors and Participants. Examples of insurance include the following:

- Director and officers (primarily for Board member issues arising in the course of *CCC* work)
- Professional liability/errors and omissions (primarily for vendors)
- Cyber liability (covering data breaches)
- Workers' compensation (if the *CCC* as an entity has employees)
- Comprehensive general liability (provides general coverage)
- Umbrella (if additional coverage is desired above underlying policies)

Milestone 2: Create Workgroups

PCCI recommends creation of one or more Workgroups to supplement the role of the Board and Administrator. A Workgroup is generally made up of committed Partners/Participants, but it may also include community residents or patients. A Workgroup is Board approved to work on any number of *CCC* topics (e.g., sustainability, best practice dissemination, funding) and can extend for the life of *CCC* or be time- or issue-limited. A Workgroup may have a formal mission statement or charter that is separate from that of the Board or it may be more loosely organized. Workgroups made up solely of Board members are sometimes referred to as a Board subcommittee. It is recommended that Workgroups, at a minimum, create agendas and minutes for their meetings in order to document issues identified, discussed, and resolved. Performing these tasks will provide the "institutional memory" that is critical to maintain momentum when inevitable changes in personnel occur. If there is wide community interest to serve on the governance body (e.g., Board), the Sponsor may wish to consider fairly short, staggered terms, with service on a Workgroup a prerequisite to governing body appointment or election.

Even if not required, the creation of one or more Workgroups is likely to receive a positive reception because it provides a vehicle for stakeholder input, promotes a feeling of broader ownership of the *CCC*, enables the sharing of best practices among Participants, serves as a means to surface and resolve disputes informally, and creates a vehicle for positive publicity and sharing of *CCC* success. Additionally, if the Board anticipates a significant need to create momentum in a particular area or believes that Partners need separate sharing vehicles, the Board can establish Workgroups specifically for these purposes (e.g., Medical Records/Health Information Management Working Group, CBO Collaborative, Council of Community, *CCC* Clinical Providers, *CCC* Funding Champions).

A Workgroup can also promote more efficient *CCC* governance. For example, a governing Board of five to seven Partners is typical for a *CCC*. If the local ecosystem requires a larger Board, then a Workgroup made up of a subset of *CCC* Partner Board members can provide some efficiency in decision-making on specific issues. If a larger Board is required, the Sponsor or initial steering group should also contemplate creation of various Workgroups arranged around functional duties, affinities, and purposes within the overall Board. For example, the *CCC* might establish a large Board but have a three-member Workgroup (made up of Board members) with decision-making authority for all but the most critical issues. It is common to establish: (1) an Audit or Finance Workgroup for reception and review of audit reports and financial oversight responsibility, (2) a Technology Advisory Workgroup to oversee the technical development of the *CCC*, and (3) a Compensation and Employee Affairs Workgroup to provide performance reviews of *CCC* executives.

Some communities may also find that affinity-based Workgroups, such as a Community Services Workgroup are well received and provide the members with opportunities to network and to share best practices. Finally, in some circumstances, it may be helpful to establish specific, purpose-driven Workgroups, such as Philanthropic Relations or Public Relations, to assure that the Board's overall direction for the *CCC* is provided in a meaningful way. In the rare circumstance where a single Administrator is providing the governance function, PCCI recommends that the Sponsor or steering group consider all these related functions as it creates the *CCC* internal processes, policies, and structures to incorporate external input and resources.

Key Task: Consider Frequency of Workgroup Reporting

The Governance Track lead should consider how often and in what format the Workgroups (including each related entity) should report to the Board (or Administrator) and include these details in the Board Resolutions and Charter (or similar vehicles). For all Workgroups, the Governance Track lead may want to determine whether to create specific or broad Charters. For example, for Workgroups that are created for a very specific purpose (e.g., kickoff funding, Health Insurance Portability and Accountability Act [HIPAA] policy reviews), the lead should consider whether to create Charters providing for dissolution of the entities upon resolution of the specific issues they were created to address or whether the Charters should be more broadly drafted so that the entity can continue to support the *CCC*. If the latter is desired, then the Governance Track lead should take that into account. For example, instead of a "Kick-off Funding Workgroup," the Governance Track lead could establish a "*CCC* Funding and Sustainability Workgroup."

PRACTICE POINTER

Consider Ways to Encourage Workgroup Commitment

Because membership and participation on a Workgroup may be voluntary, consider ways to encourage participation. For example, rather than asking potential Workgroup members to sign a "Workgroup Agreement," you could call the participation document "Workgroup Guidelines." You will still obtain an acknowledgment of expectations, but the commitment is appropriately softened given the nature of Workgroup membership.

Key Documents for Requirement 3

- *CCC* Board Charter
- Mission Statement/Statement of Purpose
- Prioritized List of *CCC*-Supported Clinical Programs and Targeted Goals
- Disclosure of Personal Conflicts Forms (see Chapter 4 Legal/Policy Track)
- Conflicts Management Plan (see Chapter 4 Legal/Policy Track)

Requirement 4: Define an Aligned, Comprehensive CCC Strategy

The demonstration (to stakeholders and the community) of the *CCC*'s value is pivotal to successful and sustainable *CCC* implementation. Strong outcomes will be critical to soliciting future funding sources and ongoing participant interest. To ensure effective and successful *CCC* implementation, it is important to define (pre-launch) a data-informed comprehensive strategy that is aligned for all Participants, community needs, and overall *CCC* goals. While the targeted clinical conditions and goals should have been identified in the readiness assessment, the Partners (and the Board) will need to sign off on a comprehensive and aligned *CCC* strategy.

The Partners will determine the *CCC* outcome measures and other information to be collected (and in what timeframes) prior to the *CCC* launch. The governance entity and Governance Track lead will also need to set target goals and update these goals as the *CCC* expands. This will ensure longevity and future funding (see Chapter 8 Program Sustainability).

Milestone 1: Establish CCC Target Goals and Evaluation Periods

A *CCC*'s success will be evaluated based on its ability to meet its goals. The goals may vary in their scope and range, from global *CCC* goals based on the intention and the purpose of the *CCC* to specific programmatic goals. Across these levels of performance, target goals should be defined as the change the *CCC* will aim to achieve in a specific goal-related measure through each Participant's use of the *CCC* (e.g., 25% increase from baseline), within a given time period.

This performance measurement approach requires the *CCC* governance entity to define the baseline and evaluation periods for any intervention:

- The baseline period will follow the initial 3 months through 12 of year 1, or some other timeframe during which Participants' history will be assessed. This data will provide a baseline for comparison of outcomes before and after *CCC* implementation.
- The implementation/evaluation period generally covers months 4 through 12 from the local *CCC* launch. During the first 3 months of the process, however, system changes will be introduced and implemented. During these 3 months, variability in usage of the *CCC* will arise due to training new users, changes in workflow, and phased rollout of

new technical functionalities, making data inconsistent and, therefore, invalid. As a result, data collected during this 3-month period should not be evaluated.

During the baseline and evaluation periods, each performance measure should be defined and calculated using a proportion representing the population evaluated. For example:

Denominator. The denominator includes the specific population of interest relevant to the measure. For example, the denominator for measure 1.a., clinical diabetes (ICD9 code 250.xx), would include all adult patients diagnosed with diabetes that have received services at both a clinical Partner clinic and a CBO.

Numerator. The numerator includes the population of interest that has met the criteria for the evaluation target. For example, for measure 1.a., clinical diabetes, the numerator encompasses all the patients that are included in the denominator who have had at least one A1c test result posted in the Electronic Health Record (EHR). Together, the numerator and denominator define how each outcome measure will be calculated.

Milestone 2: Define CCC Measures of Success

Based on the defined *CCC* target goals, the governance entity should thoughtfully select measures to evaluate *CCC* performance and its impact on the members of the community (i.e., patients/clients). These measures should be refined and updated over time based on the addition of Participants and overall *CCC* growth. Selection of a limited scope of initial measures is most feasible and allows focus on the ones with the greatest impact and value. As technical functionalities are enhanced, the network of Partners expands, and utilization of the *CCC* advances, the scope of measurable outcomes should also expand. As the targets are evaluated and potentially achieved during the initial implementation phase, *CCC* leadership should propose additional outcome measures and evaluation targets for future phases of implementation.

Key Task: Consider Criteria for Measure Selection

The Governance Track lead should take the following criteria into account when selecting measures for the *CCC*:

- *Accessibility.* The measures should be easily understood by all stake-holders (e.g., % of people in your community who transitioned out of homelessness within the past 12 months). Accessible measures not only serve as a common reference frame for all Partners but also facilitate dissemination of knowledge and positive marketing of outcomes. A good litmus test of a measure's accessibility is whether the measure would make sense in a headline of the front page of your community's newspaper.
- *Causality.* Accessibility of the measure should be determined in the context of a measure's ability to offer proof of causality. The measure should reflect a logical argument for the mission and efforts of your *CCC* relative to the overall community well-being. The closer the measure to the actual outcome, the easier it will be for the stakehold-ers to understand and accept it. For example, the percentage of clinical Partners who have undergone quality improvement activities in the last 12 months is not an effective measure to demonstrate that the *CCC* was responsible for a decline in community homelessness.
- *Feasibility.* While a measure may be desirable and easy to understand, it may be prohibitively difficult to actually obtain the data to calculate the measure. Once the *CCC* technology platform is fully implemented and adopted, more complex measurements may be made. Until then, PCCI recommends that you operate conservatively and define mea-sures supported by the data available through the initial phase of your technology implementation or through your Partners under the existing data-sharing agreements (e.g., A1c testing at least once per year among patients with diabetes can be extracted from Epic).
- *Relevancy.* Selected measures need to align with the existing standards and strategic goals (e.g., clinical and community Partners, national initia-tives). Data and measure alignment unite a community. And defining measures relevant to Partners outside of the *CCC* work builds engage-ment and enhances the accuracy of the data. As such, measures should demonstrate significant impact on patient health, functional status, and the healthcare system (e.g., A1c testing is indicator for adequate medical attention for diabetes management).

- *Credibility.* The measures should demonstrate impact on a high volume of patients/clients (e.g., large patient volume with diabetes). This is an important consideration for an innovative undertaking. Your ability to lend credence to your measurement by adopting a sound, standardized measurement discipline will enable you to publish your findings and generate positive exposure among lucrative partners and funding sources. As possible, the measures should also allow for comparison with national benchmarks.

PRACTICE POINTER

Use Data to Tell the CCC Story

The ability to tell the "story" of your *CCC* is critical to its sustainability and expansion. Qualitative accounts are important, but the data and the evidence-based demonstration of the effect that your programs have on reducing community problems are a must. When defining the measures for your programs, always approach this exercise with two questions: (1) "What value is this program bringing to my community" and (2) "What is my ROI for this program"? The first question will guide the formulation of qualitative evidence of your success, while the latter will steer you towards the quantitative evidence that Sponsors, key stakeholders, and your Partners will pay greatest attention to (and leverage) in making their strategic decisions.

The *CCC* governance entity should also consider whether to set hard objectives that must be reached as a condition of further funding to a Participant. While difficult in the short run, this accountability may encourage best efforts and avoid the demoralizing effect of lackluster Participants creating a drag on the program's momentum. Each governance entity (e.g., Board) meeting should also include a discussion of funding pipeline progress to maintain emphasis on the importance of ongoing funding to sustain the *CCC*.

Key Task: Consider Categories of Measure Selection

Three measure levels made up of six different categories of measures should be considered in evaluating a *CCC*. These categories have a hierarchical relationship and reflect the overall *CCC* framework (see Figure 3.2 demonstrating the proposed framework with example measures).

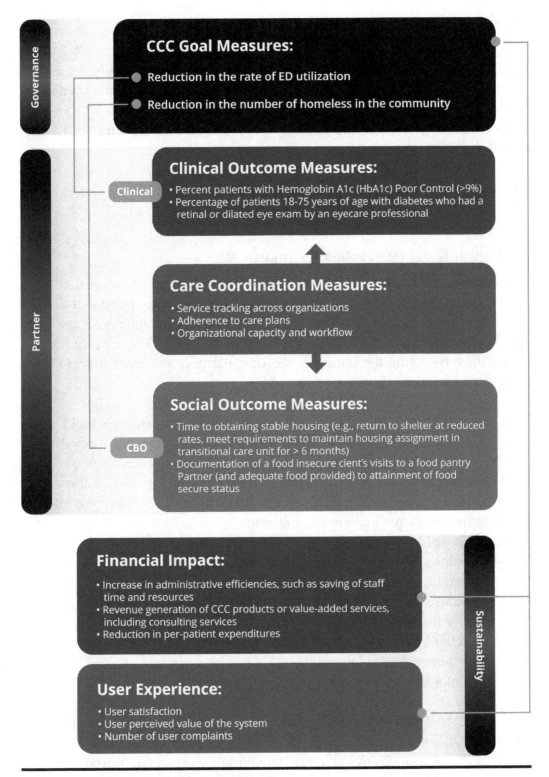

Figure 3.2   CCC Measurement Framework.

Global CCC Measures

At the highest level of this measurement framework are the global *CCC* measures. These serve as gauges of the *CCC*'s effectiveness in attaining its goals. As such, these measures should directly reflect the *CCC*'s mission statement and defined goals. These measures will be most relevant to the *CCC* governance entity, media, and the public. Examples of global *CCC* measures include the following:

- Reduction of ED utilization in the community
- Reduction of homelessness in the community

CCC Programs and Intervention Measures

The next level of the measurement framework is made up of measures that track *CCC* programs and interventions and roll up into the global *CCC* measures and, as such, reflect the effectiveness of specific interventions and programs designed to achieve the overall *CCC* goals. These categories of measures, reflecting the efforts of the *CCC* Partners and their success in aligning on the joint effort, are:

- *Clinical Outcome Measures.* The clinical outcome measures should map to the targeted clinical conditions of the *CCC* (e.g., diabetes, Congestive Heart Failure [CHF]), as determined in the readiness assessment. These measures will be determined as part of development of the clinical measures for the *CCC* as described below. Examples of clinical outcome measures include the following:
  Congestive Heart Failure (CHF):
  - All-cause 30-day risk-standardized mortality rate following heart failure hospitalization
  - All-cause 30-day risk-standardized readmission rate following heart failure hospitalization
  - Number of patients with a CHF diagnosis who have documented counseling for the following:
    - Smoking status/cessation activity level
    - Diet
    - CHF medications, weight monitoring, follow-up appointment
- *Social Outcome Measures.* The *CCC*'s value is also demonstrated through social measures directly benefiting clients in CBO programs. Measures that are common across CBO Partners should be identified,

examined, and defined, where possible. These measures will be determined as part of the CBO strategy for the *CCC*. Examples of social outcome measures include the following:

- Time to obtain stable housing (e.g., return to shelter at reduced rates, meet requirements to maintain housing assignment in transitional care unit for >6 months)
- Achievement of reporting requirements to funding agencies, such as Department of Housing and Urban Development (HUD) and the United Way
- Documentation of a food insecure client's visits to a food pantry Partner, and adequate food provided, to attainment of food secure status

• *Care Coordination Measures.* A properly functioning *CCC* will remove many of the barriers hindering current care coordination efforts by creating a network that prevents patients from falling through the gaps in the system. As such, the care coordination measures really serve as a proxy of the established *CCC* connectivity (e.g., transfers of discharge summaries that can facilitate service delivery). Typically, these measures are common to the Partner organizations. Examples of care coordination measures include the following:

- Service tracking across organizations:
  • Tracking of referrals across organizations (such as the number of referrals made or the number of referrals achieved)
  • Discharge summaries passed and received
  • Client tracking across organizations
  • Medication lists received post discharge
- Care delivery and adherence to care plan:
  • Increases in medication adherence rate
  • Increases in medication adherence and management follow-up appointment show rates
  • Increases in the total appointments achieved
  • Increases in provision of standardized treatment appointment adherence and follow-up
  • Reductions in missed appointments
  • Reductions in utilization, such as the number of ED, urgent care, or unscheduled visits
- Organizational capacity and workflow:
  • Changes in service delivery (e.g., time saved from real-time *CCC* communication methods vs. phone/fax communication)

- Measures of capacity building, such as shared community vision/mission, strong leadership structure, and organizational flexibility

The clinical and social outcomes measures and care coordination measures should be designed to roll up into—and drive—the global *CCC* measures. The global *CCC* measures in turn provide an estimate of how well the *CCC* is achieving its purpose.

Return on Investment and Social Return on Investment Measures

The last level of measures should address the downstream, lasting effects of your *CCC*. These categories should address ROI and SROI and the overall value of the *CCC* efforts to the community residents from a consumer perspective. These measures, driven by the global *CCC* measures, are the ones that will be most relevant to ensuring the sustainability of the *CCC*, both from a financial and client engagement perspective:

- *Financial Outcome Measures.* The governance entity will determine the financial measures that help to support the sustainability model by demonstrating one of the anticipated cost savings aspects resulting from meaningful use of *CCC*. Examples of financial measures include the following:
  - Health expense avoidance, such as reductions in all-cause readmission rate or duplication of services
  - Greater financial accountability, such as providing more services per dollar or serving more patients/clients per dollar
  - Cost savings from a reduction in duplication of services
  - Increase in administrative efficiencies, such as saving of staff time and resources
  - Revenue generation of *CCC* products or value-added services, including consulting services
  - Reduction in per-patient expenditures
- *User Experience Measures.* Measures that define the user perspective, as user satisfaction is critical to adoption (and meaningful use) of the *CCC*. Examples of user experience measures include the following:
  - User satisfaction
  - User perceived value of the system (i.e., willingness to recommend)
  - Number of user complaints

Key Task: Define the Clinical Measures for the CCC

The clinical and CBO Partners that are members of the Clinical Advisory Group or Board, as applicable, perform the work in this Task. Mid-level Partner leaders and those who are experienced in quantitative and qualitative data collection and analysis may also perform required actions.

The clinical Partners will need to review: (1) sources of best clinical practices, clinical quality metrics, and evidence-based guidelines; (2) local, regional, and national policy affecting the operations and finances of clinical entities; and (3) community-level clinical data to identify areas of shortcomings. The following measures should then be established based on the prioritized clinical targets and aligned strategic goals from the readiness assessment:

- *Key Clinical Outcome Measures for the CCC* based on the aligned strategic goals. Examples could include the following:
  - The change in hemoglobin A1c levels among diabetic patients in the past 12 months
  - % poor control (A1c > 9.0%)
  - % in control (A1c < 7.0%–8.0%)
  - The change in all-cause hospital readmission rates after (vs. before) *CCC* implementation
  - The community-level prevalence of diabetes after (vs. before) *CCC* implementation
- *Key Clinical Process Measures for the CCC* based on the aligned strategic goals. Examples could include the following:
  - The number of diabetic individuals screened for food insecurity on the *CCC* technology platform at a given hospital clinic within a defined time period
  - The number of hospital referrals completed through the *CCC* within a defined time period in order to address a specific social need (e.g., food insecurity)
  - The percentage of individuals with CHF referred through the *CCC* to a housing agency within the past 12 months, and who now have permanent housing
- *Key Financial ROI Measures* relevant to clinical operations and based on the *CCC* aligned strategic goals. Examples could include the following:
  - Net cost savings generated per patient per year related to reductions in all-cause ED visits

- Reduction in the total care costs per capita
- Ratio of cost of provision of community services relative to the realized savings in care costs due to avoided adverse events (ED visits, readmissions)

- *Key Patient-Centered Outcome Measures*, which are typically measured using validated instruments for self-reported patient outcomes. Examples could include the following:
  - Quality of life scores
  - Chronic pain scores
  - Other scores/means for symptom monitoring or disease severity assessment

Key Task: Define the CBO Measures for the CCC

While the *CCC* model is driven by the clinical programs designed to meet its goals, the *CCC* emphasizes that clinical programs alone are not sufficient to achieve the desired levels of health and wellness in your community. Just as the CBO programs are designed to support the clinical programs, the CBO measures should demonstrate: (1) connectivity between the clinical and community settings of care and (2) extension of clinical workflows into the CBO workflows. To design these measures, CBO Partners need to fully understand the proposed clinical programs and the associated workflows and define how these workflows will be supported in the community setting. The following measures should then be established based on the prioritized clinical targets and aligned strategic goals from the readiness assessment.

- *Key Community Outcome Measures for the CCC* based on the aligned strategic goals. Examples could include the following:
  - The number of unique social needs resolved as a result of the CBO intervention
  - The number of patients indicating a reduction in identified needs (measures created per relevant/targeted needs as identified through the readiness assessment)
- *Key Community Process Measures for the CCC* based on the aligned strategic goals. Examples could include the following:
  - The number of patients accepted as referrals from the clinical sites (measure per site)
  - The number of patients referred to a clinical site from a CBO (measure per referral to clinical site and as an aggregate)

– The range and average latency between creation of the referral and patient making it to their referral

– Percentage of referrals made among CBOs for needs identified at clinical Partner sites

- *Key SROI measures* relevant to community operations and based on the *CCC* aligned strategic goals. Examples could include the following:
  – Improvement in the selection of food choices by patients
  – Changes in the crime rate of the community
  – Changes in self-reported missed school days or missed work days for a specific patient population

- *Key Patient-Centered Outcome Measures*, like the clinical patient-centered outcome measures, are typically measured using validated instruments for self-reported patient outcomes. This set of measures, while somewhat tailored to the specific type of provider (clinical vs. community), should be standardized as much as possible and used across your *CCC* (e.g., during a clinical encounter and any CBO encounter). Examples of these measures could include the following:
  – Quality of life scores
  – Satisfaction with services received at CBOs
  – Increased mobility levels
  – Reduction in stress levels

Milestone 3: Define the CCC Evaluation Framework Supervisory and Advisory Support

The efficacy of any evaluation or performance measurement framework is dependent upon the quality (i.e., accuracy and consistency) of the data collected through the defined set of measures. *CCC* is a multilayered initiative with measures spanning in scope from the global *CCC* metrics to program-specific ones. To ensure that the *CCC* is advancing towards its defined goals, it is critical to implement a QA framework for data collection. Appropriate, dedicated resources should be assigned to carry out the QA activities both at the Partner level as well as at the broader *CCC* level. PCCI recommends assigning oversight of clinical performance and data collection to resources already familiar with the clinical operations. This same approach should be used for tracking CBO performance. The higher-level oversight should be performed by the Anchor organizations, ensuring compliance from both sets of Partners (clinical and CBO) and aligning their performance measurement with the global *CCC* goals.

The following are some general principles to follow in setting up a QA framework:

- The clinical Partners should direct the *CCC*'s clinical aspects while CBO Partners should direct the community aspects.
- The Participants must collect the appropriate data and monitor relevant outcomes.
- The Participants must promptly identify—and address—gaps in *CCC* performance.
- The Participant leaders must ensure that the *CCC* yields optimal impact in the community.

Key Task: Define Processes for CCC Supervisory and Advisory Support

The Clinical Advisory Group members and designated Workgroups should develop processes that accomplish the following:

- Clearly define roles and resources for the processes and outcomes measurement.
- Define frequency for process and outcomes monitoring and reporting.
- Conduct gap analyses/QA and periodic reviews of collected data and measures to monitor progress and identify operational issues that could impact the outcomes measured.
- Determine frequency for the gap analysis/QA activities and clearly define standard operating procedures (SOPs) for addressing any uncovered gaps. These should include the following:
  - Expected time for resolution
  - Defined chain of command, roles, and communication protocols for addressing identified measurement gaps with Partner organizations
  - Remediation steps including any additional training or certification activities
  - Proposed and supported corrective actions at the leadership level

Under one example from the Dallas IEP, a biweekly review of performance metrics indicated suboptimal numbers of referrals (relative to defined target goals) to CBOs on the *CCC* technology platform. Upon review, the Clinical Advisory Group concluded that the deficiency resulted from an insufficient number of patients screened for social needs at a particular clinic.

The Clinical Advisory Group reached out to the leaders of the clinic to perform a root cause analysis. The clinic identified the root cause of the problem and, working with the Clinical Advisory Group, collaboratively designed and implemented appropriate corrective actions, resulting in increased referrals to CBOs.

Key Documents for Requirement 4

- *CCC* Evaluation Framework, which is typically a narrative document highlighted by illustrative diagrams, such as the Input-Process-Output-Outcome diagrams or equivalent graphics for quick reference (see Figure 3.2 and the Evaluation Measures Key Document)

Requirement 5: Select Clinical Programs

The purpose of this Requirement is to create and prioritize a strategic list of programs and interventions to address the top targeted clinical problems identified in the readiness assessment. The clinical Partner leaders who are members of the Clinical Advisory Group will generally lead the work and include mid-level clinical leaders and clinical Participant data scientists (or similar roles, meaning those who are experienced in quantitative and qualitative data collection and analysis). Finally, the clinical leaders may bring in external subject-matter experts/consultants.

Milestone 1: Prioritize the Clinical Needs Based on the Estimated Impact of Interventions on the CCC Goals

The readiness assessment will have defined the most pressing clinical needs within your community, along with demographic data and community services utilization data. To formulate an effective strategy for the *CCC*, the Clinical Advisory Group needs to determine which clinical needs to address and in what sequence and then define the programs to address them. The following describes suggested steps to take to accomplish this:

- It is first important to understand the scope of the clinical needs within your community. Identify the target populations for each clinical need using data from the readiness assessment and medical claims data from the clinical Partner organizations. If medical claims data from a Health Information Exchange (HIE) or state claims database is not available, analysis of historic Centers for Medicare and Medicaid Services (CMS) data should be sufficient.
- For each target population, identify its current size, estimated growth rate, demographics, income levels, community resources available, and utilization of clinical services by the residents.
- Analysis of the medical claims data will provide an estimate of the cost of care to the target populations based on the global and key clinical *CCC* outcome metrics defined during the measure framework creation effort (e.g., ED utilization rate and associated cost of unnecessary utilization; readmission rates for the target population).
- Evaluate which resources, assets, and strategic partnerships are already in place and can be leveraged to implement each proposed clinical program. The clinical leadership team should take an inventory of any existing

interventions that are currently underway within the community (or have been previously undertaken) addressing the *CCC* goals or certain aspects of those goals.

- Develop a sensitivity table indicating the range of potential impact on the key *CCC* clinical measures (e.g., assuming 1%, 3%, and 5% reduction in ED utilization by diabetic patients, what is the estimated savings to your clinical Partners) for each of the target populations. Identify which clinical needs should be addressed first based on the greatest impact on the *CCC* goals (i.e., rank the needs in order).
- Compare the strategic goals of the clinical Partners with the prioritized clinical needs and then reprioritize, if necessary, based on the alignment of the respective strategic goals. This step is fundamental to successful engagement of foundational Partners. Engaging clinical Partners to adopt or create clinical programs that are not aligned with the Partner's strategic direction is likely to result in ineffective Partner participation and performance.

Milestone 2: Identify and Define the Clinical CCC Interventions

The *CCC* clinical leadership team should perform the following tasks:

- *Conduct Literature and Best Practice Reviews.* These reviews should identify potential interventions that can address the prioritized clinical needs of your community.
- *Compare Previous Efforts with Identified Literature-Based Interventions.* Convene the key stakeholders in a set of work sessions to determine how to leverage the identified (or preexisting) interventions to address the *CCC* goals and to drive the defined outcome measures. Include in this effort both the clinical and community staff members that lead current efforts (or led prior efforts) to learn what was done, how it was done, the outcomes, the lessons learned, and the resources/collateral generated from the work.
- *Define Clinical Interventions.* Once the clinical Partner leaders have the comprehensive understanding of best practices, the existing efforts in the community, and prior efforts to address the prioritized clinical needs, these leaders are positioned to define the interventions they feel would be appropriate to address those needs. These interventions may be simple adjustments or enhancements to existing efforts based on lessons learned from prior implementation efforts. Conversely, the

community may require a fundamentally new way to approach the clinical needs—one that aligns with best practices and has demonstrated efficacy on a smaller scale.

PRACTICE POINTER

Avoid Extensive, Prescriptive Definition of Your CCC's Clinical Programs

It is important to recognize that each clinical and CBO site (vital to the success of your interventions) will have its own, unique workflows and operating procedures. Defining a set of global SOPs may lead to pushback and some need for rework, as each site will have to incorporate some of their own procedures to meet the defined goals and implement the required interventions.

- *Define the Role of CBOs in Executing the Clinical Interventions.* The CBOs play a vital role in supporting the *CCC* clinical interventions. The *CCC* clinical Partner leaders will need to work closely with their CBO counterparts to clearly identify the roles, responsibilities, and accountability of CBO and clinical Partners for each intervention. We recommend the leaders conduct a RACI (Responsible, Accountable, Consult, Inform)[7] analysis and develop a corresponding chart/matrix. Just as with the initial definition of the clinical interventions, the definition and the scope of CBO involvement should include taking an inventory of any existing interventions that are currently underway within the CBOs (or have been previously undertaken) that relate to the *CCC* goals. PCCI recommends leveraging use cases identified in the readiness assessment to help define the interventions and CBO roles.

  For example, in the Dallas IEP, one community identified a use case applicable to CHF, an identified targeted clinical condition. In this use case, a homeless man with CHF was discharged from a community hospital at 3 pm. The patient was given a prescription for a diuretic, which was crucial to managing his CHF symptoms. However, the patient had to get in line at the Salvation Army by 4 pm to get a bed for the night. The patient had to decide whether to choose a bed or whether to get in line at the pharmacy for the medication. Based on this use case, the clinical and CBO Partner leaders determined that the Partner CBO sites would commit to modifying their existing workflows to receive information about similar patients through the *CCC* technology platform and then conduct additional referrals/interventions to enable the patient to receive both a bed and the necessary medication.

PRACTICE POINTER

Use Subject-Matter Experts as Evaluators

It can be extremely useful to include subject-matter experts (internal or external) as third-party evaluators as the clinical leaders design the clinical interventions.

Milestone 3: Select the Clinical and CBO Participant Sites

The governance entity and Governance Track lead should select the Partner/Participant clinical and CBO sites given that the guiding principles for site selection are driven by the *CCC*'s strategic goals and clinical programs.

The governance entity and Governance Track lead (with the support from business and data analysts, research leads, and others as appropriate) should perform the following actions in finalizing site selections:

- Identify clinical and CBO sites that serve the defined target populations.
- Perform a high-level (qualitative) analysis of which sites are best to include based on their level of need, strategic direction, engagement in similar initiatives, and *CCC* engagement. Obtain input from the respective sites' leadership or internal subject-matter experts.
- Work with each of the "shortlisted" sites to obtain their data in order to determine patient volumes, demographics, service utilization and cost, and overlap with the *CCC* catchment area.
- Analyze the data to determine opportunities for optimal intervention impact. For example, determine which sites have the greatest volume of the targeted population, the maximum costs opportunity, and the greatest opportunity for effective interventions.
- Translate the analysis of data provided by the clinical and CBO sites into "targets and expectations" with clearly defined performance targets for each site based on the estimated site productivity (e.g., number of patients screened or navigated per year per clinical site, number of clients served at a food pantry per year).

PRACTICE POINTER

Initially Target High-Impact Clinical Sites

Clinical program success often depends on the relationships that are in place with the clinical Partners. Certain criteria utilized in selecting clinical sites, such as culture and leadership buy-in, are not evident from a quantitative site analysis. Guidance and direction from strong senior leadership, coupled with a frontline culture built upon flexibility and problem-solving, will optimize the adoption of *CCC* workflows. As a result, PCCI recommends that the *CCC* governance entity and Governance Track lead initially select fewer—but high-impact—sites, meaning sites with a strong culture, leadership buy-in, and level of engagement. This will enable faster and more effective initial *CCC* implementation and success, which in turn will assist efforts to convince lower-impact sites (meaning those without strong leadership buy-in and a strong frontline culture) to join the effort, if needed.

CBO Participant selection is driven directly by the *CCC* goals and desired program outcomes. In addition, the categories and nature of CBO provided services and programs can impact workflow design and timelines. CBOs provide varied categories of services and programs to their residents. Some CBOs provide one specific service (e.g., food pantry services), while others provide overlapping services (e.g., utility assistance and nutrition counseling and food pantry assistance). The *CCC* governance entity and Governance Track lead should also factor in unique CBO requirements based on the categories of services provided. For example, some CBOs receiving funding from states for programs (e.g., nutrition programs) may require additional time for negotiation of more extensive legal requirements. Some of the broad CBO categories that are typically considered for *CCC* participation are included in the Supplement to Chapter 7.

Key Task: Define Measures of Accountability

From the analysis of data in the finalization of site selections, the Governance Track lead should define clear measures of accountability (e.g., performance-based reward or penalties associated with defined targets). The Partner site leaders should discuss these targets and measures of accountability to ensure that they are reasonable and that each Partner site accepts responsibility and accountability for the program deliverables. Typically, clinical sites are used to well-defined, quantitative performance targets and will welcome this level of clarity and guidance. CBO sites may appreciate an approach that emphasizes process compliance and social impact aligned with their funding goals, along with simplified quantitative performance targets.

Some communities may pursue a broad impact (e.g., address multiple health conditions) such that screening high patient volumes across all sectors of the population is a key goal. This objective calls for engagement of clinical Partners with broad catchment areas. Other communities may choose to focus on very specific subpopulations within their communities (e.g., diabetics), which would then drive the selection of care providers to accommodate the behavioral patterns and geographical spread of the targeted subpopulation.

Milestone 4: Identify Champions for Each Site

Success of the *CCC* interventions will largely depend on the level of buy-in from the clinical and CBO leadership teams. An aligned leadership team and identification of key program site "champions" can achieve the necessary buy-in. A champion is typically a knowledgeable, well-respected team member with strong communication and leadership skills, the capability to build rapport among disparate groups, and the ability to drive programmatic efforts while creatively working through barriers or challenges. Champions typically come from mid-management through executive levels, but frontline staff can also fulfill this role. What is most important is that the individual is passionate about the initiative and has the respect of peers and senior leaders, such that a champion's recommendations and resource requests are met with affirmative responses. The presence of a program champion historically has enabled the frontline staff members to optimally execute the *CCC* supported intervention requirements.

Designation of site champion(s) will serve as the foundation for the accountability framework across your Partner *CCC* sites. However, the champion(s) at each site will need strong support from their leadership to deliver on their program commitments. Specifically, each Partner's executive leadership should clearly communicate the organization-wide commitment for the *CCC* and set expectations among relevant staff for successful *CCC* implementation at their participating sites.

Requirement 6: Formalize Participation Agreements and Begin Implementation of the Governance Plan

While a comprehensive readiness assessment provides much of the information needed to begin to create and quickly implement a governance plan, the governance entity and Governance Track lead should also begin to focus on achieving the following milestones.

Milestone 1: Establish All Necessary Agreements

Prior to working with the Legal/Policy Track lead and *CCC* legal counsel (as required) to develop the necessary Participant/Participation Agreements (beyond the initial MOU), it is important to think through potential concerns and requirements that the Participants may raise. Some of these concerns can be alleviated up front. For example, the Governance Track lead can proactively consider ways to reduce Participant burden. Key areas to address include the following:

- Roles and responsibilities of Partner organizations
- Data-sharing agreements
- Terms of participation—compensation (if any), resource allocation, and any performance targets

From a timing perspective, it is important to finalize Participant Agreements (beyond the initial MOU or letters of commitment) only when you have details on the technology requirements (see Requirement 8 of this chapter and Chapter 5 Technology Platform Track).

The Governance Track lead will work with the Legal/Policy Track lead to finalize the following:

- Agreement with the Administrator (if applicable)
- Agreements with the clinical and CBO Partners/Participants
- Agreement with the technology vendor
- Participant agreements with the technology vendor (if required)
- Agreements (if needed) between clinical providers and CBO Participants

See Chapter 4 Legal/Policy Track, Chapter 6 Clinical Providers Track, and Chapter 7 Community Partners Track for details on these agreements.

Milestone 2: Implement Policies and Procedures Required by Governance Documents

Once the governance documents are adopted and contracts are signed, the Governance Track lead (working with the Legal/Policy Track lead) will implement (and provide training on) the policies and procedures contemplated (or mandated) by those governance documents.

PCCI recommends that the Board or Administrator retain experienced local counsel with expertise across the areas touched on by the *CCC* and then work with that counsel to set up a process to ensure (perhaps through quarterly calls) that no changes to the laws that affect the *CCC* (or its Participants or its funding) have taken place or are reasonably anticipated. When changes to the laws/regulations mandate contract updates or policy revisions, the Board or Administrator should implement a process to communicate (and provide training on) those changes for Participants.

Milestone 3: Develop a Publicity Plan to Publicize Successful CCC Implementation Efforts

To generate the interest of new Funders and new Participants and to raise the *CCC* profile, it is important to develop a public awareness plan through which the CBO can publicize successful implementation examples, both large and small. In addition to taking advantage of media opportunities, the appropriate *CCC* Governance Track lead should prepare and submit manuscripts, conference submissions, and other materials documenting the *CCC* successes and findings.

Leveraging local news outlets at the outset of the plan and keeping them informed throughout implementation can keep a stream of positive awareness flowing to the community, which will help support participation. Invite media members to meet participants in the *CCC* program, including CBOs and individuals who benefit. Create media opportunities, such as an Open House at a CBO or a community meeting. Having success stories and individuals who have benefited from the program available and prepared is key to attract media.

However, do not depend on intermittent media coverage to keep the *CCC* program's momentum going. A key part of the publicity plan is the use of social media. The major social media platforms can provide specific functions:

- LinkedIn: This helps attract and recruit CBOs, Funders, and other important industry partners.

- Twitter: This should be the hub for news and daily activity of the *CCC*, such as activities at CBOs, meeting notices, and service updates.
- Facebook: This is the program's retention and engagement tool, and, to a lesser degree, a location for news announcements. Facebook can serve as an ad hoc customer service platform where stakeholders, community members, and participants can interact and help answer questions they might have in moderated settings or in public and private groups. This engagement will allow higher levels of awareness and understanding while driving enthusiasm for the program.

Milestone 4: Develop Ongoing Maintenance and Sustainability Plans

It will be extremely important for the *CCC* governance group to develop plans for ongoing *CCC* maintenance and to ensure sustainability.

Key Task: Ensure Periodic Business and Legal Reviews

After the *CCC* is up and running, additional legal and operational reviews are necessary to ensure ongoing *CCC* maintenance and sustainability. See also Chapter 8 Program Sustainability Track. For example, the Board should prepare agendas and minutes of its meetings to the extent necessary to satisfy governance requirements and to document key decisions and responsibilities. In addition, the Funder may require ongoing training activities. Entities should plan to timely renew/extend contracts and policies, prepare applications for extended or new funding, and extend or wind down various components of the *CCC* in an orderly manner. If a predetermined "end date" for *CCC* funding has been set, the Sponsor or other Governance Track lead is responsible for securing new funding well in advance or making appropriate plans for winding up the *CCC*. If the Administrator has employees who will be terminated when the *CCC* ends, the Sponsor should consult with experienced employment counsel to determine appropriate next steps, which will be dependent on context and federal/state/local law.

The Board or Administrator will also periodically audit and assess how the technology is working for the overall *CCC* and each type of Participant. Often, the Funder may require an independent audit of one or more aspects of the *CCC* and its operations.

In conjunction with, or independent of, any audit schedule, the Board or Administrator, working with the *CCC* legal counsel and Legal/Policy Track lead, should set a schedule for the systematic review and update of all documents (e.g., contracts) and practices to support the *CCC*, including its technology platform. The Board or Administrator (working with the Legal/ Policy Track lead) may also want to notify Participants of key legal and regulatory changes before they go into effect.

Key Task: Develop Sustainability Principles

The *CCC* Governance Track lead should work with the Program Sustainability Track lead to develop, as part of the *CCC* design process, guiding principles for sustainability based on input from the Sponsor, Funders, Workgroups, or others as appropriate. See also Chapter 8 Program Sustainability Track. Sample principles could include the following:

- The *CCC* should be cost neutral to Participants during the first 5 years (or another appropriate timeframe).
- The 5-year (or other) implementation period should rigorously test the economic model.
- Established, firm milestones will prevent waste of resources.
- Beginning in year 6 (or other appropriate timeframe), the expected *CCC* costs should be less than, or equal to, the minimal dollar-to-dollar reduction in costs related to patient care and addressing social factors.
- The goal is a lean, efficient model increasing efficiencies in care delivery and savings while also improving the health status of the patient population.

Key Documents for Requirement 6

- Communication Strategy

Requirement 7: Define a Strategy and General Requirements for CCC Technology and Data Integration at Partner Sites

The technology infrastructure is a critical component enabling the stakeholders to achieve the defined clinical and social *CCC* goals. The technology infrastructure creates an integrated electronic platform to exchange clinical and social information securely between health organizations (e.g., hospitals, clinics) and CBOs (e.g., homeless shelters, food pantries) that are part of the *CCC* network. Through data collection and reporting, the technology infrastructure also enables network Participants and stakeholders to understand the impact and effectiveness of various programs in fulfilling their mandates.

It is primarily the responsibility of the Governance Track and Technology Platform Track leads to provide a clear, applied technology strategy for the *CCC* and its Partners. The strategy should (1) incorporate the legal considerations for the technology framework, (2) set up the primary requirements and components for the *CCC* technology platform, (3) provide key clinical requirements for successful selection of a technology vendor, and (4) work with the technology vendor to provide steps for implementation of the technology to support the *CCC* clinical and community workflows.

In order to reach its full potential, the chosen technology platform should have the capability to enhance clinical and CBO workflows through advanced analytics (e.g., predictive analytics) and decision support at the point of care/encounter. Every information exchange platform is heavily nuanced; thus, it is extremely important to clearly understand the core requirements. The database should allow Participants to maintain control of their own data, while also providing a shared central repository for important and commonly used or requested information, such as demographic information and minimal case management information, but no health information. As a general rule, the technology platform powering the *CCC* should exhibit the following characteristics:

- *Person-centered*, meaning built to be as seamless as possible for the person it is built to serve.
- *Adaptability*, meaning the ability to integrate with *CCC* Participant organizations with varying levels of technology sophistication in their respective information systems; ability to integrate with EHRs and to merge disparate data sources.

- *Consistency*, meaning the ability to provide no degradation in performance based on the number of users or the amount of data transmitted.
- *Scalability*, meaning the ability to gracefully support the *CCC* at all stages of its growth; the ability to scale based on users (new *CCC* Participants) and data.
- *Availability*, meaning the ability to run 24 hours per day, 7 days per week, except for scheduled maintenance downtime.
- *Extensibility*, meaning the capability to allow for interfaces and integration and to add functionality and custom features for all Participants, with some ability at the individual Participant level to allow for customized workflows and other components that may be unique to new service categories joining the *CCC*.
- *Accessibility*, meaning easily accessible to all users (providers, care managers, CBOs, and other stakeholders), including (at least at some future date) those users with disabilities; ability of *CCC* individuals to access only appropriate data and establish security protocols for data storage, transfer, and usage.
- *Flexibility*, meaning while maintaining case consistency for back-end reporting, the technology should have the capability to build different and unique front-end intake forms to meet evolving program needs.

Milestone 1: Analyze any Funder or Sponsor Specific Technology Requirements

The funding documents (whether a government grant, grant from a private philanthropic organization, or another arrangement) may provide the baseline requirements (along with state law) for certain technology requirements for the *CCC*. As provided in Requirement 2 of this chapter, legal counsel will need to analyze these requirements in conjunction with the Partners and the Sponsor to determine what documents are required from a legal perspective. It is rare for a Funder to mandate use of a particular software application or other technology. However, it is quite common, especially for Funder governmental entities, to outline specific privacy, security, and technical safeguards that must be utilized, along with performance standards (e.g., data transfer speed, reporting capabilities) that must be met. Funders that specify this level of detail typically certify the technology solution chosen by the *CCC*. As a result, the Sponsor or governance entity will want to ensure, during the contracting process, that the technology vendor meets or exceeds Funder requirements or is willing to conduct the necessary activities to reach the required level of compliance. The Sponsor or governance entity will need to become aware of any Funder audit plans and communicate those to the technology vendor and Administrator as far in advance as possible.

Milestone 2: Translate the CCC Intervention Workflows and Use Cases into Technical Requirements for the Technology Platform

The Sponsor and *CCC* Board, Administrator, or Clinical Advisory Group should review the information gathered in the readiness assessment surveys and focus groups conducted with patients and clinical and CBO staff, as well as the interviews with clinical and CBO leaders in order to uncover valuable information about use cases presenting opportunities for improved care coordination. In addition, this material will provide prospective user perspectives on barriers, enablers, and desired information exchange system requirements, features, and functionalities. See Chapter 2 Readiness Assessment.

The development of a library of use cases (a textual representation illustrating a sequence of events) gives clarity to how the use of an information exchange platform like *CCC* could potentially result in a better and healthier clinical or social outcome for the patient. Figure 3.3 is a sample model of common processes/workflows, providing a common framework of language to discuss use cases across diverse organizations and sectors.

The use-case analyses and the defined *CCC* interventions provide the necessary inputs for the Governance Track lead to define the necessary features and functionality of the *CCC* technology platform. As the technology strategy is shaped, consider the following questions:

- Do your *CCC* interventions allow/require your patients to provide information without assistance (e.g., taking a *CCC* survey on their own while in the waiting room)?
- What type of data will be collected and shared by your *CCC* (e.g., Protected Health Information (PHI), defined core data elements that support the workflows across all Partners or non-PHI from CBOs)?
- At what frequency should the exchange of data take place (e.g., real time or daily)?
- In what environment will patients access your data platform (e.g., public spaces or secure spaces)?
- Do your interventions require mobile access to the platform (e.g., should patients be able to self-refer from their mobile phones)?

Figure 3.3 Technology Strategy to Support the *CCC* Interventions Based on Use-Case Analyses.

- Do your interventions require integration of a patient's clinical data from an EHR?
- Do your interventions require patients to provide identification documents and determine eligibility parameters for various services (e.g., Social Security numbers or copies of identification or Medicare/Medicaid cards)?
- Do your interventions require integration of historic data from existing data sources across your community (e.g., service records from a food pantry stored on a local Microsoft (MS) Access database to prepopulate patient lists at participating clinical sites)?
- Do your interventions require formal documentation of services provided (e.g., do you have established Partner agencies, such as HUD, requiring very specific reporting and data-tracking requirements)?

- Do your interventions integrate data from external sources (e.g., state 2-1-1 services that bolster a referral network that will be part of interventions)?
- Do your interventions serve a highly diverse population (e.g., many cultures with various languages, such that multilingual support is a must)?
- Is data collection throughout your interventions prone to a high rate of errors due to self-reporting? For example, are there workflows that may be carried out in a non-digital format (i.e., using a paper-based survey tool) with the data entered into the platform later? If so, this introduces a high risk of erroneous data entry; as a result, mechanisms for correcting the data should exist.
- How will the community referral directory be initially set up and maintained for accuracy?

Answers to these and other similar questions will help define the required features of the *CCC* technology platform. To assist in effective vendor and platform selection, we recommend prioritizing these into categories, such as "critical," "enhancement," and "future." For more details on common, desired system characteristics and functionalities, see Chapter 5 Technology Platform Track.

Milestone 3: Conduct Market Research to Understand the Range of Available Technology Platforms in the Market

The market for software solutions addressing Social Determinants of Health (SDOH) and connecting the clinical and social domains of care is emerging rapidly, and it is quickly becoming fragmented. Vendors have various levels of expertise, experience, technical capabilities, and functionalities that are very nuanced. For instance, some are winning business through a robust customer experience offering, which may lack in feature depth. Others may have a highly comprehensive and complex, feature-rich platform but lack the context and expertise required to deploy this platform in a community. Multiple means of gaining a better understanding of the market include the following:

- Obtaining research reports through syndicated research organizations, such as KLAS Research and others

- Tracking the news for mentions of a successful effort to address goals similar to those of your *CCC*; you can then reach out to these organizations to gain their insights
- Attending industry conferences (e.g., Healthcare Information and Management Systems Society [HIMSS]) will provide exposure to what others around the country have done and the tools they used to achieve results
- Requesting demos from various vendors and asking them to specify who their competitors are and how they differentiate themselves

Multiple strategies are available to gain insight into "what is out there." Irrespective of which ones are utilized, the goal is to understand which solutions come closest to meeting your *CCC*'s goals and to determine whether the gap between your innovative goals and the available tools is significant.

Milestone 4: Select the Right Technology Partner

Once you have a clear understanding of your technology needs versus what is available to meet those needs, you will need to decide whether to "build versus buy." Given the complexity of the model, it is—in PCCI's experience—highly unlikely that a "build" option is financially advantageous. It may be applicable in a situation where your *CCC* is meant to function as a very narrow network. However, any scaling or expansion of the effort requires a dedicated software development and IT team. PCCI recommends that you select an existing vendor that not only offers an appropriate *CCC* technology platform but is also a good "fit" for the Sponsor and Partners. The *CCC* work is an ongoing, iterative effort that is highly dependent on trust, accountability, and collaboration. Given the innovative nature of this work, your selected technology vendor must essentially become one of the key partners of your *CCC* and should share accountability for the *CCC*'s success.

Key Task: Evaluate Potential Technology Partners

It is extremely important to select a technology partner that can stand up the data architecture to provide the system and functionality requirements and support the *CCC* organizational model's short-term objectives and long-term program goals. In addition to the inclusion of system and functionality and end-user requirements (see Chapter 5 Technology Platform Track), the *CCC* governance entity and Governance and Technology Platform Track leads should evaluate desired vendor characteristics, such as the following:

- An already well-established, robust operational technology (i.e., no or minimal building required) in place with multiple clients
- Willingness and ability to provide a clear timeline and goals for a rollout of the project
- Features an established community resource database and a demonstrated plan to keep the database up to date
- Proven ability to build a strong community network (e.g., strong user base, streamlined business processes)
- Ability to provide substantial technical assistance and training to Participants
- Ability and willingness to address issues flexibly and quickly and to approach problems collaboratively
- Proven high level of client satisfaction in performance, including problem resolution, on-time product delivery, and pricing
- High level of relevant expertise among staff. For example, are there vendor staff clinicians who can offer insights into nuances related to implementation of clinical programs? Does the vendor have a staff that is deeply connected with their community's CBOs?
- Provide not only the front-end technology but a robust back-end technology platform to manage data ingestion, storage, and ad hoc reporting; ideally have the capability to add artificial intelligence and machine learning (AI/ML)-based models for risk stratification and early warning algorithms as the *CCC* initiative matures.

The Governance and Technology Platform Track leads may want to explore vendor reviews on websites, such as Glassdoor.com to learn about the culture of the vendor and its client approach. It is important to get a sense for a vendor's rate of turnover and its approach to customer support (e.g., size of account management teams and whether the vendor outsources the function). It is also helpful to examine a potential vendor's list of existing clients to see if there is potential for a conflict of interest and to understand how the scope and magnitude of your *CCC* compares to the vendor's existing work. Finally, you may want to inquire about the vendor's road map and financial stability

(e.g., are they venture-backed and, if so, how many rounds of funding are there, and when are/have they completed?)

Key Task: Obtain Technical Readiness Assessment

The technology vendor may need to conduct technical readiness assessments at multiple *CCC* Participant sites simultaneously, in order to build the necessary interfaces across the disparate systems. This assessment may include the following:

- Technical assessment and Participant system updates, if needed, for hardware, software, or licensing, for example
- Data integrity review and cleanup
- Technical security review and readiness
- Modification of user interfaces of home systems, as needed

Key Task: Finalize the Technology Vendor Agreement

If the *CCC* contracts separately with a technology vendor, it will need to consider and address a number of key areas as outlined in Chapter 4 Legal/ Policy Track Requirement 2. As part of this process, the Sponsor or Board or Governance Track lead (working with the Legal/Policy and Program Sustainability Track leads) should consider how the documents governing the use of technology within the *CCC*'s legal and policy framework "fit" within and will contribute to the *CCC*'s sustainability. This should include identification up front of future dates for review, revision, or termination of the documents or relationships. Having completed the key actions of this requirement, the *CCC* Governance Track lead (working with the Technology Platform Track lead) will be ready to conduct a targeted search for the technology vendor. Details on desired functionalities and the actual operational steps to implement the technology platform across your Partner sites are discussed in Chapter 5 Technology Platform Track.

Key Documents for Requirement 7

- Platform Functionalities and Vendor Specifications
- Criteria for Vendor Evaluation

Requirement 8: Define and Perform Quality Assurance Activities to Ensure Intervention Integrity across the CCC

This requirement proposes a set of processes and steps both to verify the quality of the *CCC* activities (i.e., the feedback mechanism for the *CCC* governance structure) and to implement accompanying remediation steps to ensure that the *CCC* interventions progress on track towards the desired *CCC* goals and clinical outcomes. The outcomes of QA work will be used at every level of the *CCC* infrastructure:

- Key roles/stakeholders will use QA activities to gain insights into previously unknown needs and gaps within the community.
- Community and clinical leads will use QA feedback to gauge any course corrections needed.
- Frontline staff will adjust daily workflows to ensure the *CCC* interventions are delivered in the most effective way possible.

Key Roles and Responsibilities

The *CCC* Clinical Providers and Community Partners Track leads are accountable for *CCC* performance at each of the Participant sites. Examples of these leads include the following:

- Team supervisors (e.g., patient needs screening supervisor, patient navigation supervisor, supervising case manager, volunteer staff supervisor)
- Site directors

Milestone 1: Define and Create Quality Assurance Processes

The *CCC* Clinical Provider and Community Partner Track leads will perform a number of tasks to define and create QA processes.

Key Task: Consider Use of Preexisting Quality Assurance Processes

The creation and definition of the QA processes should take place in parallel with the creation of the *CCC* Clinical Provider and Community Partner workflows described in Chapters 6 and 7, since the nature of the workflow will determine the type of QA required. For instance, workflows involving the initial, first level of contact with the patients/clients for the purposes of routing or stratifying them for more intensive health-related social interventions are critical points that will require daily checks. Failure to engage patients and route them through the intake process will have a cascading, negative impact on the *CCC* goals. At the same time, these first-level processes are most intensive from a staffing and throughput perspective. Therefore, QA processes placed around these activities should be as nonintrusive as possible. Given this, it is important to utilize preexisting, validated, QA processes wherever possible. For example, in high patient/client volume environments, such as food pantries or homeless shelters, multiple reports and tracking boards are already in place to track operational metrics and to ensure compliance with various program requirements. These resources can be leveraged for the *CCC* workflows as well.

The quality monitoring process should, at a minimum, contain the following components:

- Clearly defined process measures for the workflows
- Clearly established timeliness, with exact dates, for conducting ongoing QA activities
- Identified and tested means of collecting the data for the process measures
- Established environment and strategy for sharing measures with the accountable parties
- Assigned roles and responsibilities for quality tracking

As part of any evaluation and QA strategy, it is important to position the value of the proposed processes and metrics within the context of the overarching organizational goals and strategies. Through a demonstration of the impact of the QA work on the organization's and the *CCC*'s ability to meet the desired goals (e.g., through a quantitative model illustrating how performance at each respective step of *CCC* workflow sums up to organizational and *CCC* goals), the site leaders can overcome much resistance and hesitation regarding needed QA activities. This is especially important since most CBOs do not have the staff or expertise to routinely deploy QA processes. Thus, they may not recognize the importance ascribed to these activities.

PRACTICE POINTER

*Consider Utilizing an Experienced Third Party
to Conduct QA and Evaluation Activities*

In some cases, it may be effective to utilize a third-party vendor or consultant to conduct quality monitoring activities, as they are arguably more objective and typically more experienced and less biased. For this strategy to succeed, however, that third party should have full, clear, transparent support from both the *CCC* governance group and the CBO site leadership team. The primary benefit of a third-party arrangement is that the third party is free of competing priorities and should have an objective, dedicated focus on the workflow performance. Conversely, leadership has to ultimately follow the guidance based on external recommendations; as a result, full advisory support is necessary to achieve success.

Key Task: Assign Responsibility for Monitoring Workflows

The responsibility for monitoring *CCC* workflow performance should be assigned to the same individuals who are ultimately accountable for the successful overall performance of the Partner organizations. Given their vested interest, these individuals will (1) serve as champions in integrating the *CCC* process monitoring into the existing QA reports and dashboards and (2) expeditiously remediate any anomalies or undesirable events. These individuals can also effectively address any identified barriers by effectively readjusting the frontline team's focus, as necessary.

Key Task: Develop Mitigation Strategies to Remedy Process Deficiencies

Once the quality monitoring strategies for each Partner site are defined, site staff should develop detailed mitigation strategies to remedy any process deficiencies. In addition to defining clear approaches to resolving deficiencies, this process may also consist of creating additional, redundant workflows to reach the desired outcome. The frontline and operational teams who developed the initial *CCC* workflows are best positioned to accomplish this task, with input from team members with experience in quality improvement. The mitigation strategies should be extensively detailed and resemble an SOP document, with specified timelines for completing mitigation activities. At a minimum, the strategies should:

- Clearly define the roles of those involved in mitigation processes and workflows.
- Describe all processes and technology features to mitigate the risk for inaccurate workflow implementation.
- Describe all processes and technology features to enable early identification of inaccuracies/anomalies in workflows.
- Describe reporting processes.

Mitigation strategies should also address the following criteria and questions:

- What is the chain of command and accountability if workflow anomalies are discovered? Who should be informed and by when? Who is responsible for implementing an alternative workflow until the primary workflow is remedied?
- What has to be done manually through workflow modifications or QA activities? Are there pre-established efficiencies or automations that are not sensitive enough to react to the needs of the population at hand (e.g., a preexisting screening tool in the clinical EHR does not provide the ability to ask more probing questions of the patients)?
- What can be done through technology? In other words, what existing or additional technology features might be needed to enable streamlined implementation, mitigation strategies, and QA activities? For example, is the tool used to facilitate patient data collection inefficient or requiring unnecessary amounts of interaction; can a technology-based tool be used to replace a manual process for collecting patient information?
- What should the steps be in the event of temporary unavailability of technology (e.g., should an existing, familiar, simple-to-use manual form be used to collect patient information while leveraging an automated data entry back end to capture data within a centralized location)?
- What remediation should be implemented once a process deficiency is identified? For example, should the site perform staff retraining within 7 days of an identified event, implement close, short-term supervision, allocate additional staff support to the project, or perform technology modifications? When should a return to regular QA processes take place?

- How should identified process deficiencies and mitigation strategies be captured, logged, and reported? What tool is used to log the anomaly events and does the tool track the interaction between the accountable parties? What is the process for reviewing the log of identified deficiencies upon their resolution? Who is involved in the process, how often should it occur, and who is responsible for leading the review?
- How often should specific workflows be reassessed?

Chapter 4

Legal/Policy Track

Introduction to the Legal/Policy Track

This Playbook is not intended to provide legal advice. Instead, it should help the reader identify issues to discuss with the attorneys for the local/regional CCC to be created.

Because the *Connected Communities of Care* (*CCC*) uses technology to connect patients, clinical providers, and Community-Based Social Service Organizations *aka* Community-Based Organizations (CBOs) in a way that addresses the interconnected social and health needs of a community, a legal framework is needed for the following three purposes:

- Define the parties' relationships, protect individual rights, and minimize institutional compliance risks. A well-defined legal framework is essential because the *CCC* platform requires the following:
  - Appropriate governance structures and documentation
  - The collection, transmission, and use of sensitive personal data
  - Coordination among multiple entities (via contracts and workflows)
  - Compliance with funding and legal requirements.
- Provide regulatory guidance for the concerns (or required compliance "underpinnings") for each of the other five *CCC* Tracks to ensure their smooth implementation.
- Establish a systematic basis for identification and analysis of (1) common issues that arise among clinical or CBO sites implementing *CCC* and (2) issues that are unique to each site, while minimizing risk for

CCC Participants. Once the legal issues are identified, the framework should provide the necessary legal documents and policies required by the various sites to ensure successful *CCC* deployment and operation.

CAVEAT: *While this Playbook provides a number of references or sample documents (Key Documents), it is important to consult federal, state, and local laws; requirements imposed by the Funder; and requirements of both the Sponsor and Partners as these requirements will need to be integrated with the* CCC *governance documents. The Playbook is not intended to provide legal advice;* CCC *Participants should consult with their own attorneys.*

Roles and Responsibilities

The Sponsor/initial Board or applicable governance entity should designate a *CCC* Legal/Policy Track lead to work with *CCC* counsel to establish the framework and review all documents in each Track to ensure compliance. The framework and legal considerations provided throughout this Playbook serve as a starting point for analysis and document/policy drafting. *The framework does not constitute the provision of legal advice. Each* CCC *Partner should obtain its own independent legal analysis, advice, and drafting assistance from attorneys of its choosing.* To the extent possible (to maximize efficiency), Parkland Center for Clinical Innovation (PCCI) recommends that the *CCC* rely on existing legal structures, policies, procedures, processes, and agreements already in place among the clinical and community Participants as that can vastly shorten *CCC* design and implementation timeframes.

Once a comprehensive legal framework is in place, the *CCC* will be optimally positioned to create a person-centered ecosystem that fosters the seamless, lawful exchange and use of information in multiple ways to immediately assist individuals and to enhance the ability of community programs to further coordinate care and improve individual outcomes.

Legal and Policy Framework Assumptions

The legal and policy framework assumes the following:

- The Funder is separate from the Sponsor.
- The technology vendor will sign a single contract that permits all *CCC* Participants to use the chosen technology.

- To the extent that more contracts are needed (e.g., the technology vendor requires separate contracts with Participants), this Playbook provides limited comments on considerations for those agreements, as additional individualized contracts necessarily require further negotiation and variation that should be avoided, if possible.
- Individuals will be identified for participation at the clinical provider's locations and referred to the CBOs for social services using software that is not integrated into the clinical provider's Electronic Health Record (EHR).
  - Of course, referrals could work in the other direction and in that circumstance only minor adjustments to the legal framework would be required, although this would likely require a more substantial revision of the workflows for both clinical and community participants.
- The *CCC* encompasses a closed system with referrals of patients/clients to and from clinical and CBO Participants and data sharing that does *not* include texting or calling individual patients/clients. Many highly complex federal and state laws are implicated if the *CCC* intends to include this type of patient engagement; discussion of these laws is outside the scope of this Playbook.
- If the *CCC* data will be collected outside the clinical provider's normal EHR (e.g., through a stand-alone, third-party technology platform that does not pass data between itself and the EHR), then it should not be considered part of either the Health Insurance Portability and Accountability Act (HIPAA) Designated Record Set or the Legal Health Record. Therefore, it is not generally subject to HIPAA requirements (see Requirement 2 of this chapter).
- CBOs are not HIPAA "Covered Entities" (i.e., not healthcare providers, health plans, or clearinghouses) (see Requirement 2 of this chapter).
- CBOs may share *CCC* data among themselves but Covered Entities (HIPAA defined) will not share data gathered for the community *CCC* with other Covered Entities (although they may share similar or duplicate data for HIPAA-permitted purposes of treatment, payment, and healthcare operations or for research purposes if permitted by an appropriate Institutional Review Board (IRB), all of which is outside the scope of the *CCC* (see Requirement 2 of this chapter).
- The *CCC* data is not typically shared with another Covered Entity because coordination typically needs to take place with the CBOs, not other clinical providers.

- The *CCC* will operate in an environment of goodwill and cooperation between participants; therefore, this Playbook does not provide detailed content to address dispute resolution other than to note that the contracts, especially with the technology vendor, should include dispute-resolution terms.
  - *Note*: In the rare circumstance in which *CCC* Participants engage in a serious dispute, the best course, after executive-level, dispute-resolution meetings, is likely withdrawal of one or both parties from the *CCC*.

Legal/Policy Track Requirements

The Legal/Policy Track follows the requirements below to ensure a successful and legally compliant design, launch, implementation, and sustainability of a *CCC*. As the Track leads for each Playbook Track will need to work closely with the Legal/Policy Track lead and *CCC* legal counsel, additional specifics on each of the legal framework considerations for each of the other five Tracks: Governance, Technology Platform, Clinical Providers, Community Partners, and Program Sustainability are incorporated into each respective Track.

As a general rule, the legal framework aspects for the Governance Track and the Technology Platform Track should be completed before substantive legal work begins on any of the remaining Tracks because the governance framework will help define (or even mandate) legal aspects of the remaining Tracks. In addition, the Governance and Legal/Policy Tracks oversee the work conducted in the remaining Tracks. The legal issues for developing a legal and policy framework for the technology platform (Requirement 2 of this chapter) should be resolved in parallel with the Governance Track because the technology vendor used (and its contractual requirements) will drive some of the decisions within the other Tracks. The legal work to support the remaining (non-governance/non-technology) Tracks can be prepared simultaneously or in a sequence that makes best use of the *CCC* Participants' resources and planned workflows.

The time needed to complete the Legal/Policy Track can be (and typically is) quite long, ranging from 6 months to over a year. The time it takes to complete each legal requirement necessarily depends on the following factors: (1) the availability of resources, (2) the extent to which negotiation or redrafting is required for multiparty agreements, (3) the time needed for review and approval by parties and governmental entities (if required), (4) timing for implementation of policies and procedures, (5) training time required for the technology selected, and (6) Funder timing requirements or the extent of Funder contractual requirements. Because of the multiple, time-dependent variables, PCCI highly recommends beginning the necessary Legal/Policy work as early as feasible once the Sponsor or initial governance entity has made the determination to move forward with a *CCC*. Like governance, the Legal/Policy considerations and oversight spans all four *CCC* stages of design and implementation across all Playbook Tracks.

At a high level, the Requirements needed to establish the *CCC* legal framework include the following:

1. Develop a legal and policy framework for *CCC* governance.
2. Develop a legal and policy framework for the technology platform.
3. Develop a legal and policy framework for the clinical providers.
4. Develop a legal and policy framework for the community Partners.
5. Develop a legal and policy framework for *CCC* program sustainability.

In working through the legal considerations for each Track, the Legal/Policy Track lead should focus on:

- Compliance with funding documents
- Federal law compliance (especially if a federal funding source or a federal government Participant is involved or if HIPAA is applicable)
- State law compliance
  - Generally state law will dictate corporate governance forms and rules.
  - State law may be applicable to certain aspects of the *CCC* (e.g., Medicaid data use).
  - State law will apply if state entity is a Funder or a Participant.
  - State law will generally govern contracts and Memorandum of Understanding (MOU) terms.
  - State law may apply if it applies a broader definition of Protected Health Information (PHI) or more restrictive requirements for its use than HIPAA.
- Local ordinance compliance, especially if local rules are relevant (e.g., work with homeless) or a local governmental entity is a Funder or participates in the *CCC*
- Compliance with clinical and CBO Partner policies and procedures

- Contracts with participants (e.g., Participants, technology vendor, Administrator)
- Sustainability considerations
  - Changes in law (federal, state, local)
  - New Participant concerns or requirements
  - New funding requirements (e.g., new Funders or transitions or updates)
  - Legal review, monitoring, and revision of all agreements and policies and procedures (as applicable)
  - Agreement termination dates and required notices
  - Training reviews and updates

Requirement 1: Develop a Legal and Policy Framework for CCC Governance

The "best" legal framework for governance of the local *CCC* depends heavily on its funding source, community acceptance of (and trust in) the Sponsor and Anchors, and governing state laws. In establishing governance structures for the *CCC*, the Legal/Policy Track lead will need to ensure the following (as applicable):

- Compliance with funding documents
- Compliance with federal laws (applies primarily if a federal funding source or if the federal government is a *CCC* participant in some respect)
- Compliance with state laws
  - State law will dictate corporate governance forms and rules.
  - State law may also apply to specific aspects of the *CCC*, such as the use of Medicaid data from the state Medicaid entity or its private contractors.
  - State law will apply if the state funds the *CCC* or is a *CCC* participant.
  - State law will generally govern contract terms.
- Compliance with local laws
  - Local law will apply if local rules are relevant (e.g., work with the homeless within constraints of applicable local ordinances).
  - Local law may apply if a local government entity funds the community *CCC*.
  - Local law may apply if a local government entity participates in the community *CCC*.

Milestone 1: Create Legal Documents for Early Partner Commitments to the CCC

Many Sponsors (and Funders) will require some type of MOU or letter of commitment from each potential Partner before they commit their own resources/funding. PCCI recommends that the Legal/Policy Track lead or other *CCC* legal counsel should avoid structuring these letters of commitment in a detailed, prescriptive way (see also Chapter 3 Governance Track Requirement 1). *CCC* attorneys will want to work closely with the Governance Track lead to proactively identify which Partners (especially CBOs) will have expanded legal requirements and, thus, will likely require additional time to negotiate formal agreements (e.g., CBOs that provide state funding for nutrition programs).

Milestone 2: Complete an Analysis of Sponsor and Funder Requirements for Governance

The Legal/Policy Track lead or other legal counsel for the *CCC* should examine the Sponsor or Funder requirements (e.g., grant or cooperative agreement) to determine any baseline parameters for the formal governance of the *CCC*. See also Chapter 3 Governance Track Requirement 2. Generally speaking, a successful *CCC* will have a governance function that, at a minimum, has the authority to (1) set strategic direction for the *CCC*, (2) provide oversight for operations and *CCC* budgets for Participants and vendors, (3) ensure compliance with Sponsor and Funder requirements, and (4) resolve disputes among Participants. As described in Chapter 3 Governance Track Requirement 2, the Funder requirements (e.g., grant) may provide specific requirements for the *CCC* entity (e.g., Administrator or Board). In addition to Funder requirements related to *CCC* specifics, most awards will include general "terms and conditions" that apply to all awards. The *CCC* legal counsel and Legal/Policy Track lead must carefully consider the more general terms and conditions in crafting appropriate *CCC* governance documents.

Key Task: Determine CCC Entity Requirements

The Legal/Policy Track lead, working with the *CCC* Sponsor or Anchors or other designated Governance Track lead and other legal counsel (as needed), should determine (1) if the *CCC* should be a separate legal entity organized according to the laws of the state in which it operates and (2) any legal/tax/accounting reasons to choose one form of organization over another. If separate "entity" status is necessary, legal counsel should present the advantages and drawbacks of various types of organization options and make recommendations. If the *CCC* will instead be a looser collection of separate entities operating towards a set of common, interrelated goals, then less formal legal arrangements for the *CCC* as an entity may be necessary or desirable.

Key Task: Determine Requirements for CCC Technology Platform

The funding documents (whether a government grant, grant from a private philanthropic organization, or another arrangement) may provide the baseline requirements (along with state law) for certain technology requirements for the *CCC*. Legal counsel will need to analyze these requirements in conjunction with the Partners and Sponsor to determine what documents are required from a legal perspective. It is rare for a Funder to mandate use of a particular software application or other technology. However, it is quite common, especially for Funder governmental entities, to outline specific privacy, security, and technical safeguards that must be utilized, along with performance standards (e.g., data transfer speed, reporting capabilities) that must be met. Funders that specify this level of detail typically certify the technology solution chosen by the *CCC*. See also Chapter 3 Governance Track Requirement 7.

Milestone 3: Create the Desired Governance Structure Based on Stakeholder Interests, Funding Parameters, and State Law

Once the *CCC* attorneys have reviewed the Funder requirements, the governance entity and other stakeholder requirements, and state law, the attorneys will then create the appropriate governance documents for the *CCC*.

Key Task: Draft Appropriate Governance Documents

With input from the Funder (if applicable) and consistent with state law, the *CCC* attorneys should draft the appropriate governance documents and accompanying documents (e.g., conflict of interest forms). For example, these documents could consist of (1) bylaws for a Board to serve as the *CCC*'s governing body or (2) internal policies, processes, and structures for the Administrator to provide the same governance functions that a Board would otherwise provide.

The bylaws or internal Administrator processes should be drafted in such a way to encourage continuity and change through (1) staggered terms for Board members, succession planning, and functional cross-training within the Administrator; (2) provisions for replacement of departing Board members and transitions of Administrator employees and subcontractors; (3) a means to replace derelict Board members or poorly performing Administrator employees/subcontractors; and (4) winding-up provisions in the event the *CCC* is acquired, becomes administered by a different Sponsor, obtains different funding that sets far different parameters, or terminates at the end of a funding period. See also Chapter 3 Governance Track Requirement 2.

Key Task: Determine Intellectual Property and Insurance Needs

Early in the process, *CCC* legal counsel and Legal/Policy Track lead, working with the Governance Track lead, should determine if Intellectual Property (IP) protections are needed for patentable or copyrightable or trademarked materials arising from the *CCC* operations. The Legal/Policy Track lead may also provide suggestions to the Governance Track lead on what types of insurance may be advisable, depending on the *CCC* governance and technology platform. See also Chapter 3 Governance Track Requirement 2.

Milestone 4: Establish Remaining Legal Agreements

Prior to developing the necessary participation agreements (beyond the initial MOU), it is important for the Legal/Policy Track lead, working with the Governance Track lead, to think through potential concerns and require-ments that the Participants may raise. Some of these concerns can be allevi-ated up front. For example, the Legal/Policy Track lead will need input from the Governance Track lead on key areas, such as:

- Roles and responsibilities of Partner organizations
- Data-sharing agreements
- Terms of participation, including compensation (if any), resource alloca-tion, and performance targets

From a timing perspective, it is important to finalize participation agree-ments (beyond the initial MOU or letters of commitment) only when you have details on the technology requirements (see Chapter 3 Governance Track Requirement 7 and Chapter 5 Technology Platform Track).

Key Task: Develop Clinical Partner Participation Agreements

Agreements with clinical Partners should address a number of key issues, which are outlined in Requirement 3 of this chapter. As indicated, it is important to finalize participation agreements only when the technology requirements have been established.

Key Task: Establish CBO Participation Agreement

The CBO Participant agreements should address similar issues to those of the clinical Partners and also include any appropriate consents/authorization language. See Requirement 4 of this chapter for additional details to consider with respect to these agreements.

Key Task: Establish Agreements with Administrator (If Applicable)

If an Administrator entity is selected to run the *CCC* operations, the Legal/Policy Track lead will need to work with the Governance Track lead to develop a selection mechanism, such as a Request for Proposal (RFP), and a resulting contract. It is important to provide clarity on the roles and responsibilities and reporting hierarchy for the Administrator. It is also important to include appropriate termination language to ensure flexibility and sustainability. Additional issues to consider will be similar to those identified in Requirement 3 for the clinical provider participation agreements.

Key Task: Determine the Need for Data-Sharing Agreements between Clinical Providers and Community Participants

Typically, the clinical Participant and the community Participants do not require contracts with one another, as the clinical Participant is only referring patients to the community Participant. However, the Legal/Policy Track lead, working with the Governance and Clinical Providers Track leads, will need to determine the parameters of data sharing. The agreement between the Sponsor (or other designee) and clinical Participant may provide for the Sponsor to share information from the clinical Participants with the community Participants and vice versa. If it does not, the Sponsor should consider the desirability of Participant data sharing through a separate agreement. Alternatively, data-sharing rules can be established in the agreement between the Sponsor and the technology vendor (e.g., allowing for shared use of information within the *CCC* network with the approval of each Participant, which can be secured through the individual participation agreements). These data-sharing agreements must be in place before any operations begin.

Key Task: Establish Agreement with Technology Vendor

See Requirement 2 of this chapter for details on process selection and contracting with the technology vendor.

Key Task: Establish Participant Agreements with Technology Vendor (If Required)

If separate agreements exist between the Participants and the technology vendor, there will be additional issues requiring resolution. Typically, if the Sponsor retains an Administrator, any contract between that vendor and the clinical Partners would need to address similar items to those addressed in the contract between the clinical Partner and the *CCC* Sponsor.

Milestone 5: Ensure Creation and Ongoing Implementation of Policies and Procedures Required by Governance Documents

Once the governance documents are adopted and contracts are signed, the Governance Track lead will need to create, implement, and provide training on policies and procedures contemplated (or mandated) by those governance documents. These may include policies and procedures related to a number of subjects, such as record retention, financial/accounting, security, and audit.

Key Task: Establish a Process to Communicate Changes in Laws or Funder Requirements

The Legal/Policy Track lead should work with the Governance Track lead to set up a process to ensure (perhaps through quarterly calls) that no changes to the laws that affect the *CCC* (or its Participants or its funding) have taken place or are reasonably anticipated. When changes to the laws/regulations mandate contract updates or policy revisions, the Board or Administrator will need to implement a process to communicate (and provide training) on those changes for Participants.

<u>Key Task: Update Legal Documents as Required Based on Changing Requirements and CCC Sustainability Considerations</u>

The Legal/Policy Track lead will need to ensure an ongoing review and updates of legal documents for maintenance and sustainability of the *CCC* infrastructure, including periodic reviews of contracts, state laws, and Funder requirements (see also Chapter 8 Program Sustainability).

Key Documents for Requirement 1

- MOU for Clinical Participation in a *CCC*
- Letter of Commitment for CBO

Requirement 2: Develop a Legal and Policy Framework for the Technology Platform

Central to the operation of the *CCC* is the collection and sharing of some-times sensitive personal information between clinical and CBO Participants and possibly the Funder, the Sponsor, and subcontractors of these organizations. The extent of information sensitivity depends on the scope and depth of your *CCC*'s goals and the supporting clinical interventions and whether the Funder and Sponsor permit aggregate-level reporting or reserve rights to audit at the individual level. For instance, in a small-scale implementation, it may be sufficient to collect a patient's name, address, family size, nutritional habits, smoking habits, drinking habits, and the services received at a local food pantry. On the other end of the spectrum, your clinical interventions may exchange a patient's blood pressure, lipid levels, A1c levels, insurance status, and medical and insurance IDs along with any identified social needs and social services received.

One of the first key decisions that the Sponsor or governance entity must make is what kind of patient-level clinical information will be shared with Participants within the *CCC* network, whether and what type of individual level consent is needed for collection and sharing, and how this information will be protected. Obviously, the more clinical information that is shared, the better the case management/monitoring process can be. When we speak of sharing relevant patient-level clinical information, we are not referring to information such as Computerized Tomography (CT) scans, X-rays, diagnostic test results, or similar, detailed medical information. However, providing routine medical information, such as blood pressure, cholesterol, A1c, Body Mass Index (BMI), along with commonly recognized diagnoses (e.g., diabetes, hypertension, Chronic Obstructive Pulmonary Disease [COPD], asthma), can be tremendously valuable to the Participants, especially CBOs that historically have lacked this information when trying to manage/monitor a client's health status.

The scope of data shared, the size of the network, and Partner characteristics create a number of legal challenges, especially for very sensitive data, such as information on domestic abuse or HIV. These can be minimized, however, by the *CCC*'s platform technology design, which may separate *CCC* data from HIPAA-governed medical records. When setting up a technology infrastructure, it is important to address the following legal issues:

- Determine applicability of HIPAA
- Determine requirements for individual privacy expectations, consents, and authorizations
- Determine technology requirements for nonclinical or non-CBO Partners
- Determine different levels of individual consent needed, such as:
  - Level 1: No consent to share (data/information regarding the client is invisible to any other organizations on the technology platform)
  - Level 2: Consented to share basic information (data such as name/date of birth and address, which can be used to identify a person, is shared among the organizations on the technology platform)
  - Level 3: Consented to share personal and basic information (Level 2 plus the program case management data except "safety issues"/sensitive information is shared among the organizations on the technology platform)
  - Level 4: Consented to share sensitive, personal, and basic information (Level 3 plus any other data containing sensitive information, such as safety issues, is allowed to be shared among organizations on the technology platform).

Milestone 1: Determine Applicability of HIPAA

One of the key roles of legal counsel is to identify legal and policy requirements for technology adoption at each Participant site and the applicability of HIPAA. See also the discussion in Chapter 3 Governance Track Requirement 7.

Key Task: Complete Review of Technology Vendor Requirements, Partner Policies on Privacy and Data Collection and Transfer, HIPAA, and State Law to Determine Legal Requirements

While Participants may initially automatically assume that personal information gathered in the *CCC* and concerning a patient or client is subject to HIPAA and thus is PHI under that Act, this may not always be the case with respect to information shared via the *CCC* for the reasons—and legal assumptions—provided in this section.

- If the *CCC* data is to be collected outside the clinical provider's normal EHR (e.g., through a stand-alone, third-party technology platform that does not pass data between itself and the EHR), then it should not be considered part of either the HIPAA Designated Record Set or the Legal Health Record. Therefore, it is not generally subject to HIPAA requirements (see "Fundamentals of the Legal Health Record and Designated Record Set," American Health Information Management Association, found at http://library.ahima.org/doc?oid=104008#.WnEBP03fOM8, particularly Appendix D).[8]

  - When the *CCC*'s case management/referral software is fully integrated into a clinical provider's EHR, the clinical provider's Health Information Management/Medical Records Governance Committees will need to decide whether to include the collected information into the Designated Record Set or the Legal Health Record. It is our observation that the information gathered for *CCC* purposes is in large part duplicative and, thus, need not be incorporated in either record. However, the Covered Entity's Privacy Officer should be consulted in determining if fully integrated *CCC* information is—or at least should be treated as if it was—PHI. To the extent that the information is shared among Covered Entities (as defined in HIPAA) in your specific local community, consider whether it is shared for purposes of each Covered Entity's treatment or healthcare operations (or if there is an approved IRB for research), and thus, whether it is exempt from HIPAA patient and authorization requirements.

- The *CCC* is a closed system with referrals of patients/clients to and from clinical providers and CBOs and data sharing that does not include texting or calling individual patients/clients.

- CBOs are not HIPAA Covered Entities (i.e., not healthcare providers, health plans, or clearinghouses).

- CBOs may share *CCC* data among themselves, but Covered Entities will not share data gathered for the community *CCC* with other Covered Entities (although they may share similar or duplicate data from their own medical records for HIPAA-permitted purposes of treatment, payment, and healthcare operations, all of which is outside the scope of the *CCC*).

  - To the extent clinical providers share PHI among each other via an EHR, then the process is governed by HIPAA (and they may be participating in a health information exchange [HIE]). Those requirements are well known to clinical providers and are not addressed in this Playbook.

- An important *caveat* is that some state laws define "Covered Entities" much more broadly than HIPAA and do not permit Covered Entities (as more broadly defined) the same leeway in defining their own Designated Record Set and Legal Health Record subject to state law requirements. If this is the case in your state, your legal counsel will guide you to a compliance framework for data sharing within the *CCC*. Legal counsel will also need to review any local laws to ensure compliance (although these are less likely to be applicable).

If any of the above assumptions are not applicable, the *CCC* Sponsor and Participants should consult with their respective attorneys to determine the legal ramifications. For example, if a community's state laws effectively apply HIPAA-type rules, even when HIPAA Covered Entities are not involved with the data-sharing process that necessarily takes place in a *CCC*, legal counsel will need to determine how to revise the implementation process to ensure legal compliance. If direct patient/client phone calls, texting, or similar engagement methods are to be included, this will necessarily implicate many highly complex federal and state laws regarding electronic communications. A discussion of these laws is outside the scope of this Playbook. You are encouraged to seek guidance from a legal advisor who is familiar with relevant federal and state laws, as there are potentially significant penalties for violation of electronic communications privacy and related rights.

The Sponsor should confirm, via the clinical Partners' representations, that the clinical Partners' HIPAA policies do not define the Designated Record Set or Legal Health Record so broadly as to encompass *CCC* data stored in separate software from their EHRs. The Sponsor should consider having the *CCC* Legal/Policy Track lead proactively meet with the clinical Partner's Privacy Officer (or person performing a similar function) to discuss these HIPAA (or non-HIPAA) issues. A well-informed Privacy Officer will ensure a much smoother *CCC* adoption.

If the *CCC*'s technology solution is integrated with the clinical Partners' EHR, legal counsel will have to determine how those clinical Partners define their HIPAA Designated Record Set and Legal Health Record. Legal counsel will need to determine if data collected for the *CCC* (even if duplicated elsewhere within the EHR) is considered part of these records and, thus, subject to additional HIPAA protections or whether it is outside the scope of the clinical Partner's HIPAA policies because it involves data not gathered for or stored within the EHR.

PRACTICE POINTER

Determine Partners and Compliance Requirements
with Clinical and Community Participants

It is important to remember that clinical and community Partners/ Participants are likely to have their own rules, policies, and procedures regarding patient/client privacy and data use and transfer. The Sponsor (in conjunction with legal counsel or Legal/Policy Track lead) should review these rules, and any issues should be addressed in the Clinical Provider and CBO Participation Agreements. Note also that the technology vendor's requirements should factor in those discussions as discussed in Chapter 3 Governance Track Requirement 7.

Milestone 2: Determine Requirements for Individual Privacy Expectations, Consents, and Authorizations

In order to respect individual expectations of privacy and rights to control dissemination and use of personal information (and to comply with many states' laws), regardless of HIPAA's application, it is prudent to obtain individual consents/authorizations for the gathering, use, transfer, and analysis of personal information. Funder requirements or applicable laws may dictate whether the consent must be in writing. Regardless, even if verbal consent is permitted, case managers should document the verbal consent and also read a "script" with the patient and the patient's legal representatives (as applicable) regarding exactly what the consent covers.

The form the consent must take depends on HIPAA (if applicable), other federal laws if texting/calls are contemplated, and state law if not superseded by federal requirements. A detailed discussion of HIPAA requirements is outside the scope of this Track and is so well defined that a general recitation is unlikely to be helpful. However, we note that some states require explicit written consent for the collection and use of personal information. A small number of states may permit implied consent when the individual voluntarily provides personal information to the *CCC* for purposes that would be considered obvious to the individual or when the information is used in a way that clearly benefits the individual and the *CCC*'s expectations are reasonable. Still other states permit "opt-out" consent, where the individual is given the opportunity to decline to consent. If the individual does not decline, then the individual is presumed to have given affirmative consent.

Studies have shown that "opt-out" consent policies result in substantially higher consent rates than "opt-in" policies.[9,10] The most risk-adverse practice to follow is to always obtain full written consent and authorization. If a written consent is not required, the Sponsor should weigh all relevant factors (with advice of counsel) and determine the appropriate consent format.

In some circumstances, consent/authorization is not required. In the context of the *CCC*, this is most likely to occur when a Participant is a Covered Entity and is using the data for "healthcare operations" as defined by HIPAA or when using the data for "research" as defined by HIPAA and under an IRB that waives the need for patient authorization. However, because in most circumstances consent will be required or desired (as a matter of prudence), this Playbook assumes the *CCC* processes will include a process to obtain written consents/authorizations from each affected individual. PCCI recommends a multiple-level consent structure form consenting to sharing basic demographic information up to full personal, medical, and other sensitive information.

Key Task: Review Individual Consent Form Contents

Individual consents/authorizations should account for (or include) the following (whether verbal or written):

- Competence to provide consent (if the individual is unable to do so, a legally permitted guardian or authorized party may do so)
- Specifics of the data to be shared (i.e., for what data is the consent/authorization provided)
- Scope of information to be shared (i.e., all individual information gathered at the *CCC* Participant's site or some subset of this information)
- With whom the information may be shared (i.e., all *CCC* Participants, their vendors, governmental agencies)
- What the information will be used for (e.g., research to make healthcare and social services delivery better for the individual and others, reporting to the Sponsor or Funder)
- The risks of sharing the information (e.g., data breach); this information may not be legally required but is often desired by Participants
- The voluntary nature of the request, meaning the individual does not have to consent to personal data use and will not be denied services for that reason
- Expiration or revocation of the consent/authorization
- How the consent/authorization may be revoked

Most clinical and some CBO partners are likely to have forms of consents/authorizations already in use. To the extent possible, the Sponsor and Legal/Policy Track lead should consider simply adding necessary *CCC* participation language to the existing forms. Also, if the *CCC* consent is not to be obtained upon the first touch with the clinical Partner, this should also be highlighted, as it may ease potential concerns regarding "dual consents."

In some cases, such as a federally sponsored program, the Funder may require that specific information (e.g., Privacy Act Notice) be shared with the patients. Review the *CCC* privacy considerations closely with your Funder, and if any additional information must be shared with the *CCC* patients, work with your Legal counsel and Partner site leaders to format and present the information in a simplified, accessible manner, considering the average education levels of *CCC* patients.

Finally, consider the need for photo releases. If your *CCC* seeks to use a particular patient/client for publicity or for fundraising, you will need to obtain a legally compliant photo/media release as well as the consent/authorization for data sharing.

Key Task: Reconcile Necessary Consent Process with Technology Platform Capabilities

The consent and privacy notice requirements have significant implications for your *CCC*'s technology platform. Depending on the privacy framework defined, the *CCC* technology platform may need to feature the ability of controlling progress through the workflows based on consent status of the patient. In some cases, it may be mandatory to require an upload of a signed, written consent into a patient's profile within the technology platform. The level of data access that a certain consent provides across your *CCC*'s Partners needs to be clearly defined and discussed. That is, consider whether all Participants should use a *CCC*-wide consent document, allowing for the Patient to consent once at their first interaction with a *CCC* Partner or should the platform prompt the end user to consent the patient at every encounter. Further, the duration of consent and the process for its expiration or revocation must be fully supported by the technology platform.

Milestone 3: Determine Requirements for Nonclinical or Non-CBO Partners

In addition to your Clinical and CBO Partners, the *CCC* goals may require partnership and data-use agreements with other entities, such as the State Health and Human Services Commission (HHSC) or local data from HIE, to gain access to Medicaid claims data.

Key Task: Determine Need to Obtain State Medicaid Data or Other Payer Data for ROI Purposes

To conduct an effective assessment of your *CCC*'s Return on Investment (ROI), you will likely need data reflecting financial expenditures (e.g., medical insurance claims data), which may come from either commercial or government entities. Depending on the scope of your *CCC* and current environment, partnering with commercial entities may not be feasible at the onset of the effort, as these entities often require a well-defined ROI and value proposition. Therefore, it may prove more effective to partner with your state's HHSC or Insurance Department to gain access to its Medicaid claims data for the initial phase of ROI analysis. Also, once the initial—and compelling—*CCC* ROI analyses are completed, commercial payers and partners may be more open to collaboration.

Key Task: Complete Requirements to Obtain State Medicaid Data or Other Data for ROI Purposes

If it is advantageous to obtain access to Medicaid data from the state's agency managing the program, the Sponsor and Legal/Policy Track lead should expect to see the following:

- A privacy and security initial screening questionnaire for the Sponsor or its technology vendor
- If the screening is satisfactory, an extensive (and likely nonnegotiable) State Data Use Agreement
- Once the State Data Use Agreement is signed, an audit of the technology vendor to determine actual "in use" technical, privacy, and security safeguards
- A requirement that the *CCC* subcontractors/vendors agree in writing to the terms of the Data Use Agreement

The Medicaid agency may also require policies and training that exceeds baseline HIPAA-compliant policies and training or (in some cases) signed certifications from the individual employees/subcontractors who are accessing the Medicaid data, certifying that they have read and will comply with the policies and have taken any state-mandated training. The Sponsor's legal counsel should carefully review the Medicaid agency agreement and work with the *CCC* program leads to develop any necessary new policies, training, or certifications.

Many states have extremely extensive technical and security requirements that may go beyond what clinical providers typically require. States may also prohibit the housing of data offshore. For these reasons, if you believe your *CCC* will want access to Medicaid data, the Legal/Policy Track lead should obtain the state's data use agreement and make compliance with its terms a condition for bidding by the *CCC*'s administrative/technology vendor. Similar issues may exist with commercial payer data and will need to be addressed.

PRACTICE POINTER

Consider Need for Federal Medicare Data

Federal Medicare data is typically not shared outside the context of a federal cooperative agreement or grant, which is generally a "take it or leave it" proposition for the *CCC*. It is possible to partner with an agency that is considered to be a "qualified entity" by the Federal Government (or conversely, one of your Partner agencies may apply to become a qualified entity). However, annual costs associated with this arrangement are significant. While inclusion of Medicare data may provide a more comprehensive analysis, the Sponsor should weigh the cost and benefits of this approach and identify potential alternative data sources to support the desired measures. Accordingly, Medicare data access rules are not described in this Playbook (but see www.data.cms.gov).[11]

Milestone 4: *Finalize Agreement with Technology Vendor*

If the *CCC* contracts separately with a technology vendor, it will need to consider and address a number of key areas as shown in Table 4.1, as well as other issues identified by the *CCC*'s independent legal counsel. As part of this process, the Legal/Policy Track lead, working with the Sponsor or Board or Governance Track lead and Program Sustainability lead should consider how the documents governing the use of technology within the *CCC*'s legal and policy framework "fit" within and will contribute to the *CCC*'s sustainability. This should include identification up front of future dates for review, revision, or termination of the documents or relationships.

Table 4.1   Eighteen Key Issues in a Technology Vendor Contract

1. Parties (Whether the *CCC* is able to contract on behalf of its participants)	2. Term and termination (Should extend at least to the anticipated *CCC* end date unless terminated for cause)	3. Pricing (Consider caps on price increases during the term)
4. Software, services, and support/ warranties (Performance guarantees and penalties for less-than-promised performance/service interruptions or upcharges for enhanced support)	5. Authorized users (Numbers and instances of the software)	6. Confidentiality of data and security requirements (Passwords, authentication)
7. Data-related provisions between/ among the Sponsor, technology vendor agreement parties, and other *CCC* participants (Data use, transfer, storage, warehousing, with possibly no firewalls between entities' data, and data sharing among participants. Considerations should include factors, such as protocol for minimum necessary for routine disclosures, role-based access controls, restrictions on functionalities (e.g., community-based organizations cannot alter medical information/data)	8. Transfer outside the technology vendor's platform (Likely to be desirable for further analysis and reporting, depending on the vendor's capabilities)	9. Liability for data breaches

(*Continued*)

Table 4.1 (*Continued*)   Eighteen Key Issues in Technology Vendor Contract

10. Insurance (Cyber liability, professional services/E&O at a minimum)	11. Indemnification	12. Limitation of liability
13. Subcontractor usage and rights and corresponding assignment provisions	14. IP license and ownership (Vendor may want to create/own derivative works from the *CCC* data; most Sponsors will want exclusive ownership of any IP created from the *CCC* data; vendor will also retain sole rights to its existing IP)	15. Ownership of usage data (Aggregate-level data)
16. Legal compliance representations (e.g., that consent was obtained before individual data was stored on the vendor's system, prohibited actions)	17. Governing law (Sponsor will want its state law to apply)	18. Detailed dispute resolution procedures

The Sponsor or Funder may wish to include, in the bid conditions, the right to review all vendor contracts to ensure that appropriate data use/sharing protections, insurance, indemnity, and other provisions are sufficiently strong to protect the *CCC* in the event of default or mismanagement by any vendor.

PRACTICE POINTER

Consider Pros and Cons of Contract Periods

The Sponsor should weigh the potential benefits of new technology against stability and predictability of costs. Term length in contracts with technology vendors should not be so long that the *CCC* is locked into obsolete technology when other, more nimble or cost-effective technology solutions are available. Conversely, short-term technology contracts may create instability as Participants must learn new software packages if the technology vendor is able to terminate the agreement on short notice. Technology vendors know that participants may be reluctant to learn new technology and, thus, have an advantage to negotiate a higher price than the market would otherwise bear upon renewal of a short-term agreement; a longer term agreement permits the Sponsor to lock in technology costs (or at least limit the rate of increase).

Rather than having multiple contracts between the technology vendor and each Participant, it is generally more advantageous to have one contract with the technology vendor on behalf of all Participants, for the following reasons:

- This arrangement allows the Sponsor or Administrator to negotiate price, service terms, and other provisions on behalf of the larger group. This both simplifies the process and gives the Sponsor or Administrator more bargaining power.
- If a change in technology is needed at some point, only one contract between the two parties must be renegotiated.
- Simplifying the vendor relationship promotes sustainability because it avoids creating situations where Participants may become frustrated with a repetitive need to negotiate and sign new contracts.

If the *CCC* wishes to go this route, it should include the single contract requirement as a condition of the bid. In the alternative, if the technology vendor insists on a separate contract for each instance of its software, the Board, Administrator, or Sponsor can still include language in the RFP or otherwise require that the Sponsor and technology vendor must agree to that contract's terms as an initial matter to avoid further negotiations that could slow implementation. In other words, while the Participants would have to separately sign up to the agreement, the basic terms would already be negotiated and be the same across all Participants.

Having completed the key actions of this requirement, the *CCC* Governance Track lead (working with the Legal/Policy and Technology Platform Track leads) will be ready to conduct a targeted search for the technology vendor. The actual operational requirements to implement the technology platform across the Partner sites are discussed in Chapter 5 Technology Platform Track.

Key Documents for Requirement 2

- HIPAA and related policies, procedures, and schedules—not included in this book
- Individual Consent/Authorization Forms (in addition to any necessary HIPAA authorizations and notices)
- Data Usage Agreement, which will vary based on state requirements, but examples are provided

Requirement 3: Develop a Legal and Policy Framework for the Clinical Providers

The *CCC* clinical Partners and Participants are likely to have many questions centered on consents and data sharing, necessary platform functionalities, and additional work related to the use of the *CCC* technology platform. The Legal/Policy Track lead and *CCC* legal counsel should ensure:

- Compliance with *CCC* funding and clinical Partner governance documents
- Compliance with applicable federal, state, and local laws
- Consideration of how the clinical Partner documents created as part of the legal framework will contribute to *CCC* sustainability, and whether there is a need to identify future dates for review, revision, or termination of these documents

Milestone 1: Ensure Completion of Requirement 2 Milestones

This work includes the following:

- Complete review of clinical Partner policies on privacy and data collection and transfer, HIPAA, and state law to determine legal requirements
- Determination of requirements for Individual Privacy Expectations, Consents, and Authorizations

As indicated, most clinical Partners are likely to have forms of consents/authorizations already in use. To the extent possible, the Sponsor and Legal/Policy Track lead should consider simply adding necessary *CCC* participation language to the existing forms. Also, if the *CCC* consent is not to be obtained upon the first touch with the clinical Partner, this should also be highlighted, as it may ease potential concerns regarding "dual consents."

Milestone 2: Finalize Agreements with Clinical Partners/Participants

An important step in the development of the *CCC* Legal/Policy framework is to formalize agreements with clinical Partners.

Key Task: Develop Clinical Partner Participation Agreements

Agreements with clinical Partners should address a number of key issues outlined in Table 4.2, which include appropriate consents/authorizations, if required, as well as any additional issues identified by local legal counsel engaged by the *CCC* to ensure compliance with applicable federal, state, and local laws.

Table 4.2   Thirty-Three Key Issues in a Clinical Participation Agreement

1. Parties (and authority of the Partners to bind affiliates (e.g., those in its network)	2. List participating locations	3. Specific intervention obligations of the Partner
4. Software as a Service (SaaS) license (if needed)	5. Insurance (if needed)	6. Data use, transfer, and sharing (including whether separate community Partner consents/ authorizations must be obtained; including data warehouse (if applicable))
7. Maintenance of commercially reasonable privacy policies, technical safeguards for data	8. Defined data to be gathered	9. Reporting obligations (of the parties)
10. IP ownership definitions for Partners	11. Use of Partner and Sponsor's name, logo, trademark in the other's materials (consider also a photo/media release)	12. Payment (if any) for *CCC* participation generally or for specific activities (e.g., navigation/referral) and payment limitations based on funding source, timely submission of payment claims, etc.
13. Payment for software and support services (if any)	14. Resources for data gathering	15. Governing or Advisory Board participation requirements; monthly operation calls; periodic networking events with other Partners, etc.

(*Continued*)

Table 4.2 (*Continued*) Thirty-Three Key Issues in Clinical Participation Agreement

16. Training – roles and scope	17. Eligibility criteria for patients to participate in *CCC* (residence; social needs; insurance status; any disqualifications; etc.)	18. Technical requirements (from Funder or technology vendor), if any
19. Software provided and promises to use only for permissible uses	20. Services and support to be provided	21. Individual consents/ authorizations (to the extent required; authorization maintenance by Sponsor or Partner, or both)
22. Business Associate Agreement (only if Sponsor or Administrator is providing HIPAA covered work on behalf of the Covered Entity (most likely health care operations)	23. Use of ancillary staffing resources (i.e., Interns, community health workers, volunteers)	24. Availability of records or other information for audit (if required by Funder or Sponsor)
25. Confidentiality provisions (if warranted and permitted under state law)	26. Notice provisions and points of contact	27. Term (until end of funding or indefinite with an annual rollover provision, absent notice of termination or as otherwise desired)
28. Termination (consider requiring some notice and opportunity to cure if a particular clinical Participant is critical to *CCC* success)	29. Appropriate disclaimers if needed (e.g., no partnership or joint venture; will not represent any agency relationship)	30. Representation of compliance
31. Anti-assignment clause (if warranted)	32. Governing Law and Merger clauses	33. Dispute Resolution (typically require an executive level meeting and no other terms)

PRACTICE POINTER

Address Use of Interns or Volunteers Up Front

If interns or volunteers will be used to provide any services connected with the *CCC*, then the Participation Agreements should address intern and volunteer use and supervision consistent with the Participant and internship or volunteer program rules, payment (if any), and liability. Note that many entities will require interns or volunteers to take the entity's "new hire" or compliance training if the interns or volunteers will see patients/clients.

Consider the use of cooperative and collaborative language regarding resources issues (e.g., "The Sponsor and clinical Participant will explore multiple avenues to obtain independent case managers/patient navigators/ interns or funding for additional employees to provide *CCC* navigation"). If the Funder and applicable law permit verbal consents to be documented by the case manager, highlight this fact for the clinical Partner.

Key Task: Determine the Need for Separate Clinical Partner Agreements with Vendors or CBOs

As outlined in Requirement 2 of this chapter, the Legal/Policy Track lead and legal counsel will need to determine the need for separate agreements between a clinical Partner and the technology vendor or a *CCC* Administrator. In addition, while typically there is no need for a contract between the clinical Partner and the CBOs given that the clinical Partner is only referring patients to the CBO, in some instances, the agreement between the *CCC* Sponsor and clinical Partner may provide that the Sponsor can share information form the clinical Partners with the CBO Partners (and vice versa). If it does not, then the Legal/Policy Track lead and Governance Track lead, working with the Clinical Partners Track lead, may want to consider the desirability of sharing participant data through a separate agreement.

Requirement 4: Develop a Legal and Policy Framework for the Community Partners

Enthusiastic participation by CBOs is necessary for *CCC* success. The *CCC* legal and policy framework should avoid overly complex legal documents or significant revamping of workflows and existing policies and procedures unless absolutely necessary. As with the clinical providers, CBOs are likely to have many questions centered on consents and data sharing, necessary platform functionalities, and additional work related to the use of the *CCC* technology platform. The Legal/Policy Track lead and *CCC* legal counsel should ensure:

- Compliance with *CCC* funding and CBO governance documents
- Compliance with applicable federal, state, and local laws
- Consideration of how the CBO Partner/Participant documents created as part of the legal framework will contribute to *CCC* sustainability and whether there is a need to identify future dates for review, revision, or termination of these documents

Milestone 1: Ensure Completion of Requirement 2 Milestones

This work includes the following:

- Complete review of CBO policies on privacy and data collection and transfer, HIPAA, and state law to determine legal requirements
- Determination of requirements for Individual Privacy Expectations, Consents, and Authorizations

Milestone 2: Finalize Agreements with Community Partners/Participants

Another important step in the development of the *CCC* Legal/Policy framework is to finalize agreements with CBOs.

Key Task: Establish CBO Participation Agreement

The CBO Participant agreements should address some of the same/subset of the issues outlined in the clinical provider agreements and also include any appropriate consents/authorization language. It is beneficial to use collaborative language, especially with respect to resource issues (e.g., the Sponsor and Participant will explore multiple avenues to obtain patient navigators or funding to support additional CBO staff to provide navigation services). Agreements (or guidelines) with Participants should address.

PRACTICE POINTER

Utilize Existing Consents, Where Feasible

If the CBO has existing consents/authorizations, the Sponsor and legal counsel should work with the Participant to add any required *CCC* language to the existing document, rather than mandating a separate consent form for *CCC*.

In addition to the information in Table 4.2, CBO participation agreements should address:

- Acknowledgments and confirmations if an umbrella CBO has the authorization to sign on behalf of the individual service delivery organizations
  - For CBOs, it is important to carefully consider whether binding legal agreements are necessary or whether general guidelines will suffice. Any agreements with community Participants should be short and avoid legal jargon to the extent possible. It may be more feasible to utilize an acknowledgment form (if sufficient under state law) that permits umbrella organizations to sign agreements binding their smaller community delivery organizations. The smaller delivery organizations can then sign one-page acknowledgments binding them to the main agreement terms.
- Additional details on what services the Sponsor or governance or technology vendor will provide, such as (1) use of free software, (2) assistance in client navigation, (3) reports suitable for sharing with the CBO board and funders, (4) publicity rights/recognition,

(5) training and support, (6) possible Board or Workgroup participation, and (7) meetings and community calls for additional Participants.

- Additional details on what services the CBO will provide, such as (1) the same services they provide under existing policies, (2) additional required consents/authorizations (if any), (3) reporting using the software provided, and (4) no shows and other information, as appropriate.
- Details on intern and volunteer use and supervision, consistent with both the CBO and internship/volunteer program rules, payment (if any), and liability requirements.

Requirement 5: Develop a Legal and Policy Framework for CCC Program Sustainability

The legal and policy framework to support *CCC* sustainability requires a combination of legal savvy and astute project management skills. The *CCC*'s legal counsel and Legal/Policy Track lead should identify areas that require ongoing legal review based on (1) anticipated or actual changes to the law, (2) contract and policy renewal and termination dates, and (3) funding expiration. Once identified, *CCC* legal counsel and the Legal/Policy Track lead should ensure all documents are updated as required.

Milestone 1: Review Sustainability Requirements for Each Track from a Legal Perspective

As part of an examination of sustainability considerations and requirements from a legal perspective, *CCC* legal counsel and the Legal/Policy Track lead should consider sustainability aspects for all aspects of the work under the Legal/Policy Track requirements, such as the following:

- Draft bylaws or internal Administrator processes to encourage continuity and change via staggered terms for Board members, succession planning for the Administrator, winding-up provisions if the *CCC* is acquired or is administered by a different Sponsor or receives funding from a new Funder requiring different parameters, etc.
- Revisit bylaws and meetings schedules as needed to ensure that any necessary changes are promptly implemented.
- In addition to legal requirements of corporate formalities, encourage the governance entity to retain agenda and keep detailed minutes in order to readily identify decisions made, issues determined, and work completed.
- Review *CCC* progress to determine if the corporate form should be modified and to determine if inventions have been created or materials developed that warrant patent, trademark, copyright, or related legal protection.
- If there are winding-up activities or employment terminations, ensure an analysis of appropriate federal/state and local laws.
- Set periodic review dates with Governance Track lead and Sponsor to review documents and practices generated through the Legal/Policy

Track for governance, technology platform, clinical providers, and community partners to determine if changes are needed.

- Establish periodic calls with the Sponsor and Governance Track lead to go over any changes in the law requiring new or revised contracts, policies, or processes and subsequent training.
- Encourage the Sponsor to meet with its insurance broker on a regular basis to update insurance coverage or requirements as needed.
- As an iterative process, consider the need to identify future dates for review, revision, or termination.

Chapter 5

Technology Platform Track

Introduction to the Technology Platform Track

The technology infrastructure for an information exchange platform, such as the *Connected Communities of Care (CCC)*, is a critical component enabling the stakeholders to achieve clinical and social goals to fulfill the *CCC* requirements. The technology infrastructure creates an integrated electronic platform to exchange clinical and social information securely between healthcare organizations (i.e., hospitals, clinics) and Community-Based Social Service Organizations Community-Based Organizations (CBOs) (i.e., homeless shelters, food pantries) that operate within the *CCC* network. Through data collection and reporting, the technology infrastructure also enables network Participants and stakeholders to understand the impact and effectiveness of various programs in fulfilling their mandates.

The Governance Track provides a framework for a strategic assessment of the *CCC* technology needs, ranging from required features to market analysis. The Technology Platform Track builds off that strategy and explores in depth the nuances and critical activities necessary to ensure a successful deployment of the *CCC*'s backbone—the data-sharing platform. Specifically, the Technology Platform Track will (1) set up the primary requirements and components for the *CCC* information exchange platform, (2) outline key requirements for successful selection of a technology vendor, and (3) provide requirements for implementation of the technology to support the *CCC* clinical and community workflows.

Integral to the work in the Technology Platform Track is the work in the Legal/Policy Track Requirement 2 centered on:

- Determining applicability of Health Insurance Portability and Accountability Act (HIPAA)
- Determining requirements for individual privacy expectations, consents, and authorizations
- Determining technology requirements for nonclinical or non-CBO Partners
- Determining different levels of individual consents needed

Prerequisites to the Technology Platform Track

The work in this Track can begin once the *CCC* key decision makers have completed the following actions as part of the Chapter 3 Governance Track Requirement 7:

- Develop a clear applied technology strategy for the *CCC* and define the general requirements for *CCC* technology and data integration at Partner sites.

Roles and Responsibilities

Key roles associated with the Technology Platform Track include the following:

- The *CCC* Board, Funder, and Sponsor
- Governance Track lead
- Assigned Technology Platform Track lead and the technology vendor providing the technology powering the information exchange platform
- Partner site leads

Requirements to Establish the *CCC* Technology Platform

The Technology Platform Track lead should address each of the following requirements:

1. Define the underlying business requirements supporting the technology platform.
2. Determine desired system characteristics and requirements.
3. Define required application functionalities.
4. Stand up the technology platform.
5. Develop a short- and long-term user support strategy.
6. Ensure the technology platform is sustainable.

Requirement 1: Define the Underlying Business Requirements Supporting the Technology Platform

The *CCC* should facilitate technology support for the Participants and users of the *CCC* technology platform. After the technology strategy is defined in Chapter 3 Governance Track Requirement 7, the next step is to translate that strategy into specific needs and requirements, starting with the business requirements of your *CCC*'s interventions.

Milestone 1: Know the Partner/Participant Organizations

It is extremely important to understand the number and function of organizations that will be involved in your *CCC*. For example, there may be stand-alone Participants performing case management for their own clients and having no interaction or information exchange with other organizations other than sending or receiving referrals. Conversely, networked organizations perform case management for their own clients but also share appropriate client information and activity with a network of other organizations. Umbrella organizations, such as a centralized food bank or the United Way, may oversee the efforts of multiple organizations and are involved in defining how the case management workflow will occur across these organizations. Umbrella organizations typically have access to all of their member organizations' information for reporting and analysis purposes.

Milestone 2: Contemplate User Factors Affecting CCC Technology Adoption and Use

For *CCC* site users and their environments, there are associated factors that can impact adoption and widespread use of the technology platform. The Technology Platform Track lead should incorporate these factors into decisions regarding selection of the technical solution and fit to the needs of your *CCC*. Examples of these types of user factors can include the following:

- *Availability and Commitment of Resources at Each CBO Setting.* The *CCC* Sponsor or governance entity could consider subsidizing participation costs or providing personnel to assist with implementation needs.
- *User Trust of the Technology System.* Establishing and maintaining a conservative privacy and data-security approach will facilitate end user trust of the system.

- *System Integration and Support of User Workflow.* Design efforts should include workflow studies and continue to engage end users in iterative system design modifications.
- *Management of User Expectations.* Ensuring close collaboration in goal-setting discussions and timelines leads to aligned expectations and activities.
- *Perceived Value Benefits to the End Users.* Providing ongoing and consistent evaluation and demonstration of outcomes increases the technology's perceived value.
- *Varying Technical Skill Levels among End Users.* Providing training tailored to end-user skill levels, with ongoing skill development opportunities promotes technology use and acceptance.

Milestone 3: *Know the Users of the System*

It is also important to understand the system users and their functionality needs and data access needs.

Key Task: Classify Users by Their Roles and Function

There will be several users of the technology platform at the Participant sites, such as:

- Administrators
  - At clinical sites, these are typically lead clinical investigators or clinical administration staff members.
  - At CBO sites, these are typically executive staff members or program administration staff members.
- Case Managers
  - At clinical sites, these are typically care managers, case managers, behavioral/mental health counselors, social workers, or care coordination staff members.
  - At CBO sites, these are typically case managers, behavioral/mental health counselors, social workers, or intake specialists.
- Service Delivery
  - At clinical sites, these are typically billing personnel, medical assistants, or nurses.
  - At CBO sites, these are typically case manager assistants, social workers, or service delivery specialists.

- Program Managers
  - At clinical sites, these are typically the lead clinical investigators or clinical administration staff members.
  - At CBO sites, these are typically executive staff members or program administration staff members.
- Data Access/Reporting User
  - These include any staff members with access to specific data types, as described below.

Key Task: Ensure the Technology Supports Specific User Roles

The Technology Platform Track lead should ensure that the system supports the roles that can be assigned to users within the application. Each user may have one or more of these roles, such as:

- Administrative Roles
  - *Organization Administrator.* Has the ability to configure the application to tailor the system for the specific needs of the organization and to add additional CBOs as needed.
  - *User Administrator.* Has the ability to add new users and to define each user's level of access to features and programs.
  - *Program Administrator.* Can authorize access for specific programs and has the ability to configure new or existing programs, including defining the data-collection workflow and the services and data to be collected. Program administrators also provide support for those who oversee the program outcomes and analyze the results through reporting.
- End User Roles
  - *Enrollment Specialist.* Has the ability to engage (and obtain consents from) patients and clients and register them for the *CCC*'s programs. These are typically frontline or administrative staff at the sites of care.
  - *Case/Client Manager.* Like enrollment specialists, case managers have the ability to collect relevant client information and enroll clients in programs. In addition, these individuals operate in depth on *CCC* interventions and leverage their experience to work with the patients/clients on the case managers' specific intervention goals (e.g., tracking of social care needs, performing additional client assessments, making referrals to other organizations, entering and

tracking client tasks and appointments, creating client case notes, and providing other services for clients).

- *Patient/Client.* The *CCC* may offer the patients/clients themselves the ability to participate in the interventions directly through portals or engagement tools.

Key Task: Define User Data Access Roles

In addition to general user roles, it is important to understand which subsets of the *CCC* or organizational data that each user needs access to in order to perform necessary tasks.

Classify extent of *CCC* data required

- All *CCC* data
- Multiple organizations' data
- Single organization's data
- Subset of an organization's data (individual level or another subset)

Classify data sensitivity

- Restricted information that is to be accessed on an exception basis by a limited number of individuals
- Sensitive information (such as Protected Health Information [PHI])
- Personal information that is personal but is not PHI
- Basic demographic (or similar) information not derived from (and not) PHI

Key Documents for Requirement 1

The key document associated with Requirement 1 includes the List of User Roles and Functions. The Parkland Center for Clinical Innovation (PCCI) has provided examples in the narrative of this Requirement.

Requirement 2: Determine Desired System Characteristics and Requirements

Once the *CCC* governance entity and Governance Track and Technology Platform Track leads have defined the technology strategy as part of governance (see Chapter 3 Governance Track Requirement 7), the clinical and CBO Partners will define the requirements for *CCC* technology deployment and data integration, specific to their sites, to achieve optimal clinical and operational outcomes. However, technology requirements are a well known source of frustration for site staff, primarily due to technology's perceived interference with the provision of care and services. Therefore, it is important to systematically introduce the *CCC* technology in a way that assuages concerns, minimizes workflow disruptions, and encourages technology adoption by frontline personnel. The Clinical Advisory Group and Technology Platform Track lead will need to coordinate with clinical Partner sites to define the operational requirements for deployment of the technology.

Milestone 1: Conduct Technology Inventories at Partner Sites

The Technology Platform Track lead, in close collaboration with the Clinical Providers and Community Partners Track leads, should inventory all technology and data storage/sharing platforms relevant to clinical and CBO operation activities across all participating sites. While the inventory efforts conducted by the governance entity (as part of the readiness assessment process) and the Governance Track lead (as part of Governance Requirement 7) covered technology at a high level, the work to be done here is significantly more detailed. The Technology Platform Track lead needs to ensure examination of specific requirements, such as data formats, field definitions, and security protocols for each of the participating sites. It is important to review the diverse technologies that might need to integrate with the *CCC* technology across all of the clinical and CBO sites.

Milestone 2: Define the Functionalities Needed for Identified Use Cases

Use-case categories determined through the readiness assessment analysis help define and prioritize the technology functionality requirements. It is a worthwhile exercise to plot the use cases against corresponding functionalities to ensure the technology solution will be able to provide the

Table 5.1   Sample Functionalities that Support Use-Case Categories

Required CCC Functionality	Use-Case Categories			
	Demographic Information	Standard Documents	Service Eligibility Identification	Personal Eligibility Criteria
Notifications	✓			
Secured messaging	✓			
Referral request	✓			
Appointment calendar			✓	
Document tagging and storage	✓			
Real-time alerts		✓		
Query service eligibility and availability	✓		✓	✓
Reporting and analytics	✓			
Decision support			✓	

functionality or, alternatively, whether customization is required, which can cause delays. For example, many information management systems provide functionalities to support many use-case categories. However, some use-case categories require the ability to query service eligibility or availability of resources (e.g., available beds), which requires additional databases of services and query and logic functionality that may not be available in some systems. Those cases would require additional technical development or customization. Table 5.1 depicts a sample plotting of use-case categories and corresponding functionalities.

Milestone 3: *Align Clinical and CBO Needs with CCC Technology*

The Clinical Providers and Community Partners Track leads must coordinate with the *CCC* technology vendor to align the *CCC* workflow needs and key functionalities (identified through use-case analysis) with the *CCC* technology offerings and roadmap. This process ideally results in a defined "minimum viable product" for technology and data integration that is acceptable to the clinical and CBO Partners. The Partner leads will then coordinate across all of their participating sites to define standard acceptance criteria, certification processes, and any other requirements.

Technology should enable the user to know the required criteria and collect and store eligibility documents (e.g., birth certificates) that are sent electronically with the referral.

Key Task: Reconcile Technology Requirements with Planned Features of the Technology Platform

The Clinical Providers and Community Partners Track leads will work with the Technology Platform Track lead to create detailed technology requirements for *CCC* integration at all Partner sites.

PRACTICE POINTER

Utilize Seasoned Product Managers

PCCI recommends leveraging the skills and expertise of seasoned product managers (on a contract basis, if necessary) to create the detailed technology requirements. Remember, this effort is most likely not only novel to you and your Partners, but it may be to the technology vendor as well. Technology vendors are largely accustomed to well-defined, clearly scoped requirements. A successful set of requirements results from close collaboration among the clinical and CBO business leads, Technology Platform Track lead, and technology vendor, driven by the product manager responsible for detailing the requirements. Ensure a clear communication channel between the product managers on both sides to avoid miscommunications and consequent delays. Be sure to clearly define acceptance criteria for each of the requirements, as well as the desired timeframe for meeting them.

The Technology Platform Track lead will reconcile the technology requirements with existing and short-term planned features of the *CCC* technology platform. The Technology Platform Track lead will also determine, for each requirement, whether or not it is currently available in the *CCC* technology and, if not, whether or not it is a planned feature of the *CCC* technology (with an associated short-term timeline). The Clinical Providers and Community Partners Track leads may then negotiate with the technology vendor to ensure that all the critically required functionality will be available in a timely manner to launch the *CCC*.

PRACTICE POINTER

Create a Reconciliation Document

The process of determining specific technology requirements and aligning them against the technology vendor's current set of offerings and roadmap requires frequent and significant decision-making. PCCI recommends a very thorough system for tracking all of the communications with the technology vendor to avoid any potential confusion or disagreements. It is also good practice to create a reconciliation document that describes, for each requirement, whether that functionality is currently available or its status on the vendor's future development roadmap.

Key Task: Obtain a Consensus of "Must-Have" Technology Requirements

The Clinical Providers and Community Partners Track leads will next negotiate with clinical and CBO Participant site leads to obtain a consensus list of "must-have" technology requirements that will be provided to the technology vendor and Technology Platform Track lead for review. This is an iterative process. The Clinical Providers and Community Partners Track leads require bargaining and creative thinking skills in working with the clinical and CBO Partners and the technology vendor in order to define practical clinical and operational workflow workarounds to supplement *CCC* technology shortcomings. They should also build trust through transparency and management of expectations for the following reasons: (1) It is essential to create—up front—an expectation that the *CCC* technology may not provide all desired features (meaning the Partners will need to assist in providing optimized clinical workflows around the technology features), and (2) the technology vendor needs to be prepared to make some reasonable enhancements that will be required for technology implementation and adoption at Participant sites. Success in convincing the technology vendor to incorporate these changes (ideally at no cost) will depend on whether or not the requested change/enhancement can be utilized by all of the vendor's existing (as well as new) clients. To the extent that the requested requirement is unique to your *CCC*, you should expect some amount of pushback, an up-charge for the functionality, or a delayed technology-build timeline.

While no two *CCC*'s are identical, in PCCI's experience, there is a set of core platform requirements necessary to enable the initial phases of any *CCC* implementation. The following is a list of these core system requirements:

- *Accessibility.* The technology platform should be offered as a hosted, software-as-a-service (SaaS) solution offered via a secure, private, cloud-based environment that has the ability to act on (and process) information in real time, while providing organizations with privacy and control over sensitive information, with integrated, secure data protection.
- *Privacy and Security.* The technology platform should support appropriate authentication for increased security and provide additional multiple levels of protection, such as:
  - Strong access control
    - Access to production system is restricted to Developer Operations Engineering (DevOps) and security personnel.
    - Access (check-in) to the source code is restricted to developers only. DevOps or security cannot check-in the code.
    - Dual Control principle requires an action from more than a single person to perform important operations. Dual Control mitigates human errors and intentional insider threats. Dual controls are granting and auditing access to applications and systems.
  - System should meet any legal requirements for data, such as segregated and role-based access to sensitive health and financial information.
  - System should support a strict identity verification protocol to restrict system access to authorized users; single sign-on capabilities should be offered to Participant organizations who wish to provide a seamless user interface from within their own systems if the vendor software is integrated into Participants' existing information systems.
    - Role-Based Access. Restrict access to pre-defined roles; this access works in concert with authentication to ensure appropriate access based on various user roles.
  - Protection against unauthorized access using intrusion detection and prevention systems

- Zoning and network segmentation (i.e., splitting into subnetworks) to control access and enhance security
- Encryption of all databases and all external and internal communications to meet legal and security encryption requirements for data stored and transmitted
- Network and web application firewalls
- Continuous automated security code testing and web application vulnerability scanning
- Patient matching should be automated and demonstrate a high level of accuracy to prevent unintentional or unauthorized access to patient records and to minimize errors. The solution should be based on proven algorithms and technologies. Patient matching is also of critical importance in preventing duplicative records.

- *Adaptability.* The system should allow for a seamless exchange of information across disparate systems and databases to create a case record that includes medical/health and social information. The integration engine will support multiple data exchange standards and enable new organizations to rapidly join the network of Participants. It should also provide both real-time and batch-processing capabilities with the ability to scale as the *CCC* network expands.

- *Consistency.* The system should have the necessary tools to monitor system activity, determine when failures occur, and provide timely resolution. The system will have failover and disaster recovery procedures in place that will ensure little to no downtime in the event of a system failure due to sabotage; disaster; or basic network, hardware, or software failure.

- *Scalability and Reporting.* The technical system should meet existing record retention laws (e.g., 6 years) as determined by the Legal/Policy Track lead. For performance improvement purposes, the system should maintain audit logs of consent records, user activity, each data request, each record request, each violation of security policy, etc.

  - In addition to secure retention of records and data, the system needs to allow a flexible engine for data extraction. Some vendors offer this functionality as customizable report-generator tools (often powered by a third-party, white-labeled application). This approach is sufficient and appropriate for the initial *CCC* phases, as there may be a lack of resources with technical expertise to configure your own reporting capabilities. More complex *CCC* instances may have reporting requirements that surpass the capabilities of the tools included within your technology platform. In such cases, it is vital that your data teams are given access to the platform's databases to extract the raw data required for you to create the necessary reports.

Key Documents for Requirement 2

- Platform Functionalities and Vendor Specifications
- Criteria for Vendor Evaluation

Requirement 3: Define Required Application Functionalities

Once the core system requirements have been defined, the next requirement is to specify the necessary platform functionalities to support the *CCC* workflows. The technology platform should include application functionality to address various data inputs, outputs, and essential program outcomes. This process should include a focus on the following: (1) how each Participant will use the technology functionality, (2) how the Participant defines programs and workflows, (3) what information should be collected for each service for optimal client/patient and program outcomes, and (4) appropriate forms for data collection.

Functionality 1: Define Notification Requirements

The Technology Platform Track lead should determine notification requirements for the technology. Notifications constitute messaging within the *CCC* network to convey information to intended recipients. These messages are typically triggered by an action or change of status within the technology system (e.g., document expiration) signaling the requirement for recipient action. Notification methods may include email, Short Message Service (SMS), voice, flag, or some other indicator.

Functionality 2: Define Secured Messaging Functionality

Secured messaging should be established based on the security privileges of each Participant. Secured messaging is the ability to communicate information (e.g., confidential information) via free text with one or more *CCC* Participants, in a secure manner based on each Participant's security privileges. One example is a secure message to alert a case worker that a patient needs to be quarantined. Another example is a secure message to alert a shelter that a client needs to pick up a prescription.

Functionality 3: Define Requirements for Appointment Calendars

An appointment calendar captures and displays information about a client's appointment history and present and future appointments. This data should include both scheduled and kept appointments. This allows Participant organizations to send reminders to patients/clients and to track the clients (i.e., to know the facilities the client has visited and the services provided).

Functionality 4: Define Needs for Document Storage and Tagging

Document storage and tagging may be used in conjunction with notifications to push alerts when a document is up for renewal or expiration. This is helpful when retrieving information for clients who have lost documents or for alerting a case worker that a client's insurance is expiring.

Functionality 5: Define Need for Real-Time Alerts

Real-time alerts are issued when immediate action is required by an alert recipient. Both the system and the individual user should be able to issue the alert. For example, a real-time alert may be issued by one Participant to alert other Participants that a client should be quarantined.

Functionality 6: Define Query Service Eligibility and Availability

A service eligibility query enables a Participant to query the *CCC* network for available services and to determine client eligibility for these services. One example is a service query to: (1) locate a shelter allowing a patient to use a nebulizer, (2) determine shelter eligibility criteria, and (3) determine space availability.

Functionality 7: Define Reporting and Analytics Functionality Needs

In some cases, a Sponsor or Funder may have specific reporting requirements. In such instances, the platform reporting functionality must accommodate the requested reporting frequency, format, and reporting data logic.

The technology vendor may offer reporting functionality as a set of predefined reports, or it may offer a tool that allows for reporting customization. Generally speaking, at a minimum, the system must provide the ability to extract all of the data fields being collected and do so retrospectively for a user-defined time period. Be mindful that the data likely to be collected through *CCC* interventions will have errors due to user input and user interaction. The platform should enable the program administrators and Quality Assurance (QA) staff to retrieve affected records and make the necessary adjustments in the data to correct the errors. Per Sponsor or Funder requirements and for your own performance measurement efforts, the reporting functionality of the platform should have the ability to export the entire history of the data record, including the erroneous data that was entered.

In general, the analytics reporting functionality should allow a *CCC* Participant to generate reports (both in electronic and print-ready formats) at various levels of resolution, ranging from client-specific to aggregated organizational-level views (e.g., client, program, site, and system levels). Both predefined and custom reports should support the functionality to create custom views and the ability to export the data in a variety of formats (e.g., Excel, PDF, Word) for further analysis and evaluation. Report examples include the following:

- *Unduplicated Service Delivery Report.* Total number of families served— Single count of every individual who has been served in a program within a given timeframe
- *Services Provided by Encounter Date (Families).* A report of every service provided for an entire family and filtered by encounter date
- *Services Provided by Encounter Date (Individuals).* A report of every service provided for an individual and filtered by encounter date
- *Services Provided by Type (Families).* A report of every type of service provided for a family (e.g., report on how many diabetes test strips have been delivered in a certain timeframe)
- *Services Provided by Type (Individuals).* A report of every type of service provided for an individual (e.g., report on how many hours of physical activity or hours of nutrition classes completed)
- *Client Enrollment Reports.* How many people are enrolled in a program within a period of time
- *Timeliness Reports.* Case management efficiency report
- *Goal Attainment Report.* Identifies how many patients/clients have achieved their established care or Social Determinants of Health (SDOH) goals; provides quantitative evidence regarding the degree of progress (or lack thereof), which is essential for successful care or case management
- *HMIS Reports.* If applicable—all standard reports required by Homeless Management Information Systems (HMISs)
    Example: Use of an HMIS system is required by all agencies and care providers that receive U.S. Department of Housing and Urban Development (HUD) funding to provide services to homeless clients. Most *CCC* technology platforms, including Pieces Iris®, are working to address HUD HMIS requirements to enable homeless care providers to share enrollment data, encounter data, and other information with other care providers within the network.

- *Custom Reports.* As requested by the health system or CBO. Examples could include the following: number of referrals, what referrals were made, referral outcomes, feedback, timeliness, all services a particular client is currently receiving within the *CCC*, or *CCC* usage by a CBO over a specified timeframe.

Both standard and custom reports should provide a high level of drilldown capability allowing users to fully understand their ecosystem. As your *CCC* grows, the complexity of reporting requirements will grow and will exceed the ability of the available reporting tools. To avoid challenges and barriers to reporting at a more mature stage of the *CCC*, it is important to ensure that your technology platform (and the policies of your technology vendor) allow for direct access to the raw dataset. If this access is in place, your analytics teams will be able to craft the required reports on their own and not be limited by the functionality of the technology platform. Another option, especially for CBOs, is to establish a contract for advanced data analytics with the technology vendor, if the vendor is the keeper of the data. Such arrangements are much more efficient for CBOs that only need custom reports on a periodic basis and do not have expert data analysts on staff.

Functionality 8: Define Decision Support Needs

Decision support functionality aggregates, simplifies, and presents targeted information in a manner that supports decision-making activities. This typically requires a more sophisticated technology platform that incorporates Artificial Intelligence (AI) and Machine Learning (ML) mechanisms to identify patterns and predict needs. While more complex (and expensive), these decision-support functionalities can be of tremendous value, especially for high-risk populations, with individuals experiencing mental/behavioral challenges or individuals suffering with chronic conditions, such as diabetes and asthma. One example of decision support is a recommendation for services based on a patient's level of risk or history of referrals and services. Another example might be a summary of a patient's health and social assessments provided at the points of care.

Functionality 9: Define Beneficiary Registration Information

The technology platform must be able to record patient demographics, including (at a minimum) name, date of birth, address/addresses, phone numbers, insurance status, family size, transportation status, and primary language.

Functionality 10: Define Ability to Identify and Merge Patient Records

The technology should have the ability to identify and merge duplicate patient records. Technology solutions can discourage duplication through "fuzzy" client list searches to pull potential duplications in enrollment based on variations of a client's name. The system can also offer additional pieces of information (e.g., name, birthdate, address, gender) for the case manager to determine whether to proceed with a new enrollment or utilize an existing client profile. The system may also have a Master Data Management (MDM) process to identify duplicates after entry.

Functionality 11: Determine Eligibility Identification Functionality

The technology should offer functionality to determine an individual's eligibility for certain benefit programs (e.g., Supplemental Nutrition Assistance Program [SNAP] or Women, Infants, and Children [WIC]). Eligibility information can be included in the referral directories. It is ideal if the technology has the ability to take a screening tool (e.g., WIC) and embed this information in the technology solution.

Functionality 12: Customize SDOH Screening Questions

The technology platform should have the ability to be customized to allow for various screening questions. For example, the Pieces Iris® screening tool includes a customizable ontology of over 600 data fields. It uses logic-based questions to filter for social and resource needs that can be further filtered by location (filtering nearest to where the beneficiary resides or the organization making the referral is located). Once an individual's needs are identified either via a screening tool or through conversation with the individual, the case manager or CBO staff member can access the *CCC*'s Resource Directory to specifically match client's needs with availability of local resources that are convenient and accessible.

Functionality 13: Define Referral Needs

Referrals are requests made for services on behalf of a patient/client by one *CCC* Participant to another. Generally, there should be an ability to generate referrals to community and clinical resources and provide feedback loop functionality, whereby a provider can make a direct referral to a CBO, such as a food bank, and the CBO can respond back to the referring provider with the resources provided (e.g., pounds of food provided, service-related notes such as "patient received nutrition counseling") and the outcome of the referral (e.g., confirmation of receipt, appointment made, individual served). In addition, the system should allow CBOs to refer individuals to other CBOs (e.g., a food bank can refer an individual to a homeless shelter) and clinical providers within the *CCC* network.

Receiving Referrals

The technology software and its applications should have the ability to connect all members of the clinical and service communities, irrespective of their selected technology platform. As such, referrals can be made and received by those who are on the *CCC* platform, as well as to those who are not, by way of system-generated email notifications. Organizations wishing to participate in this endeavor may have their own legacy Customer Relationship Management (CRM) systems and may not be ready, for a number of reasons, to make the transition to a single platform. As a result, the technology may require configuration to interface directly with other systems.

Providing Referrals

The technology platform should provide closed-loop referrals, meaning that the referring entity receives information on the outcome of the referral from the entity that received the referral. Depending on the scope of data sharing determined to be necessary by the Sponsor or governance entity and Technology Platform Track lead, the platform should share confirmation of receipt of a referral, if an appointment was made, if an appointment was kept, if the individual was served, if the resource or service was provided, etc. Additional information to be captured and shared includes the type of resource (e.g., taxonomy code, dosing information, service-related notes, Current Procedural Technology (CPT) code), and what resource, if any, that was requested and not provided (with justification).

Case Study: The Pieces Iris® Referral Process

For referrals made in Pieces Iris®, a notification appears in the case management dashboard at the receiving CBO. During implementation, CBOs can select if they would also like to receive an email notification in addition to the alert in the dashboard. The case manager can choose to accept or decline the referral, as well as to communicate whether or not the client was a "no-show" or canceled the referral. The organization originating the referral will be notified of the patient's referral status (i.e., remove Referral, No-Show, Accept, or Cancel). Notes between case managers at both organizations can be shared, and if a client has consented to share their information, this information may immediately populate at the receiving organization's end once the client has been accepted at intake. Information is segmented into three different levels and can be shared, depending on beneficiary consents and agreements between participating organizations on the platform.

- If **Basic** information has agreed to be shared, Pieces Iris® will seamlessly transfer the agreed-upon data (usually), name, DOB, race, ethnicity, sex, veteran status and information, and address. If **Personal** information is being shared, the basic information, along with data on when an appointment was made, if the appointment was kept, the resource of service provided to the individual (metrics on services such as pounds of food, bed-night stays, counseling sessions, and service-related notes) and program exits/enrollments will be visible to both case managers at each organization. **Sensitive** information can also be shared at a heightened level of restriction and includes data such as HIV status, domestic violence data, diagnoses, and other PHI. Pieces Iris®_can_link family members within the system and track whether a service was provided to an individual or a family.

- Within Pieces Iris®, a client profile user interface contains an "Activities" module containing a "New Referral hyperlink," which directs a care provider to the referrals page. As such, the care provider will search the Referrals page based on the patient's previously described needs. A patient will be engaged in the referral making process by determining the zip code range from the patient's home or the referring organization in addition to describing the desired program enrollment or service provisions.

- Once an organization has been selected, the "Add to Referral" is selected and a user can proceed to the "Referral Checkout," which displays the "Referral Summary" containing the organization's name, physical location, and hours of operation. A specific care provider name at the organization is also provided in order to foster a "warm referral" and establish the mechanisms for a closed-loop referral. While viewing the completed referrals, a care provider can select to email the referral summary document to the patient's email address in either English or Spanish or another language as appropriate.

- If the organization receiving the referral is within the Pieces Iris® network, the care provider will access the referral from within the "Referrals" module. The care provider will then select the patient's name and decide to (1) Remove Referral, (2) No-Show, (3) Accept, or (4) Cancel the referral based on the patient's behavior or communicated preferences. If the care provider is not within the network, an email containing the "Referral Summary" will be emailed to the person listed as the organization's contact.
- Organizations receiving the referral and operating within the network will process the referral based on the activities described above. The organization originating the referral will receive notification of the patient's referral status (i.e., Remove Referral, No-Show, Accept, or Cancel). This status is also displayed in the patient's client profile within the "Activities" module. Referrals are confirmed in four different categories: (1) Remove Referral, (2) No-Show, (3) Accept, or (4) Cancel based on the patient's behavior or communicated preferences.
- If the care provider is not within the network, an email containing the "Referral Summary" will be emailed to the person listed as the organization's contact. Based on consortium-level data-sharing agreements, an external care provider may choose to share the referral process with an in-network care provider. This information would be recorded in the patient's "Encounters."
- Pieces Iris® allows for highly configurable social service encounters. As such, organizations can choose to collect a (1) Measure and Measure Type (e.g. Days, Dollars, Hours, Items, Miles, Minutes, Pounds, or Units), (2) Note, (3) Resource Assignment, (4) Resource Check-In, and (5) Service Start/ End Date. These details are then captured in patient intake workflow and recorded in the "Encounters' module.
- Pieces Iris® also allows for establishment of family relationships. Care providers can either add or link a family member to a patient's client profile. Family members who are added are simply listed in the patient's profile, whereas those who are linked will be linked with a live client profile, thereby streamlining future reporting measures.

Secure Referral Communication

The technology platform should ensure that secure communication about a person can be shared between the referral source and the CBO as part of the referral process and feedback loop. Information shared via the platform should allow all case managers with proper permissions to see pertinent client service and program information in order to coordinate care. Non-PHI-related comments can also be shared, through individual profiles, by case managers. The need for HIPAA compliance is a product of the legal framework established for the community and depends largely on the type of data being shared. Ensuring client data privacy begins with the required step within the application workflow of acquiring client data-sharing consent prior to the software user having access to any other client-relevant software functionality. The platform should ideally offer multiple tiers of consent, ranging from restricting client data sharing, to limited data sharing within a program, to broader data sharing across multiple organizations. See also Chapter 4 Legal/Policy Track Requirement 2. Further, the platform should be configured to accept written and signed consent documents, which are stored securely, along with any other additional client documents that may be desired, within the platform.

The amount and the type of information that can be shared should also be configurable (e.g., only demographic information about a client may be shared among organizations that were identified as part of the data-sharing group). Additionally, during the creation of a program for a specific organization, a program may be designated as "sensitive," indicating that no other organization in the data-sharing group would be able to access any information of the clients within the "sensitive" program. For example, CBOs serving vulnerable populations, such as those who are HIV positive or receive domestic violence-related assistance, often use this feature.

Finally, the platform should have additional security criteria around actual access to client records. The system should also feature an automated log-out period due to system inactivity to prevent exposure of sensitive information if a system is left unattended.

Client Profile

Each client registered on the platform should have an associated profile. Depending on the client-provided level of consent and the data-sharing rights established for the program and the organization, the client's profile and related information would be accessible/viewable by other organizations. Information about a client, or a specific client encounter, can be captured in a case notes field. Once entered, the information is immediately viewable by other organizations with proper data-sharing rights. This type of shared information also includes any client documents that have been uploaded into the system—these too would be accessible and viewable by organizations with proper data-sharing rights. To further foster care coordination, the platform should offer a case manager summary view listing all clients within a selected program, across participating sites. The summary view should be configured to highlight the desired client attributes and to also support custom flagging functionality. This functionality enables the system user to create up to a specified number of custom flags (e.g., high-risk patient, high Emergency Department [ED] utilizer patient). In cases where multiple organizations provide a client service to a shared pool of clients, staff from the participating organizations are able to interact with (flag, update, edit) the summary view and associated client profiles to avoid duplication of efforts and care gaps.

Enabling Patient "Self-Referrals"

The governance entity or Sponsor and Technology Platform Track lead should determine the need for beneficiaries to self-refer utilizing the CCC. In some instances, it may be sufficient for the receiving organization to receive all pertinent information about the referral, while the individual receives a "Referral Summary" containing the organization's information and the name of a specific contact who the client should ask for when arriving at the resource center. This type of "warm handoff" personalizes the experience and makes navigating the system's vagaries easier. When the beneficiary completes the referral, all documentation on the beneficiary can be shared within the technology platform, thus minimizing the need for patients, providers, or CBOs to complete new intake forms and carry around documentation like proof of insurance or utility bills. Conversely, there may be a preference (by the Sponsor or Funder) that an individual have the ability to seek and self-refer. This functionality is typically beyond that included in most standard information exchange platforms though more and more Sponsors and Funders are requiring it. If so, this functionality should be delivered in the technology platform.

Functionality 14: Determine Data Elements, Definitions, and Requirements for a Resource Database/Referral Directory

The technology platform should have an established resource database/referral directory and the ability to supplement the database/directory quickly, as by accepting feeds from a resource like 2-1-1 or other local, state, or national resource directories. The resource database should be designed to accommodate all users based on language and reading level (e.g., written at fifth-grade literacy level and offered in various languages).

Defining the data elements and definitions of a resource is extremely important to ensure consistency across services. In addition to program descriptions, services offered, contact information, and geo-mapping the resource database, the technology should use a North American standard for indexing and accessing human services. For example, the Alliance of Information and Referral Systems (AIRS)/2-1-1 Los Angeles (LA) County Taxonomy is a hierarchical system containing more than 9,000 fully defined terms covering the complete range of human services.[12] It serves as a common language facilitating interoperability between different IT resource databases. All resources in the database can be tagged using this system to ensure consistency across services.

Functionality 15: Define Required Support for Organizations Offering Multiple Programs

In essence, the *CCC* technology platform functions as an expanded case management system extending beyond the clinical setting and enabling real-time data transfer among all Participants in the care network, irrespective of the types of services provided. As such, the platform should support (and be based on) well-established case management workflows and principles. One of these is the creation and management of clinical programs. In the case of the *CCC* technology platform, the programs are not limited to clinical ones but are extended to include the CBO programs. Each program in itself will have specific services that are offered, as well as an associated data-tracking structure (e.g., quantity of service given, units of measurement, time of service provided, location of service provided, case manager notes).

The platform needs to accommodate data-sharing functionality (and control of this functionality) across all programs and *CCC* Partners. Additionally, the platform should present a framework for curating all of these programs as a list of resources available for clinical and CBO Partners for patient and client referrals. The resulting *CCC* resource database should be program-centric, such that multiple programs and service areas can be set up to allow referral of an individual to a specific program linked to an organization, rather than simply to the organization (e.g., ability to refer a patient for a specific food need at a local CBO, rather than simply a general referral to a local CBO). This type of framework for managing the *CCC* programs will also facilitate a robust resource-referral database that can be filtered and searched based on the specific needs of the patients/clients.

Functionality 16: Account for Resources Outside the CCC Referral Network

A community may need to make referrals for resources that are offered at organizations not currently on the *CCC* platform. For resources that are offered to these types of organizations, referrals may need to be communicated using current email addresses of key points of contact (on file in the resource directory) at those organizations. While this is not optimal, it does allow other service providers to participate in the *CCC* network until they are transitioned onto the *CCC* technology platform.

Functionality 17: Support the Resource Database Updates at Any Desired Frequency

The Technology Platform Track lead should determine how often to update the resource database (a/k/a referral directory) with new information (e.g., program and contacts). An up-to-date, reliable resource database is essential to building user trust. The Technology Platform Track lead will also need to determine how often to update public-benefit information (e.g., once per year) and how often to update community-based resources (e.g., twice per year). Ideally, when external programs or organizations are added to the referral directory, the system will send a verification ensuring deliverability and receipt as well as confirming the data. If the data is not accurate, the technology vendor should update the listing. In addition, the referral directory should be manually verified/audited at least twice per year, as stated above.

The verification process of the referral directory is not a trivial matter, as it requires coordination with the *CCC*'s community engagement resources and dedicated staff who will curate and conduct quality checks on the data. PCCI recommends that staff perform checks on subsets of the referral directory at least on a quarterly basis. To accommodate these quality assurance efforts, the system functionality should allow program administrators to make the necessary changes. This can either be done through a centralized approach, whereby access to modify the referral directory rests with a few program administrators, or it can be done through a "crowdsourcing" approach, whereby each authorized user (or site platform administrator) is able to edit the directory. PCCI encourages the latter with a centralized QA effort. Allowing for individual sites to update their own program information in the referral directory (or update information of their most commonly referred-to partners) enables a nearly real-time, self-correcting process to maintain referral directory accuracy.

In addition to the aforementioned functionality for referral directory management, the platform should also support batch uploads of referral directory information. This is particularly important to the ingestion of external referral directories of *CCC* Partner sites (e.g., ingesting the referral directory information of your State's 2-1-1). In addition to the ability to ingest external data, the system—or the technology vendor—needs to offer a process for reconciling any duplicate referral directory listings. This is a nuanced process requiring prioritization of the accuracy of one data source over another. The system should also have the ability to flag, or otherwise indicate, the sources of the referral directory entries (e.g., a flag or a tag indicating that the resource is from 2-1-1).

Functionality 18: Define the Process for Curation and Selection of CCC Resources for Referrals

Selecting a Resource

The technology should offer a single, standardized, user-friendly referral process irrespective of the type of user or desired resource. The designed process of locating the appropriate resource should be intuitive and familiar to a person with basic computer and digital media acumen. The users should be able to select the desired resource based on, at a minimum, the first four bulleted default resource criteria (PCCI recommends the addition of the fifth bulleted criteria) below:

- *Service Category.* A drop-down listing of the types of services (e.g. mental health, healthcare provider, housing) that are provided by the organizations within the referral directory.
- *Network.* Whether or not the desired resource is (1) within the existing user network enabling real-time referrals and data tracking, (2) not on the technology platform but is still able to receive the referral, and (3) internal to the user's organization.
- *Program Status.* Ability to select whether the resource is an active program. Programs with the resource and funding capacity to receive referrals will be listed as active. Programs that no longer have capacity to receive referrals or that have exceeded their allotted funding cycle may be listed as inactive. The status is defined by the organization receiving the referrals.

- *Proximity to Client.* Display of the resources meeting all the desired criteria within a desired radius of a specified zip code, either in relation to the individual's desired zip code or the organization's zip code.
- *Custom Research Criteria.* Ability of the referring organization to tag the organization within their resource directory based on their preferences (e.g., affiliate-specific organizations or "favorites" or a 2-1-1-sourced program). This custom tagging should be established during implementation of the technology platform.

Resources in the search results are typically ordered based on their distance from the desired reference zip code, from closest to farthest away. Users should also have the ability to select for referrals both within the *CCC* network and external to it. Here too, referrals will be ordered by distance from the desired reference zip code. Ideally, the platform should also offer the ability to indicate which resources are recommended (by a provider, payer, or government program). Indication of a resource as "Recommended" is achieved through the use of a custom tag (bulleted above).

Once the resource search yields the desired results, the user is able to select any desired resource from the search results list and add each desired resource to a "shopping cart." Additionally, upon selection of each resource, the user should see specific detail about the resource, such as resource description, description of provided programs, zip codes served, age/gender requirements (if appropriate), and, most importantly, eligibility criteria for those seeking this resource along with any required documentation needed. Once the desired resources are selected, the user should simply proceed to a virtual resource "checkout," and then in a single click request the desired resources. Once the referral is completed, users should have the ability to print it out in English or Spanish or other applicable language or email it directly to the beneficiary from the system.

Requirement 4: Stand Up the Technology Platform

A cloud-based application requires no on-site installation effort. However, as with any other software system, successful deployment is directly dependent on the training provided to the end users. In the case of the *CCC*, effective frontline staff training is paramount. Therefore, it is best to define technology implementation as the site-specific configuration, robust training, and support processes.

Milestone 1: Define Roles and Responsibilities for the Platform Implementation

It is critical to define roles and responsibilities early on to avoid potential misunderstandings or potential implementation delays.

Key Task: Agree on the Scope of Training with Your Technology Vendor

Your *CCC* will be built upon unique workflows designed by the clinical and CBO Partners. Your technology vendor will have a strong grasp of how the platform supports the designed workflows but will likely not be best positioned to address any workflow-related nuances or situations that may be outside of the specified parameters of the software. For example, a patient's caregiver may express interest in participating in a clinical intervention offered to the patient. A software vendor would not have enough insight to determine if this is within the scope of the *CCC* interventions. Therefore, it is necessary to establish a robust plan and approach for training at the Partner clinical and CBO sites. This plan should incorporate a number of items:

- The implementation plan should clearly delineate who provides training for which aspects of user experience. PCCI recommends that the implementation team comprises vendor experts and frontline *CCC* power users or *CCC* intervention experts.
- The implementation team should construct a detailed training agenda with estimates of the required time commitment for each training component.
- In addition to the agenda, the implementation team should also create a list of required attendees (e.g., case managers, site directors).

- Finally, the plan needs to clearly detail any operational and logistic requirements (e.g., access to a laptop computer for each trainee, access to a specific browser, reliable Wi-Fi connection, access to a room with a projector).

PRACTICE POINTER

Define Training Roles and Responsibilities in the Vendor Contract

PCCI recommends that the agreement with the technology vendor delineate the *CCC* training requirements. Even if specific details of training requirements are not available during the contracting period, the contract should spell out broad-level accountabilities and expectations (e.g., training timelines and broad topic areas).

Key Task: Develop Supporting Training Materials

Your technology vendor will likely have multiple training resources ranging from electronic manuals to training videos to user community blogs and forums. While these are important to ensure end-user technical proficiency, these materials alone are insufficient to support the work required for the *CCC* interventions. The Clinical Providers and Community Partners Track leads and other implementation team members accountable for workflow trainings will need to develop user-friendly, detailed resources to support your *CCC*'s frontline staff. Required actions may include the following:

- Develop step-by-step workflow walk-throughs in digital format, including screenshots of the technology platform, with clear instructions for each step.
- Record workflow execution examples with detailed narration. Make these recordings easily accessible for playback to the end users.
- Consider creating, for frontline staff, one-page "cheat sheets" or "reference cards" that help them with critical platform functionality and with workflow nuances.
- Plan training activities to also include user "certification" steps to ensure that frontline staff have reached the necessary technology platform proficiency levels to successfully carry out the *CCC* workflows.

The certification activities may require creation of a test or workflow simulation for frontline staff to complete under supervision of the technology implementation team.

PRACTICE POINTER

Repetition is Key to Success

Although the technology vendor will perform extensive technical training on the various capabilities and uses of the platform, PCCI recommends that the Technology Platform Track lead reviews an additional set of functionalities during workflow training. These functionalities relate to the basic operation of the software and troubleshooting procedures. This review should include the following:

- The steps for accessibility controls, such as two-factor authentication (if your platform offers this feature) and user login reset procedures
  - While a temporary issue and seemingly trivial, user inability to access the system is one of the greatest barriers to smooth workflow execution. Users at all levels should receive training to assist one another in gaining access to the platform in the event of user profile lockout or forgotten login credentials.
- The process for submitting bug and malfunction reports and assistance requests. Vendors tend to be very specific with their help procedures and if these are not followed, users could experience significant delays in problem resolution.
- Basic troubleshooting steps to resolve the more commonly encountered functionality challenges.

Key Task: Tailor Application Configuration for Each Site's Functionality

Each of your *CCC* Partner sites will play a unique role in carrying out the *CCC* interventions. There are aspects of the *CCC* intervention workflows that will be ubiquitous across all sites, while there are other workflow and service aspects that will differ among sites. The technology platform instance at each Partner site should accommodate both the common and the unique functionality and needs of each site.

The technology vendor should complete the basic configuration of the software instance. Typically, this would include the following:

- Configuration of the basic, default user interface and case management environment
- Configuration of basic, default reporting tools
- Assignment of user roles and administrative rights to desired users
- Configuration of the environment to support data and analytics (e.g., custom reporting features or access to the software database, if applicable)
- Configuration of data-sharing control and consent handling

Software configuration may be labor-intensive, especially if the workflows and the interventions are complex. Although each Partner site will have nuances requiring some level of instance customization, the general configuration of the system will be the same across the *CCC*. For instance, your *CCC* may require clinical sites to administer a survey to patients to determine if the patient has any health-related social needs. Following the survey, the sites are to refer the patient to an appropriate CBO. In this example, as the survey to be used is the same across all sites, configuring the same survey multiple times is inefficient. Instead, request that the technology vendor allow for replication of instance configurations.

The configuration of the platform to accommodate custom needs of each site should be completed by the Partner site team members who are assigned program administrator privileges and also the Clinical Providers and Community Partners Track leads and implementation team members who are well versed in the *CCC* workflows. Custom configuration typically involves:

- Organization-specific configuration of the offered programs
- Definition and configuration of services offered under each program
- Determination and configuration of information to be collected for each service for both client/patient and program outcomes
- Configuration of the data-sharing framework and permissions
- Configuration of any workflow-specific forms (e.g., surveys)

PRACTICE POINTER

Complete Configuration Prior to Training Sessions but Ensure that Program Administrators Are Trained to Perform Configurations

Workflow training conducted for each site should use that site's pre-configured instance of the software platform. This allows for the training session to focus exclusively on the work to be done using the software. This also allows the users to become comfortable with all of their site-specific features and functionality. For this reason, members of the implementation team need to perform configuration and testing of the site's software instance well in advance of the training day. The designated program administrator at the site should also receive training on how to configure their software instance. It is, thus, a good practice to include the program administrators in the configuration process or to train them and then have them configure their instance as a test of competency.

Key Task: Include a Referral Directory

The technology will usually include a customizable ontology of data fields. It uses logic-based questions to filter for social and resource needs that can be further filtered by location (e.g., filtering nearest to where the beneficiary resides or the organization making the referral is located). Once an individual's needs are identified, either via a screening tool or through conversation with the individual, the case manager or CBO Participant staff member can access *CCC*'s referral directory to specifically match a client's needs with availability of local resources that are convenient and accessible.

In addition to specific workflow features and functionalities, the referral directory will likely require configuration as well (i.e., community-wide, updated resource database including at a minimum food, housing, transportation, and interpersonal safety resources). The need to perform this activity is dependent on the size and the setup of your *CCC*. For instance, a small *CCC* within a narrow geographical area will have a few clinical and CBO Participants. As a result, Participants will refer to one another with fairly equal frequency. Larger *CCC*'s with many diverse Participants will find that certain Participants have established referral patterns that accommodate the needs of their specific populations (e.g., a certain set of zip codes or CBO Participants that have historically collaborated with one another).

In such cases, the referral directory of CBO resources should be tailored to reflect each site's preferences.

PRACTICE POINTER

Incorporate Existing Site Referral Directories

The case managers at Participant sites typically have their own referral directories. During the Participant site onboarding process, PCCI recommends that the implementation teams request these referral directories, which may come as Excel spreadsheets, three-ring binders, Word documents, etc. The implementation teams can then work with the technology vendor to integrate those resources into the *CCC* referral directory. Once integrated, these resources should be tagged or marked as "favorites" for that specific site to enable the site's team members to easily locate their preferred Partner organizations.

Key Documents for Requirement 4

- Steps for Technology Implementation
- Operational Guidelines for *CCC* Data Sharing

Requirement 5: Develop a Short- and Long-Term User Support Strategy

Successful technology vendors will pride themselves on having well-established and effective account management services. However, your Participants will likely require support services beyond standard technical assistance. For example, plan for ongoing training during regular intervals due to high volunteer and staff turnover at CBOs. One-time training is definitely not enough.

Milestone 1: Define and Document the Terms for Technical and User Support

To avoid confusion, disruption, and Participant dissatisfaction during the execution of the *CCC* workflows, it is vital to discuss the scope of support services that your technology vendor will offer under the *CCC* contract:

- Clearly define if the vendor is accountable to provide any assistance relevant to workflow execution.
- Define the process for how the vendor should handle requests for assistance that are outside the scope of their support services.
  - These processes may include handoffs to designated implementation team members who are not affiliated with the technology vendor but who are either program administrators or system "power users" at Participant sites.
- Discuss and document the various levels of support that the vendor is willing to provide and how quickly the vendor will respond to requests (e.g., tiered support levels ranging from web-based support tickets, to email requests, to 24/7 telephone support).
- Clearly define the expected duration of support-service availability included with license fees (e.g., 1 year, 3 years, indefinite).

The defined support roles and strategy should be included in the contract with the vendor. Support needs will change or the needs may become clearer as the *CCC* evolves. Renegotiation of the contract at the end of the contract term provides an opportunity to address any unmet support needs with the vendor and to establish additional processes, if needed.

Milestone 2: Define and Document the Short-Term, Post-Launch Requirements for Technical and User Support

The first few months (or quarters) of your *CCC*'s operation will likely require heightened levels of oversight and user support, until all Partner sites get accustomed to, and proficient in, the workflows. The ability to quickly resolve any issue and barriers is essential to maintaining the staff buy-in and momentum at the Partner sites. There are a number of implementable strategies to ensure expeditious problem resolution, including:

- Establish a help line or a similar direct process to seek assistance to address any workflow questions.
- Work with the technology vendor to establish a process for prioritization of Partner issues.

Key Documents for Requirement 5

- Expectations for User Support

Requirement 6: Ensure the Technology Platform is Sustainable

Following the initial implementation, all Participants may drive further product and system enhancements and changes as the *CCC* network continues to grow. The technology vendor should remain actively engaged in iterative implementation and evaluation processes to continue augmenting system performance and value. This should be stipulated in the technology vendor's contract. To ensure sustainability, the technology vendor and the Technology Platform Track lead should ensure that the following requirements are in place:

- A reliable method of recording ongoing technology issues and reporting those issues to the technology vendor and the Board or Administrator; this includes methods of capturing (and reporting) user feedback, issue tracking, and resolution
- Active and ongoing system maintenance and backup
- A secure information system that can accommodate changing policies and legal requirements
- A system that can evolve with the growth of the *CCC*
- A system that can adjust to new Funder requirements

The technology needed for *CCC* must be supported by a robust and state-of-the-art, back-end infrastructure that is built to accommodate and support advanced analytics (including AI/ML methods) for current and future applications, such as risk-stratification, early-warning notification algorithms and sophisticated reporting functionality.

Key Documents for Requirement 6

- Project Orders for Functionality Change
- Quality Assurance Processes

Chapter 6

Clinical Providers Track

Introduction to the Clinical Providers Track

Although clinical *Connected Communities of Care* (*CCC*) workflows will vary across your selected clinical sites, they need to converge on the common goals of the *CCC*. Numerous nuances and key factors to consider in establishing the clinical consortium of your *CCC* include executive sponsorship, clear definition of roles and responsibilities, handling of clinical information, compliance framework, and integration of the new workflows. The purpose of the Clinical Providers Track is to set out the stakeholders and processes required to integrate clinical entities, insights, programs, interventions, strategies, and measurement for the *CCC*.

Prerequisites to Clinical Providers Track

The work in the Clinical Providers Track can begin once the *CCC* key decision makers have completed the following actions as part of the Governance Track and Legal/Policy Track:

- Identify and prioritize key health-related needs to be targeted as part of a *CCC* (via a readiness assessment).
- Develop a comprehensive and aligned clinical strategy for the *CCC*, including defined clinical measures for the *CCC*.
- Select clinical programs, including defined clinical interventions and selection of Participant sites.

- Define technology strategy and general requirements for *CCC* technology and data integration at Partner sites.
- Define and address the legal needs for clinical Partner engagement
- Define the *CCC* evaluation framework.

Requirements to Implement the Clinical Providers Track

The four key requirements for the Clinical Providers Track implementation are:

1. Develop relevant and practical workflows for the selected *CCC* clinical programs.
2. Convene and engage frontline clinical staff to support the *CCC* at the clinical sites.
3. Develop and perform clinically relevant training for the *CCC*.
4. Coordinate and support the launch of the *CCC* at pilot clinical sites.

Requirement 1: Develop Relevant and Practical Clinical Workflows for the Selected CCC Clinical Programs

The first requirement in implementing the clinical workflows of your *CCC* is to translate the strategic direction of the *CCC* and the supporting clinical interventions into a tactical plan. To achieve this, the assigned Clinical Providers Track lead will work with individuals at the clinical Partner/ Participant sites and Community Partners Track lead to define cross-organizational workflows supported by the *CCC* framework and technology.

Key Roles and Responsibilities

The key roles for this Requirement will be performed by the following individuals at the clinical Partner/Participant sites:

- Mid-level clinical leaders
  - Medical director or similar lead provider with quality improvement or research background or role
  - Clinical site operations lead and champion (identified in the Governance Track)
- Frontline and operations staff: social workers, outpatient intake staff, population health nurse
- Community engagement staff: community health worker

Milestone 1: Develop Standard Operating Procedures for the Workflows

Once the clinical interventions are clearly defined (see Chapter 3 Governance Track), the Clinical Providers Track lead will need to develop the detailed standard operating procedures (SOPs) and workflow descriptions for each of the clinical interventions. While it is advantageous to standardize your *CCC* clinical workflows across all participating sites to the extent possible (given that the SOPs are a key resource and alignment tool for the work performed across clinical sites), be aware that global SOPs can lead to staff pushback. It is important to recognize that each clinical and Community-Based Social Service Organization *aka* Community-Based Organization (CBO) site (vital to the success of your interventions) will have its own unique workflows and operating procedures. Therefore, global SOPs may need to be structured with some flexibility to allow for sites to accommodate their internal workflow requirements while still meeting the common defined goals and implementing the required interventions.

PRACTICE POINTER

Track and Archive Each SOP Version

The SOPs are a dynamic resource and will undergo revisions and updates as your *CCC* evolves. As a result, each SOP version should be tracked and archived to maintain a record of the evolution of the SOPs, especially for knowledge-sharing purposes. All SOPs should be stored in a centralized location that is accessible and transparent to *CCC* clinical site stakeholders. A dedicated *CCC* website is a good location. The development of SOPs is a significant work thread requiring input and content development from the clinical frontline and operations staff.

Key Task: Convene Staff to Review Existing Workflows

Clinical leaders should convene frontline, quality, and operations staff from each of the participating clinical sites to:

- Review their existing workflows.
- Clearly diagram existing workflows through work sessions and in-person discussions.

For work sessions, it is best to leverage the quality improvement and operations staff members who are skilled in facilitating group discussions and who are skilled in process documentation and improvement activities.

To standardize the workflow development across the *CCC* sites, you may want to develop or use a common template for the workflows, where possible. Workflow diagrams, at a minimum, should describe:

- Staff members involved in the existing process, including their names, titles, roles, and functions
- Data capture and sharing points, including each step where input of any patient information takes place (e.g., insurance status, residence, demographic data, clinical data)

- Physical resources required, including where each step of the workflow takes place and any facility dependencies (e.g., Wi-Fi connectivity)
- Mitigation processes, if needed, to resolve any conflicts between potential *CCC* clinical workflows and existing workflows

Once the existing workflows are documented, it is important to review the captured workflow diagrams and descriptions with the key stakeholders to ensure accuracy and to maintain buy-in, build trust, and further the frontline staff engagement.

The *CCC* should complement existing programs (where possible) rather than duplicate what is already done or introduce counter-effective activities. The goal should be to develop a *CCC* network across all Partners and Participants that is seamless and delivers effective and efficient outcomes. Despite the best of intentions and planning, from time to time, conflicts or cross-sector issues may develop requiring mitigation. Consider creation of a document that illustrates in detail how any conflicts between potential *CCC* clinical workflows and existing workflows will be mitigated. The process of thinking through the conflict-mitigation process may actually help in workflow design (or redesign).

Key Task: Define Required Modifications to the Existing Workflows to Achieve CCC Outcomes

The clinical leaders should next clearly define, through an iterative process requiring multiple drafts of the SOPs, the required modifications to the existing workflows to achieve the clinical intervention outcomes. Activities making up this process include the following:

- Empower the frontline staff members to guide the process for the new workflow creation (i.e., make it their own idea and achievement)
- Examine multiple outcomes/possibilities of the proposed processes and consider possible barriers and challenges and associated mitigation strategies
- Clearly define what roles will perform each step of the new workflows
- Follow the same rigorous approach used during the documentation of the existing workflows.

The process of breaking down the workflows into a phased approach allows the team to focus and test one step at a time, where possible. Clinical workflows may include (1) patient enrollment, (2) registration, (3) screening, (4) referral, (5) navigation, and (6) closeout. Each of these phases may lend themselves to separate testing. For example, for patient enrollment and screening, members of the staff can assume the role of a patient during the draft workflow process. Observers in place can note the challenges and successes with each step. Modifications can then be made on the spot and retested, resulting in refinements to the SOPs and new insights that will help optimize the approach.

Key Documents for Requirement 1

- List of Participant Clinical Sites and CBOs
- SOP That Details a *CCC* Workflow

Requirement 2: Convene and Engage Frontline Clinical Staff to Support the CCC at the Clinical Sites

Once the workflows have been defined, the next requirement is to assemble a dedicated staff of individuals who will own the processes required to carry out the *CCC* clinical interventions at each clinical Participant site. The guidance offered in this section is meant to ensure adequate buy-in from the clinical Partner organizations and their staff. The process of obtaining buy-in and acceptance of disruptive changes is one of the key barriers to any initiative. Given this, the tasks and guidance provided in this Requirement support strategies to help clinical leaders navigate and circumvent some of the common challenges associated with the adoption of disruptive change and innovation.

Key Roles and Responsibilities

The key roles and stakeholders for this Requirement include the following:

- Executive-level (C-Suite) and senior-level leaders at clinical Participant sites
  - CEO (Chief Executive Officer), CMO (Chief Medical Officer), CIO (Chief Information Officer or Chief Integration Officer), and other C-Suite members as appropriate (i.e., those who have direct influence over the strategic direction and clinical operations and who can leverage influence to align Partner sites with the *CCC* goals)
  - SVP (Senior Vice President) or VP of Clinical, SVP or VP of Strategy, SVP or VP of Operations, and other VP-level members as appropriate (i.e., those who are able to align the clinical site leadership with the strategic direction and *CCC* goals as defined by the C-Suite leaders)
- Mid-level clinical leaders
  - Medical director or lead providers with quality improvement or research backgrounds or roles
  - Clinical site operations lead and clinical site *CCC* Champion (if different)
  - Frontline and operations staff (e.g., social worker, outpatient intake staff, population health nurse)
- Patients, families, and caregivers

Milestone 1: Convene Senior and Mid-Level Leaders to Review the CCC Clinical Programs and Goals

The first step in bringing together the right stakeholders is to convene the executive, senior, and mid-level leaders from Participating clinical sites to review the *CCC* clinical programs and goals. Staff members who are ultimately responsible for the execution of the *CCC* workflows are likely to be involved in multiple other initiatives and have competing priorities, to which they have adjusted and optimized their existing work processes. Implementation of the *CCC* workflows, as with any innovative initiative, will undoubtedly impose a level of disruption. For the frontline staff members to accept, embrace, and act to effectively implement the new clinical programs, the clinical site must ensure the following:

- Complete alignment at the leadership level on the importance and the level of priority of the *CCC* clinical programs to the organization
- A leadership directive (to the entire organization) to implement the clinical workflows and, in parallel, leadership's assistance in clearing organizational barriers and clearly deprioritizing competing projects
- Organizational, team, or individual goals to reflect the importance of the *CCC* clinical program implementation
- Empowerment of the frontline staff to execute workflows through a level of ownership and personal accountability

Complete alignment begins at the top of the organization and cascades throughout the organization. Therefore, before any conversations with senior- and mid-level leadership, executive leaders must buy-in to the program and prioritize the goals of the *CCC*. While in most cases this is the least time-intensive aspect of the process, it is a vital step that should be completed before any others. There may be instances during the *CCC* implementation process where staff members reach an impasse on how to proceed. The organization's C-suite executives will be the ones to break that impasse and help reposition their teams for further effective discussions and issue resolution. It should also be expected that such impasses or instances requiring C-suite intervention for realignment may occur on multiple occasions. Such instances are a natural part of conducting innovative, disruptive, and complex work.

Key Task: Compromise with Frontline Staff to Alleviate Technology Restraints

Technology interoperability constraints are a common barrier to engagement. The medical industry suffers from a fragmented IT landscape dominated by a few larger Electronic Health Record (EHR) vendors. Due to this fragmentation (and the proprietary interests of the EHR vendors), it is often difficult for clinical providers to receive the benefit of efficient data-sharing interoperability among their various software systems and tools. The result of this impediment is added burden on frontline staff in the form of workflow and data entry redundancies.

Depending on the technology exchange platform selected, direct and complete integration (two-way data exchange) with the Participants' EHR may be a primary goal. However, in many cases, (1) complete integration with the predominant EHR requires additional and significant development efforts by the technology vendor or (2) the information exchange community lacks a predominant EHR platform (i.e., integration would be required with many different EHRs). Both of these factors may negatively impact the timeline to implement the *CCC* (or other information exchange platform). The best solution to this constraint may be to compromise with affected frontline staff by offering a resource or technology support to alleviate the added workflows and data redundancy efforts. Specifically, this compromise would:

- Allow the frontline staff to carry out the clinical interventions according to their specified workflows while their leadership or the *CCC* governance entity provides staffing resources to assist with data entry efforts.
- Require the *CCC* leadership to work with their data and IT teams to develop an ad hoc process to execute synchronized data transfer between the EHR and the chosen information exchange platform on the back end (i.e., independent of the clinical provider's IT function and Health Insurance Portability and Accountability Act [HIPAA] requirements).

Key Task: Secure Commitment on Clinical Program Implementation from Partner Sites

While every organization has its own nuances and political structure, Parkland Center for Clinical Innovation (PCCI) notes that the following tactics are commonly effective and fundamental to securing consensus on the approach and a commitment to the *CCC* clinical program implementation:

- Utilizing the previously defined *CCC* value proposition (see Chapter 3), prepare and present a clearly defined value proposition of the *CCC* clinical programs, which should be referenced at the onset of each meeting with organizational leaders. The value message is not a one-size-fits-all and should be tailored according to the audience. Consider having a colleague (who is a peer to the specific leadership team) communicate the value of the work. For instance, clinical leaders highly respect and value input from other clinicians and place heavy emphasis on the potential impact of work on patient outcomes. Financial leaders resonate with factual, data-driven messages that clearly define the financial opportunity of a proposed program. Strategy leaders tend to engage when the discussion includes the long-term potential impact of the program on other key organizational initiatives.
- Stress the fact that the *CCC* is a large, highly visible program with multiple, high-profile partners and, thus, will likely receive a significant amount of local or national attention within the industry and from popular press and media. The importance of effective partnership can be a powerful catalyst for action. Therefore, it is beneficial to emphasize that the level of contribution to the effort will be transparent not only to other *CCC* Participant sites but also to a much broader audience through this higher level of exposure.
- Obtain staff initial reactions to the proposed programs through proactive outreach to document staff member concerns and barriers and to allow hesitant parties to feel heard. As with any complex program, there will be disruption and a solution and path forward. Through this proactive approach, some of the organization's primary "nay-sayers" or "resistors" will become the project's greatest champions if they are engaged in a diligent and cooperative manner. Once the resistant parties have been heard, it is helpful to continue the discussions with them by including the resistor's peers who are supportive of the initiative and maintaining the "how, not if" environment during the discussions.

Milestone 2: Develop the Clinical Workflows Staffing Model

The sustainability and success of the *CCC* platform depends on the ability of the Participants to integrate the *CCC* activities into their daily operations. Once the key leaders of the participating organizations have all agreed on the importance of the work and have committed to implement the *CCC*, the leaders will need to develop the staffing model to support the clinical programs. At this point, senior-level leaders should invite mid-level leaders to the table to engage them in the conversation and to enable them to take ownership of the implementation work. Functional staff, such as the Directors of Operations, Emergency Department (ED) Directors, and Program Managers are typically best positioned to make decisions about staff allocation since they have implemented the most effective and efficient workflows within their organizations.

Key Task: Define Functional Program Teams

While the exact titles and staff structures are unique to each organization, you may want to consider using the following tactics to successfully define the functional *CCC* clinical program teams:

- Clearly articulate to mid-level leaders what is expected from each team. Assuming the site has obtained leadership buy-in, the functional staff at each site will have to define the clinical pathways for program implementation given that there will be no universal solution or workflow for every site. For this audience, the value proposition is less important than the "what is expected and how" discussions. The functional staff at each clinical site will ultimately be the ones defining the successful and effective means of implementing the clinical programs. One way to successfully achieve this task is to share a detailed framework for achieving the goals of the clinical programs and demonstrate an ideal-case workflow solution for getting there. Expect a lot of detailed questions about the proposed workflows and aspects of the program. The mid-level leaders will expect to see a level of expert proficiency regarding all aspects of the clinical programs.
- Propose an "ideal state" workflow and position it as the "art of the possible"—this should serve as a seed for ideation and a starting point for discussions. During the discussions, leaders should engage key stakeholders to describe the current workflows and how these

workflows deviate from the ideal state. Allowing the mid-level leaders to voice their concerns and talk through potential challenges will leave the conversation open to problem-solving and will ensure that the key stakeholders feel heard. Ultimately, the goal is to enable these leaders to propose solutions that will meet the goals of the clinical program and incorporate fairly easily into existing processes.

- Maintain a focus on two specific goals of the process: (1) What will your workflow look like and (2) who is best positioned to implement the workflow. In discussions, Participants may want to focus on complex, broader aspects of the project and challenges versus the "what needs to be done" and the focus should be on the latter.

- Choose functional site team members who are best positioned to ensure success of the program, such as champions selected on each team to serve as the point of contact. In some cases, a mid-level leader may be the *CCC* team champion.

- Provide consistent and regular communications and updates to senior leadership, key stakeholders, mid-level leadership, and functional teams to ensure everyone is on the same page. This process will help to avoid misunderstandings and loss of alignment or delays, to pre-emptively avoid additional challenges, to promote engagement, and to maintain momentum.

- Share the latest developments and celebrate successes at all levels.

PRACTICE POINTER

Leverage Existing Staff Where Possible

Staffing constraints can be a common challenge throughout all aspects of the *CCC* clinical workflows as existing staff are likely already dedicated to multiple projects and are now asked to engage in this new effort. However, simply hiring temporary staff to alleviate the burden on clinical sites is not sustainable in the long term and it conflicts with the spirit of the *CCC*. Consider a staffing support model that may require some additional staffing during the initial *CCC* implementation but then transitions the workflows into the existing set of operations.

Key Task: Determine Root Cause of Staffing Constraints

For any identified staffing constraint, determine its root cause and conduct a thorough analysis of the affected workflows. Once this process is completed, if a modification to alleviate the constraint is not feasible, clinical leadership is better positioned to develop a detailed task list and desired skill requirements for additional staff based on the specific workflow components that need support. For example, if existing clinical staff members indicate that they are unable to screen patients in the ED, the identified requirements for additional staff would include motivational interviewing skills, multilingual status, and experience working with members of the community. The workflow analysis would also yield the capacity (i.e., timeframe) that additional resources are needed. Given the capacity and skill-set requirements, leadership may wish to consider the following staffing sources:

- Community Participant sites as some of these sites may have community health worker staff that clinical Participants can leverage into the work.
- Local educational institutions as these entities may offer free internship opportunities for their bachelor's- and master's-level social work students. This strategy can also provide greater visibility to the clinical provider staff drawing in talented students. Two shortcomings of this approach are the fact that (1) many interns are only available when school is in session and (2) use of interns on this short-term basis means constant turnover, a lack of consistency, and the need for close supervision and retraining.
- Contract or directly employ community workers or licensed social workers to both provide full-time support and to manage the part time or intern pool of resources.

PRACTICE POINTER

Use Certain Strategies with Caution

A couple of strategies have proven effective in the right circumstances. But these strategies also include specific risks so clinical leaders should carefully weigh the risks and benefits:

- The Sponsor provides financial support to clinical Partner staff to conduct the required interventions and workflows. The new resource effectively becomes a full-time member of the clinical provider organization and reports directly to the provider's management. However, the organization may then assign competing priorities to this new resource, limiting resource effectiveness for the *CCC*. This means that the *CCC* Administrator, for example, may no longer control the resource's work schedule.
- The clinical providers leverage community volunteers or students/interns to fill the staffing gap. While this strategy bears no additional financial burden, the challenges associated with interns or volunteer-level resources may quickly outweigh the financial benefit. Volunteer or intern resources typically have high turnover rates and often demonstrate a lessened level of reliability in terms of performance and commitment.

Key Documents for Requirement 2

- Each site's list of designated frontline and operational staff accountable for *CCC* execution at each clinical site (e.g., site champion, social workers, case managers, clinic directors, outpatient staff, population health nurse)
- A tool, such as a Responsible, Accountable, Consulted, and Informed (RACI) chart, clearly defining the roles, responsibilities, and chain of accountability[13]

Requirement 3: Develop and Perform Clinically Relevant Training for the CCC

The training of clinical partner sites is not a one-time event. Rather, it is an extension of the engagement and integration of each clinical site's frontline staff into the clinical interventions of the Clinical Providers Track. Although the interventions can be categorized as "clinical workflow" and "technology," the nature of the *CCC* requires them to be interdependent, which has significant implications on how the frontline staff should be trained.

The purpose of Requirement 3 is to develop and implement, for your *CCC*'s clinical Partners, a training curriculum that ensures their ability to:

- Independently and accurately execute your *CCC*'s defined clinical workflows using the supporting technology platform.
- Transfer knowledge to other clinical *CCC* Participants to ensure uniform *CCC* operations irrespective of staffing challenges or other unforeseen events.

Key Roles and Responsibilities

The key roles and stakeholders for this Requirement include the following:

- The clinical lead responsible for execution of the *CCC* clinical workflows
- Clinical site *CCC* intervention lead
- Clinical frontline staff executing the *CCC* clinical workflows

Milestone 1: Deliver the Training

The training team (e.g., designated *CCC* super users and a technology vendor representative), as covered in the Technology Platform Track, should deliver the training either in person or by live webinars using audiovisual tools to enhance the learning experience. Training should be documented and tracked through administration of tests and surveys via a survey platform (e.g., Survey Monkey). These include the following:

- A self-paced, post-training test
- A satisfaction survey
- A completion certificate, delivered to trainees who complete the training, pass the test, and complete and submit the satisfaction survey

Training Frequency

Training activities should be ongoing throughout the life of the *CCC* and consist of:

- Initial training completed prior to the initiation of any *CCC*-related clinical activity (e.g., patient enrollment, screening)
- Ad hoc training, as needed to support new staff, or to remediate discrepancies or inadequacies in clinical workflows, or at the request of a clinical site
- Annual refresher training to ensure optimal compliance with clinical intervention requirements and prevention of quality gaps

Staff should demonstrate proficiency in the clinical workflows under direct supervision of the clinical site's supervisory staff or experienced staff at the clinical site until at a minimum each staff member has satisfactorily completed at least five patient encounters. Estimated completion time for *CCC* staff onboarding is 7–10 days.

Key Documents for Requirement 3

- Training Objectives

Requirement 4: Coordinate and Support the Launch of the CCC at Pilot Clinical Sites

Prior to the official launch of your *CCC*, the participating clinical Partner sites will need to pilot the defined workflows to ensure staff readiness and ability to carry out the required work. Based on PCCI's experience in the Dallas Information Exchange Portal (IEP), we found that piloting efforts should be iterative, involving at least two rounds.

Key Roles and Responsibilities

The key roles and stakeholders for this Requirement include the following:

- *CCC* leadership (*CCC* clinical leads and *CCC* program leads)
- Leadership staff at the Partner clinical sites
- Frontline staff at the Partner clinical sites

Milestone 1: Select a Subset of Sites as Pilots

Although the goal is to pilot at all Partner sites, the first round of pilots (almost as proof-of-concept activities) may need to be conducted at a subset of sites as a demonstration of feasibility and a way to give other sites confidence. The initial subset of pilot sites should comprise the most engaged ones. Additionally, the selected subset should vary in defined workflows in order to provide the greatest test of program readiness. The *CCC* and clinical leaders should avoid selection of similar sites, such as outpatient clinics in the same zip code, as these sites will likely have similar workflows and patient needs. Rather, select vastly different sites, such as a pediatrics site, an outpatient clinic, and a behavioral health site.

Milestone 2: Conduct a Pre-Launch Visit to Pilot Sites

It is important for the Clinical Providers Track lead to conduct a visit to the pilot sites prior to the pilot to ensure that all logistic and operational requirements are in place (e.g., staff are clear on what they need to do; sufficient amount of printed materials are ready; if the platform is cloud-based, pilot sites have adequate Wi-Fi connectivity and a robust internet access).

Milestone 3: Determine Time Periods for the Pilot

The *CCC* clinical and program leads should work with the frontline staff at clinical sites to determine the most effective times to carry out the pilot of the full clinical workflows and also to assign pilot leads. Depending on the population that is served, patient volumes may vary throughout the month based on patient type and needs. For example, patients on social support programs tend to show up towards the end of the month as their resources become depleted. Further, there may be "peak hours" during the day for patients who would benefit from interventions.

Multiple days (4–6 days) covering various times over a workday should be sufficient to provide enough feedback to make workflow adjustments, as needed. This shorter pilot period may be more effective than a longer one, as it would provide an opportunity to quickly uncover unforeseen challenges and promptly test the workflow solutions. Depending on the specific profile and needs of the population, piloting activity does not have to take place on consecutive days. Rather, it is best to prioritize "peak" days and times for the pilot work to "stress-test" the workflows. If the clinical site will be operational on weekends, include at least one weekend day in the piloting session.

Milestone 4: Define Measurement and Success Criteria to Evaluate the Pilot

Prior to initiating a pilot, the pilot sites' leadership staff should define and commit to a set of measurement and success criteria for evaluation of the pilot. Consider development of a template for pilot evaluation.

Sample metrics for pilot:

- Number of patients approached for the *CCC* intervention
- Number of patients that agreed to receive the *CCC* clinical intervention
- Specific outcomes of the *CCC* clinical intervention (e.g., if the intervention is a screen for social needs, then what needs were identified)?
- Duration of the *CCC* clinical intervention from initial patient approach to the conclusion of the intervention visit
- Qualitative/observational data on what worked well, what did not work well, and how to improve the workflow
- Patient willingness to recommend *CCC* intervention

Sample success criteria:

- Seventy-five percent of encountered patients were able to progress through the desired workflows
- Error rate with respect to the captured information was less than 10% (be clear in the definition of "errors")
- The pilot continued for the scheduled duration, unless terminated for a valid, documented reason (be clear in the termination criteria)
- Post-pilot surveys of the frontline staff demonstrated that 75% or more of staff members were confident in their ability to execute the required workflows
- Willingness to recommend *CCC* intervention (90% or greater)

Key Documents for Requirement 4

- Evaluation Measures
- Communication Strategy

Case Study: Engaging Patients— Location and Relationships Matter

As part of our *CCC* history, PCCI has developed and tested a number of approaches to identifying individuals within the population of vulnerable and underserved Parkland patients who could benefit from screening for health-related social determinants, engaging them in the completion of a brief risk assessment and subsequent linkage to available community resources. As with many of the elements of the *CCC*, this proved to be a learning experience in which initial, more conventional approaches gave way to new and more innovative approaches of engaging this population to optimize goal attainment.

RECRUITMENT

Much of the initial work began with screening in the outpatient setting. Parkland has 12 Community-Oriented Primary Care (COPC) clinics located throughout Dallas County to serve local residents. Because the COPCs see a large number of patients on a daily basis, many of whom are considered vulnerable and underserved, these COPCs were determined to be a great location to conduct the social determinant risk assessments. When a patient checked in for a visit, the office staff would provide the patient with a paper-based screening tool to self-administer. Trained community health workers were available in the waiting area to help, if required. Initially we felt like this approach made sense since the large number of COPC patients translated into large numbers of completed screening surveys. However, while there were a large number of initial screenings, the number was very low of patients that agreed to engage with a PCCI community health worker to connect with local community services. Many stated they were not interested or needed to leave the facility for another commitment. Other patients completed the needs assessment but left the COPC before staff members were able to connect with them. Of these, very few responded to follow-up phone outreach and the ones that did were hesitant about referral to community-based services. The team attributed this gap to the lack of personal engagement at the point of initial screening.

As a result of this initial experience, the team made some changes to the screening protocols. Three concurrent workflows focusing on different points of patient encounters were designed and tested. The three new points included: (1) engagement while the individual was in the ED, (2) engagement of individuals that had already left the ED, and (3) engagement of hospitalized patients on the medical/surgical floors of the hospital.

For the direct engagement while the individual was in the ED, licensed social workers conducted initial face-to-face screenings with patients awaiting care. The social workers were provided a list of eligible patients (those with multiple ED visits in the past year) and went room to room to conduct the screenings and determine if the patients were interested in connecting with community resources. Because many of these patient interactions took place while the individual was in the middle of an ED care visit, the PCCI team member was mindful of this and stepped aside, as needed, to ensure they didn't interrupt the patient's care.

For those individuals that left the ED before screening, the PCCI team placed these individuals' names and contact numbers on a sheet and later reached out to them by phone to explain the program and ask if they were interested in receiving information on community resources. Finally, for those individuals undergoing an inpatient stay in the hospital, PCCI personnel obtained census data reports with information about eligible patients and then staff visited these patients in their rooms to conduct one-on-one conversations to implement the screening tool and to determine if the patients were interested in receiving more information about navigation services to community resources.

Table 6.1   Case Study Screening Conversion Rate

Care Setting	Screening Output	Conversion Rate[a]	Patient Engagement
Outpatient (in person)	High	Very low	Low
Outpatient-post discharge (calls)	High	Very low	Low
ED (in person)	Low	High	High
ED-post discharge (calls)	Low	Low	Moderate
Inpatient	Low	High	High

[a] Number of patients screened that proceeded to seek help/resources from PCCI staff.

As shown in Table 6.1, a key learning from this undertaking was that the site matters in conducting the screenings and successfully connecting people to local programs for support. We learned that engaging patients during their inpatient stay was the optimal care setting in which to conduct screenings and then connect those patients to the appropriate community resources.

Establishing trust with patients early in the process was essential, both for completing the initial screening tool and for facilitating connection to community services. During our initial approach, we relied on self-administered screenings that provided little in the way of opportunity to establish a relationship with patients. Our modified workflow allowed our social workers and community health workers to verbally administer the screening tool and provide additional explanations as part of that exchange. This process also made the transition to navigation services virtually seamless and much more effective. Feedback from patients has also been positive; most indicated that the information received was useful and many said they would share this information with other family members and close friends.

THE SCREENING PROCESS

The PCCI community engagement team consisted of six community health workers and two master's-level, licensed social workers. Initially, the team consisted entirely of social workers, but our experience taught us that a blended staff model was more cost-effective. PCCI physician leaders coached all team members on how to be flexible and professional when working in the ED, where care moves at a rapid pace. The team needed to take cues from medical staff on where and when to step in to conduct the screenings. Similar trainings were delivered to those staff visiting patients in the hospital.

Over the course of the 6-month pilot, we were also able to identify a number of key elements that increased both the effectiveness and efficiency of the screening process. For example, we learned that it took on average 15 minutes to complete the assessment tool when it was facilitated by a team member but only 10 minutes when self-administered. While the self-administered survey took less time to complete, we found a much higher percentage of incomplete and inaccurate responses, making many of the screens useless. As would be expected, we also found that older patients— those 65 or older—took on average 20 minutes to complete the facilitated screening survey while younger individuals completed it in half the time. The difference was attributable to the amount of questions asked and attendant conversations, which were much more prevalent with older patients. Finally, once we began to work more closely with the patients and they developed a better sense of the purpose of the work, we encountered very few issues with obtaining consent from the patients to share their information with others.

Chapter 7

Community Partners Track

Introduction to the Community Partners Track

The Community Partners Track provides the requirements for the workflows and the tools needed for Community-Based Social Service Organizations *aka* Community-Based Organizations (CBOs) to achieve the goals of the *Connected Communities of Care (CCC)*. For example, lack of transportation may be identified as a *CCC* social need connected to missed medical appointments. To address this pressing need, the CBOs should coordinate efforts across the community to manage and provide transportation services for these residents. To achieve large-scale, lasting solutions, the CBOs will need to coordinate their efforts with Partners across the community, including local municipal elected officials, to align insights, activities, and workflows around clearly established *CCC* goals.

Just as with the clinical provider workflows, community workflows require consideration of a unique set of circumstances, relationships, and nuances. Even more so than the clinical provider workflows, community workflows will vary widely across CBOs but ultimately need to align to support the global *CCC* goals. Leadership, staffing, and management models may be vastly different from those of the clinical Partners and will, thus, require dedicated, deep expertise from the Sponsor or Community Partners Track lead working to engage the CBO Participants. For many of your CBO Participants, this program will require a significant change in their workflows and in the scope of their influence in the community. To ensure CBO Partner readiness, specific roles should be defined for the organization staff and training activities should cover consent workflows, case management workflows, and technical interface and functionalities.

The workflows created as part of the Community Partners Track should:

- Create and facilitate coordinated and aligned relationships (service referral and data sharing) across diverse CBOs and across CBOs and clinical providers.
- Clearly define the processes and workflows for supporting the *CCC* interventions.
- Monitor progress and results to ensure the diverse populations served are receiving the designed *CCC* interventions promoting better health and greater self-sufficiency.

It is important to note that not all CBOs need to adopt the *CCC* technology for their operations, but strong efforts should be made to ensure that they are listed in the referral directory, and that they can still receive referrals via email outside of the *CCC*.

Prerequisites

The work in the Community Partners Track can generally begin once the *CCC* key decision makers have completed the prerequisites of the Clinical Providers Track. Other prerequisites include:

- Defined roles of CBOs in executing the clinical interventions
- Selection of CBO Partner/Participant sites
- Defined requirements for technology and data integration at Partner/Participant sites

Requirements to Establish Community Workflows

The four key requirements for the Community Partners Track implementation are as follows:

1. Develop community interventions and workflows to support the *CCC* clinical programs.

   Note that this will include identification of the unique workflow requirements of CBOs and associated programs to be included in the *CCC*.
2. Convene and engage staff or volunteers to support the *CCC* at the CBO sites.
3. Conduct training at CBO sites.
4. Conduct pilots at CBO sites to ensure readiness for *CCC* launch.

Requirement 1: Develop Community Interventions and Workflows to Support the CCC Clinical Programs

The purpose of this Requirement is to develop a tactical plan for CBOs to address the goals of the *CCC* and, specifically, the use cases identified as part of the readiness assessment process. To achieve this, the Community Partners Track lead will work with the Clinical Providers Track lead to define cross-organizational workflows supported by the *CCC* framework and technology. It will be important to adapt workflows to technology offerings, meaning that workflows may need to adjust if the technology evolves.

Key Roles and Responsibilities

The key roles for this Requirement will most likely include the following individuals at the CBO Partner sites:

- CBO leaders
  - Program directors
  - CBO site operations lead
- CBO frontline and operations staff: social workers, volunteer staff, navigators

Milestone 1: Convene Staff to Review Existing Workflows

The Community Partners Track lead, working with the leaders of the participating CBOs, should convene frontline staff from each of the CBOs to review existing workflows to better understand how the CBOs currently operate and what changes may need to be made going forward. Existing workflows should be diagramed and reviewed in detail during in-person working sessions conducted between the CBO staff and the Community Partners Track lead.

Key Task: Leverage Appropriate Staff for Work Sessions

For the joint work sessions, it is preferable to engage the frontline staff and management personnel who are tasked with operating the CBO. These individuals are likely the most knowledgeable and experienced within the CBO with regard to how the entity actually works. Because of the high turnover rates among CBO personnel, to gain the best historical perspective, it is critical to engage those within the organization who have the longest tenure. Most CBOs have at least one or two individuals with enough firsthand experience to be able to articulate the workflows as they know them. To facilitate the review process and insure uniformity of approach, the Parkland Center for Clinical Innovation (PCCI) recommends that the Community Partners Track lead create a template standardizing the workflows across the participating CBO sites. The workflow diagrams and review should at a minimum identify the following key elements:

- All staff members involved in the existing process workflows, including their name, role, and job description
- Physical infrastructure or resources required for the workflows, including where each step takes place, any facility dependencies (e.g., high-speed internet connectivity), and the time-dependent sequencing of each step
- Data flows with emphasis on where data is captured, shared, or consolidated, including all steps where patient-level information is collected or comes into play. Special attention should be placed on data elements, such as demographic data, residence, insurance status, and all appropriate clinical and Social Determinants of Health (SDOH) data.
- Those CBO processes or operational requirements that are mandated or highly inflexible and that may conflict with the necessary *CCC* requirements call for the development of mitigation plans or legal guidance.

PRACTICE POINTER

Use Conflict Mitigation Analysis to Assist in Workflow Design

To the extent possible, all *CCC* interventions should complement existing programs rather than duplicate offerings or services or worse, generate counterproductive practices. A thorough understanding of those elements identified above requiring the development of mitigation plans will promote the establishment of workflows that are additive and supportive rather than detrimental to the CBO, its staff, and its clients. If the number of potential conflicts between existing CBO workflows and proposed *CCC* workflows is material, the creation of a document that describes the nature of the potential conflicts and how they will be addressed may be helpful for reference and to ensure consistency and efficiency going forward.

Milestone 2: Identify and Document Required Modifications to Existing Workflows to Achieve CCC Outcomes

Once sufficient joint work sessions have taken place, the resulting depiction of the existing workflows will serve as the basis for the design of the *CCC* specific workflows. CBO leadership should review the current workflows diagrams and descriptions with their teams for accuracy and to maintain buy-in, build trust, and further frontline staff engagement. CBO leaders should clearly define, through an iterative process of multiple drafts, the required modifications to the existing workflows in order to achieve the outcomes of the interventions with minimal to no disruption of existing operations. Specific activities included in this review process should include at a minimum:

- Clearly define what roles and individuals perform each step of the new workflows.
- Empower CBO personnel, especially mid-level managers and the frontline staff, to guide the process for any new workflows (i.e., make it their idea and achievement).
- Propose an "ideal-state" workflow and position it as the "art of the possible" as this will serve as a starting point for discussion from which ideation can take place. During these discussions, CBO leaders will need to engage key CBO staff to describe their current workflows and how these workflows deviate from the ideal state. Allowing mid-level managers to voice their concerns and talk through potential challenges will (1) facilitate open and frank dialogue, (2) encourage actionable problem-solving, and (3) ensure that CBO personnel feel heard and valued. Ultimately, the goal is to develop workflow solutions that will meet the objectives of the community program and be easily incorporated into the CBO's day-to-day operations.
- Examine multiple outcomes/possibilities of the proposed processes; consider all known and potential impediments and how they will be dealt with if encountered.
- Ensure that a consistent and rigorous approach is used both through the review process of the existing workflows and the development of the proposed workflows.

PRACTICE POINTER

Break Down the Workflows into a Phased Approach

Breaking the workflows down into a phased approach will allow the team to focus, ideate, and test one step at a time. Community workflows will likely include all of the following elements, which should be considered individually and as a whole to optimize outcomes: (1) client enrollment and consent, (2) screening/information gathering, (3) making referrals and accepting referrals, (4) provision and documentation of services delivered, and (5) closeout activities. In testing these elements, staff should assume a client role to simulate the newly required steps for the draft workflow process. Observers in place can note the challenges and opportunities with analysis of each element. Teams can then suggest modifications and retest, resulting in refinements to the workflows and new insights around the new process.

Key Documents for Requirement 1

- List of Participant Clinical Sites and CBOs
- Standard Operating Procedure (SOP) that Details a *CCC* Workflow

Requirement 2: Convene and Engage Staff or Volunteers to Support the CCC at the Community Sites

The purpose of this Requirement is to identify a key group of staff who are accountable to execute the CBO workflows at each CBO site. The actions set out in this section offer guidance to ensure adequate buy-in from the community Partners and Participants and their staff.

Key Roles and Responsibilities

The key roles and stakeholders for this Requirement include the following:

- Senior-level CBO leaders
- Mid-level CBO leaders
  - Program director
  - Community site operations director
  - Community engagement/marketing manager
  - Frontline and operations staff (e.g., case managers, service manager, social worker, community health worker, volunteer coordinator)
  - Community site *CCC* Champion (if one exists)

Milestone 1: Convene Senior and Mid-Level Leaders to Review the CCC Community Programs and Goals

As with any innovative initiative, implementation of the *CCC* workflows will undoubtedly impose a level of disruption to the status quo. As is the case for the clinical Partners and Participants, in order for staff to accept, embrace, and act to effectively implement the new community programs, each CBO site must ensure the following:

- Complete alignment among CBO senior leaders and Funders as to the importance of the *CCC* initiative and its prioritization among existing programs and service offerings
- A senior leadership directive to the entire organization to implement and support the *CCC* community workflows while, in parallel, leadership also assists in clearing organizational barriers and deprioritizing competing counterproductive programs and services
- Empowerment of frontline staff to deliver workflows through a level of ownership and personal accountability

- Establishment or adjustment of goals at the organization, team, and individual levels to encourage success of the *CCC* community programs

Complete alignment begins at the top of the organization and cascades throughout the entire organization. Therefore, before any *CCC* announcements take place with mid-level managers or frontline staff, senior leaders (including the CEO or President) must buy-in to the *CCC* and prioritize its goals by linking them to the organization's own goals. Even the slightest bit of trepidation on the part of the senior leadership team in conveying the importance and value of *CCC* to the organization and its clients may be sensed by staff and taken that *CCC* is just another "flash in the pan" idea and not to be taken seriously.

Achieving complete alignment at the leadership level may require multiple iterations of the workflow effort conducted in proper sequence and with varying subsets of leaders. While every organization has its own nuances and political structure, PCCI has identified the following tactics to be effective and fundamental to securing consensus on the approach to a *CCC* community workflow implementation:

- Assuming the site has obtained leadership buy-in, the frontline staff at each site will have to define the pathways to implement the workflows defined in Requirement 1. There is no universal solution or process for every site. Leaders should share the detailed framework of the defined workflows and demonstrate an ideal-case workflow solution to get there. Leaders should expect a lot of detailed questions with respect to the proposed workflows and aspects of the program. The mid-level leaders should expect to see a level of expert proficiency with respect to all aspects of the community program.
- Choose functional site team members, such as team champions, to serve as points of contact as they are best positioned to ensure success of the program. At CBOs, these will be individuals who have been with the organization for a few years and, more importantly, have established a good reputation and respect among their peers. CBO environments typically comprise tightly knit groups of people who share the passion and the vision of the CBO. The process of securing buy-in and adopting a new disruptive process often requires inspiration and confidence from "one of their own."
- Maintain a focus on two specific goals of the process: (1) What will your processes to execute the defined workflows look like and (2) who is best

positioned to implement the workflows. While it is typical for the staff to focus on complex, broader aspects of the project and challenges versus the "what needs to be done," the focus should remain on the latter.

PRACTICE POINTER

Position the Workflows to Support Current Efforts

When engaging this audience, learn about the key drivers and values of the current work and look for ways, where possible, to position the workflows as ways to support or improve what the teams are already doing. While the process will primarily involve the frontline staff, it is important to provide progress updates to leadership teams. This helps to ensure that everyone is on the same page in order to avoid misunderstandings, loss of alignment, or project delays.

Staffing constraints are a common challenge at CBO sites. While some larger CBOs have dedicated, fully funded staff, most rely on a mix of full-time employees and volunteers. Simply hiring additional staff to address the needs of the *CCC* workflows will not be sustainable unless the *CCC* is able to fund these new resources. Consider leveraging community health workers, additional volunteers, or social work interns to support the CBO sites that need added support. Working with local colleges and universities and your clinical Partners to secure interns or to tap into the Partners' community development/community health resources may be a good place to start. These strategies have proven effective in the right circumstances. But the Community Partners Track lead should carefully consider the following risks and benefits:

- The Sponsor provides partial to full financial support to the CBO to deliver the required *CCC* programs, interventions, and workflows. As explained earlier in the Clinical Providers Track, this approach essentially makes the new resources full-time employees of the CBO. Thus, they are subject to the directives of the CBO, which may include partial assignment to competing programs. While this may not be problematic, it does remove control of the new resources from the *CCC*, possibly limiting the resource's effectiveness to achieve the *CCC*'s objectives.

- Many CBOs make use of community volunteers to fill staffing gaps. While this strategy entails no additional financial commitment on the part of the *CCC*, the challenges of using volunteers may prove to outweigh the cost of hiring dedicated staff as volunteer resources typically have high turnover rates or demonstrate a lessened level of performance and commitment, especially in difficult times.

Key Documents for Requirement 2

- Each CBO site's list of designated frontline and operational staff responsible for *CCC* execution, the site's *CCC* Champion, and other staff that will interface with clients on behalf of the *CCC* (e.g., social workers, community health workers, any part-time or full-time clinicians, or other health professionals and community development specialists).

Requirement 3: Conduct Training at CBO Sites

The training of CBO sites should not be viewed as a one-time engagement. Rather, it should be viewed as an integral part of the *CCC* initiative and incorporated into the administration of *CCC* on an ongoing basis to ensure optimal engagement of CBO's frontline staff and management in the delivery of the community interventions. While the interventions are clinical or community in origin, the nature of *CCC* requires them to be viewed as interdependent, which has significant implications for how the frontline staff should be trained.

Milestone 1: Deliver the Technology Training

The technology training is best delivered by a team consisting of a representative from the technology vendor and a *CCC* team client relations staff member who is designated a "super user." Ideally, the training should be delivered in person, although live webinars using audiovisual tools to enhance the learning experience may be substituted if the number of CBOs requiring training is extensive or if the CBOs are located in areas which are difficult to access (e.g., remote rural locations). Experience has shown that breaking up the training into two shorter sessions (1.5 hours each) rather than one longer session produces better engagement and learning, though the logistics of the training may become more challenging (i.e., setting up two sessions vs. one session). All trainings should be documented and tracked through the administration of tests and surveys via a reputable survey platform, which includes the following:

- A self-paced post-training test
- A satisfaction survey using at least a five-point response scale
- A certificate of completion provided to each trainee who successfully completes the test (at least 80% correct) and submits a completed satisfaction survey

Milestone 2: Deliver Training on Patient Engagement to CBO Staff

These training sessions begin where the technology training ends and focus on the initial interaction with the client. Experience has shown that staff can benefit from regular and ongoing "refresher" training, ensuring that the programs, interventions, and services delivered by the *CCC* are in alignment with the initiative's processes and goals as articulated by the *CCC* governance group or Administrator. It is surprising how quickly the required processes of a program, such as *CCC*, can be individually "modified" by frontline staff to make the workflows simpler and less time-consuming. This practice, which is far more common than most program administrators will acknowledge, can do serious damage to the program by removing uniform practices, compromising results, and generally making the program less effective and efficient.

At a minimum, training activities should include the following:

- Initial client contact (explanation of *CCC*, enrollment and consent process, assessment of needs, and provision of services)
- Ad hoc training as needed to support new hires, or to remediate discrepancies or inadequacies in workflows, or to address inconsistencies in outcomes reporting
- Annual refresher training to ensure optimal compliance with community workflows and overall *CCC* requirements

It is expected that all CBO staff should demonstrate a basic level of proficiency in the community workflows (80% achievement on standard tests) and operate under the direct supervision of the CBO site's supervisory staff or other experienced staff until at a minimum, each staff member has conducted at least ten patient/client encounters. Estimated completion time for *CCC* staff onboarding is typically 7–10 days from completion of initial technology training.

Milestone 3: Deliver Training on Programs, Interventions, and Services

Once training has addressed how to use the technology and engage patients in the *CCC*, the final topics that must be covered with CBO staff involve the programs and specific interventions to be offered, as well as any additional services provided by the CBO or its partners to benefit the individual. This training begins with a review of the programs offered (e.g., smoking-cessation classes, behavioral counseling, basics of managing money), so that frontline staff can quickly and correctly identify those that best align with an individual client's needs. This means that the program offering overview must be detailed enough that the staff person understands what the programs are intended to do, any eligibility requirements that might exist, and the elements of the programs (i.e., the interventions). Staff should be encouraged to consult standard descriptions of each program that has been previously developed at each CBO.

PRACTICE POINTER

Standardize and Centralize Information for Clients

PCCI recommends that CBOs keep standard descriptions of each program offered in a central file location easily accessible by frontline staff. This process will help to (1) ensure consistency in what gets communicated by staff, (2) provide a hardcopy of the program description/interventions for clients, and (3) allow for easy updating should the program or its eligibility requirements change.

In addition to training staff on the programs and interventions offered by the CBO, it will be beneficial if staff have a basic understanding of any supplemental services either provided by the CBO or offered at the CBO's primary partner organizations. These services cover things like transportation services, medication-disposal services, or possibly childcare services.

Because programs, interventions, and services change over time, it is essential that all documentation be kept updated and that CBO staff members become familiar with the changes through mandatory training sessions conducted either in groups or individually via self-paced reviews. While most CBOs do not require a post-learning quiz, PCCI sees great value in developing a simple five to ten question quiz to assess whether the learning objectives were accomplished. As each CBO operates differently, we believe it is best left up to each CBO to determine how often to conduct the trainings.

Key Documents for Requirement 3

- Training Objectives

Requirement 4: Conduct Pilots at CBO Sites to Ensure Readiness for CCC Launch

As much of this work may be new to your CBO Partners and Participants, PCCI recommends that prior to the official launch of the *CCC*, all CBO sites undertake a brief pilot of the defined workflows and other operational requirements to ensure CBO staff members are ready and able to undertake the required work. Our experience in the Dallas Metroplex suggests that piloting should be iterative in nature and consist of a minimum of two rounds of testing.

Key Roles and Responsibilities

The key roles and responsibilities for this Requirement include the following individuals:

- Community Partners Track lead
- Leadership (however defined) at the Partner CBOs and participating CBOs
- Frontline staff and mid-level managers at the Partner CBOs and participating CBOs

Milestone 1: Select a Subset of CBOs as Pilots

Although the goal should be to pilot the new workflows at all CBO sites before formal launch, testing the processes at a limited number of select CBO sites represents a good first step in deploying the *CCC*. Success with the pilots should serve to confirm the validity and applicability of the new workflows and to give the remaining CBO sites confidence when it becomes their turn to test the new workflows. Initially, the subset of pilot CBOs should be selected from among the most engaged and supportive organizations. CBOs that meet these criteria and tend to be larger, serve a more diverse population, and have more varied workflows, are good candidates for the initial piloting. *CCC* leaders should avoid selecting similar sites, such as all food banks or homeless shelters, or those CBOs located in the same zip code as they will likely have similar patient/client profiles and needs.

Milestone 2: Conduct a Pre-Launch Visit to Pilot Sites

It is important to conduct a pretest visit to the pilot sites to ensure all logistic and operational requirements are in place (e.g., staff are clear on what they need to do, sufficient amount of printed materials are ready, pilot sites have adequate Wi-Fi connectivity, and a robust internet access if the technology platform is cloud-based). The *CCC* Community Partners Track lead should meet with CBO leadership to identify which staff will be involved in the pilot testing and who will coordinate or manage the effort. Once these requirements have been addressed, the actual pilot test can proceed.

Milestone 3: Determine Time Periods for the Pilot

The *CCC* Community Partners Track lead should work with the CBO sites' mid-level managers and frontline staff to determine the best times to conduct the pilots. Depending on the populations served, patient/client volumes are likely to vary throughout the day, week, and possibly month, potentially having a material impact on the number of cases available for testing. For example, those on Supplemental Nutrition Assistance Program (SNAP) or Women, Infants, and Children (WIC) benefits tend to show up towards the end of the month as their resources become depleted. Understanding these flow patterns before beginning the pilots will be valuable in managing the case volumes during the pilot period.

Experience suggests that 3–6 days a week (depending on case volume) covering various times over a normal 8-hour workday should be sufficient to provide feedback, to adjust if needed, and to retest. Depending on the specific patient/client profiles and needs of the population served by the CBO, piloting activity does not need to take place on consecutive days; rather, experience has taught that identifying "peak" days and times is far more important and results in a more predictable assessment of the "stress-tested" workflows.

Milestone 4: Define Measurement and
Success Criteria to Evaluate the Pilot

Prior to initiating a pilot, the *CCC* Community Partners Track lead should work with CBO leaders to arrive at a set of performance measures to be used in evaluating the pilot test. The *CCC* Community Partners Track lead should also create a simple data-collection tool (a simple Excel spreadsheet will suffice) to capture key data needed for the evaluation of the new *CCC* workflows. Listed below are several sample performance measures and success criteria that should be considered by the CBO/ *CCC* team:

Measures

- Number of clients eligible for program services
- Number and type of SDOH needs reported by clients
- Number of clients approached to participate
- Number of clients actually participating
- Number and type of interventions/services included on care plan
- Number of clients with a defined goal plan

Success Criteria

- Number of clients willing to recommend the program
- Specific outcomes desired (e.g., reduction in Emergency Department [ED] visits and hospitalizations, fewer missed clinic visits, more prescriptions filled)
- Number of clients completing the entire program
- Error rate for data collected <2% ("error rate" defined as two or more missing data fields per data record)
- Eighty percent or more of CBO staff feel confident in their ability to execute the *CCC* workflows

Key Documents for Requirement 4

- Evaluation Measures
- Communication Strategy

Case Study: Building CBO Partnerships

A cornerstone of the *CCC* is the CBO. The community food pantries, homeless shelters, crisis centers, and transportation service providers are the lifeline for many vulnerable and underserved community residents. In addition to providing essential services, these organizations help the individuals cope with the challenges of daily life. For far too long, these organizations were excluded from the clinical care plan process for a host of reasons. Communities Foundation of Texas (CFT) (the initial philanthropic funder of the Dallas Information Exchange Portal [IEP]) and PCCI recognized the vital role these entities play in the health and well-being of the individuals seeking care at Parkland. As part of the design of the Dallas IEP, PCCI began an ongoing effort to establish meaningful partnerships with local CBOs to foster their involvement in (and support of) the Dallas IEP, through linkages to each other and to Parkland.

PCCI recognized early on that given the large geography covered by Dallas County, more than a couple CBOs would be needed to make the IEP robust and meaningful. In the past, efforts to engage CBOs typically involved recruitment at the individual CBO level, something that in the case of the IEP would likely prove problematic given the number needed. Instead, the PCCI team, with support from CFT, proposed a new approach of engaging the major Sponsors of the CBOs, which in this case included the North Texas Food Bank (NTFB), which worked with many local food pantries, and the Metro Dallas Homeless Alliance (MDHA), a large umbrella organization coordinating services for dozens of smaller homeless shelters. By working directly with these umbrella organizations, PCCI only needed to execute two contracts rather than multiple contracts with the individual CBOs. The NTFB and the MDHA were then responsible for recruiting their members in sufficient numbers to increase the IEP's scale.

While this approach proved successful, it did not remove the need for PCCI to "make the case" for the IEP with the NTFB and the MDHA. In addition to explaining how this program would involve NTFB's food pantries and MDHA's homeless shelters, it was imperative to make the business case for their involvement—how will this work benefit them and their members and what will be needed from the membership. In addition to helping improve the health and well-being of community residents, we found the following to be key incentives for CBO participation: (1) ability to provide funding to support the IEP or its usage, (2) enhanced reporting and analytic capability—either through the technology platform software itself or through PCCI analytical staff, (3) opportunity to participate in future research projects that would bring visibility to other sources of funding, and (4) greater operational efficiency.

Once the list of participating CBOs was shared with PCCI, the team installed the software at the participating sites, trained CBO staff, and communicated expectations and next steps. This process proved to be one of the critical success factors behind the initiative. CBO staff members that reported training as helpful and beneficial were more likely to use the IEP than those for whom training was deemed less helpful. Feedback from those receiving training suggested that two shorter training sessions (each 1.5 hours) and involving hands-on practice exercises was far more helpful than one longer training session (3 hours). When PCCI staff members (1) set clear expectations of what was expected of the CBO and how the IEP was to be used and (2) reinforced that message through follow-up question and answer sessions and individual consultations, CBO use of the IEP (as it was intended to be used) was materially higher than where less emphasis was placed on expectations.

With the software installed and training completed, PCCI implemented several short pilot test periods to ensure that the technology was performing as expected and that the CBO staff felt comfortable in using it. These short pilot test periods, lasting from 2 to 4 weeks, were critical in a successful launch of the broader IEP implementation. As anticipated, the pilot work uncovered some software issues that needed to be addressed to ensure optimal use by the CBOs. The work also revealed some modifications to the CBO and clinical/CBO workflows that needed to be made. It is important to note that all pilot testing was done without involving any patients or residents in the testing phase.

While the preparatory work helped to ensure a successful launch of the IEP both with Parkland and the participating CBOs (whose numbers grew appreciably after the launch due to continued recruitment into the network), we found that additional steps were needed to ensure ongoing success. Much like processes that are measured regularly as part of an improvement campaign and then ended abruptly when the campaign ends, we found that to optimize the effectiveness of the IEP and maintain its momentum, we needed to institute a continuous monitoring process with both the CBOs and Parkland. This ongoing involvement with the IEP Participants proved to be a greater time commitment than we had originally foreseen. While the frequency of challenges declined with the length of time since launch, we continually uncovered new issues or new opportunities to strengthen the initiative. This was especially true for the CBOs, where most staff members include volunteers and the turnover rate is quite high. Because of this, we employed a train-the-trainer model, which proved largely effective. Again, most CBOs have a very small staff. Thus, the departure of a manager or experienced frontline worker often proved a major disruption to the use of the IEP. Constant contact with the CBOs (even when the number of CBO Participants approached 100) helped ensure that any challenges could be addressed as quickly and effectively as possible.

The key takeaway from the past 5 years of working with the CBO community in Dallas is that relationships matter, and that these relationships need constant, open and honest, two-way communication and nurturing to bring about success. We believe that these lessons apply far beyond this initiative.

Community Partners Track Supplement: Sample Stakeholder Categories, Programs, and Services

Types of CBOs and Services

Housing

Housing services vary widely among CBOs. As a result, successful CBO engagement requires knowledge of the types of housing assistance provided, regulations, and populations served. Some of the programs offered through housing CBOs include the following:

- U.S. Department of Housing and Urban Development (HUD) Programs contributing to building and preserving healthy neighborhoods and communities, such as:
  - Neighborhood Stabilization Programs (NSPs)
  - Housing Trust Fund Organization (HTF)
  - Housing Opportunities for Persons with AIDS programs (HOPWA)
  - Home Investment Partnership programs
  - Continuum of Care programs (CoC)
  - Community Development Block program (CDBG)
- Public Housing and Voucher Programs, providing safe and affordable housing for eligible low-income families, the elderly, and persons with disabilities. Examples include the following:
  - Housing Choice Vouchers
  - Mixed-Finance Public Housing
  - Public Housing Agency (PHA) Plans
  - Rental Housing Integrity Improvement Project (RHIIP)
  - Section 8 Management Assessment Program (SEMAP)
  - Supportive Services Programs
- Shelters services offered depend on program regulations and length of stay. Thus, when engaging shelters, some shelters will be better suited to meet desired workflow outcomes tied to specific timeframes. Examples of shelter categories include the following:
  - Long-Term Housing services typically have no time limit on length of stay or receipt of assistance.
  - Short-Term Housing services are intended to be for a duration of up to 30, 60, or 90 days.

– Emergency Shelters provide overnight sleeping accommodations, the primary purpose of which is to provide temporary shelter for a specific population experiencing a housing crisis or unsafe housing accommodations.
– Transitional Housing provides temporary accommodations with prescribed limits (e.g., 24 months per HUD).
– Domestic Violence Shelters.
• Group Homes serve as private residence models to assist individuals with complex needs, such as transitional homes for teenagers aging out of foster care or veteran residential group homes.

Nutrition

Access to nutrition services will depend on the funding available under a specific program at a CBO. You should first research the type of services available in your community, such as food pantries, meals on wheels, or nutrition education classes and then proactively identify what restrictions or barriers may affect *CCC* participation. For example, the culture of food pantries widely varies, and it is essential to understand the dynamics between workflow, workload, resources, and program capacities in order to correctly define workflows. Smaller food pantries have the capacity to generate a stronger rapport with their clients and community when compared to larger food pantries.

Examples of Food Sources include the following:

• Feed America Food Banks
• Local Food Banks
• Soup Kitchens
• Hunger Relief Organizations

Examples of nutrition programs offered by CBOs include the following:

• United States Department of Agriculture (USDA) Food and Nutrition Services
  – Supplemental Nutrition Assistance Program (SNAP)
• State Services Programs, such as:
  – Texas Department of State Health Services:
    • Women, Infant, Children (WIC) nutrition classes
    • Farmers' Market Nutrition program

Education

Two factors are critical when working with a CBO focused on education: (1) time constraints and (2) funding. Time constraints will be determined by the type of CBO you engage with. For example, CBOs providing services based on a school calendar will be limited to the types of programs they can provide outside of the school hours. As another example, CBOs providing educational services for adults will tend to function on an evening and weekend schedule. Funding plays a major role in determining how a CBO providing education will function and could potentially limit the capacity of clients served. Examples of educational programs provided by CBOs include the following:

- Child Development
  - Early Head Start and Head Start: The Office of Head Start (OHS) at the U.S. Department of Health and Human Services (HHS) helps young children from low-income families prepare to succeed in school through local programs. Head Start and Early Head Start programs promote children's development through services that support early learning, health, and family well-being.
  - Early Childhood Intervention (ECI): Statewide program within the Texas Health and Human Services Commission for families with children birth up to age 3, with developmental delays, disabilities, or certain medical diagnosis that may affect development.
- General Education Diploma (GED) programs: Information for GED programs can be found in Public Libraries and through School Districts
- Community Skills Training Programs
- English as a Second Language classes
- Citizenship classes

Financial Stability/Assistance

CBOs in this category provide programs focusing on services to alleviate financial strains of targeted populations. Because the goal is to teach habits that can lead to stability, it is important to consider that program outcomes are not produced as quickly as with other types of programs. In working with these CBOs, you will need to carefully consider desired timelines and reportable outcomes. When engaging these types of CBOs, you may want to select those who provide multiple service encounters across longer periods of time. This will allow for an effective outcome evaluation of your *CCC*'s desired goals. Examples of programs or assistance offered by these CBOs include the following:

- *Utility Assistance*. CBOs providing these services tend to have funding restrictions that affect how often or how many clients they serve. Typically, these types of services are on a first come, first served basis and are not consistently available throughout the year.
- *Financial Crisis Assistance*. CBOs providing these services do not focus on longer-term sustainability for the client. The primary focus for financial crisis assistance is to eliminate or minimize unforeseen one-time barriers for clients; therefore, financial literacy services are not necessarily the focus of these organizations.
- *United Way Services*. This CBO offers programs to empower individuals to achieve financial stability, with proven methods like job training, financial wellness classes, and more.

Safety (Abuse, Violence)

Abuse can be categorized as: physical, sexual, emotional, economic, and psychological. Typically, CBOs providing shelter for individuals or families suffering from abuse give limited information about location, population, and logistics due to the sensitive nature of the services they provide. Before engaging these CBOs, carefully identify desired outcomes and how this can be achieved through this type of CBO. Consider the possibility of having limited access to qualitative data and personal interviews. When engaging CBOs focusing on safety, including state and local services (e.g., domestic violence shelters, Child Protective Services), limit the size of your team to the smallest possible number of group members as this will demonstrate your understanding of the need for client privacy.

Mental/Behavioral Health

Engagement with Mental/Behavioral Health CBOs also requires a clear view of the desired target population and work in advance to determine the diagnosis that the *CCC* intends to work with in order to uncover barriers for proposed workflows in an effort to achieve better informed conversations, proactive identification of barriers (and potential solutions) to proposed workflows and desired outcomes, and avoidance of misunderstandings.

Examples of entities offering mental/behavioral health services include the following:

- Federal Government
  - Substance Abuse and Mental Health Services Administration (SAMHSA)
- Self-Help, Peer Support, and Consumer Groups

Correctional Systems/Jails

Before you engage a CBO that works with prisons to alleviate recidivism, you may want to conduct some preliminary research on these types of program resources, such as:

- Mental Illness of prison populations (e.g., Community Bridges Fact Team offering help in coordinating treatment plans and locating housing)
- Social Factors (e.g., Horizon Prison Initiative, under which volunteers spend time chatting with inmates to provide social support and an opportunity for inmates to engage with members outside the prison community)
- Education and workforce skills training (e.g., Prison Entrepreneurship Program (PEP) providing resources and values-based business skills to inmates through an immersion program consisting of 1:1 inmate training with executive volunteers, and 1:1 business plan inmate mentoring by seasoned professionals)
  - GED programs (e.g., Safer Foundation)
  - The Last Mile, providing instruction for inmates on technology and digital communication
  - Diversion and reentry brokerage networks (e.g., Unlocking DOORS), providing a community-based reentry platform through coordination and collaboration with state agencies and community CBOs
- Substance Use Disorders and Rehabilitation Services
- Advocacy and Legal Assistance
  - Anti-Recidivism Coalition. Provides a support network for formerly incarcerated young men and women and advocated for fairer criminal justice policies.

Elderly

CBOs that offer services for the elderly may each define "elderly" differently. Some CBOs offer services based on the following age criteria: 50+ years, 55+ years, 60+ years, and 65+ years. You will want to identify your target population and verify which CBOs serve individuals within your desired parameters. CBOs providing services for the elderly can range from national funded programs to locally funded senior centers. The following are a few agencies that can provide information on already established programs offered by CBOs in your community:

- *Administration on Aging (AOA).* This HHS agency is designated to carry out the provisions of the Older Americans Act of 1965. It promotes the well-being of older individuals by providing services and programs designed to help them live independently in their homes and communities.
- *Aging and Disability Resource Centers (ADRCs).* ADRCs are designed to streamline public access to long-term services care programs. These centers serve as a key point of access to person-centered specialized information, referral, and assistance and provide one-stop access to information for individuals who need help finding long-term care services.
- *National Council on Aging (NCOA).* NCOA partners with nonprofit organizations, government, and businesses to provide innovative community programs and services, online help, and advocacy to help individuals aged 60+ meet the challenges of aging. Areas of focus include economic security, healthy aging, and public policy and action.
- *National Institute of Senior Centers (NISC).* This institute supports a national network of over 3,000 senior centers dedicated to help older adults remain active, engaged, and independent in their communities. Areas of focus include the following:
  - Strengthening senior centers to improve the lives of older adults
  - Engaging NISC members in NCOA's social impact goals of enhancing economic security, improving health, and advocating for older adults, especially those who are vulnerable and disadvantaged.

Individuals with Disabilities

To effectively engage a CBO providing services for individuals with disabilities, it is important to identify the CBO's source of funding and possible restrictions for alternative funding and program deviations. Examples of programs offered include the following:

- State Programs: Some states grant funding directly to the CBO; others grant funding to a third-party agency that regulates and manages the distribution of monies across grantees/CBOs.
- Federal Programs: Eligible individuals with disabilities may qualify for federal and state programs that pay benefits or health care costs or that provide food.
  - Medicaid: Provides health coverage; each state has its own rules covering eligibility and coverage.
  - Medicare: In addition to covering those aged 65 or older, Medicare also covers individuals with certain disabilities or permanent kidney failure.
  - Supplemental Nutrition Assistance Program (SNAP): Allows beneficiaries to buy nutritious food at their local grocery stores.
  - Social Security: Pays a monthly benefit to older Americans, workers who become disabled, and families in which a spouse or parent dies.
  - Supplemental Security Income (SSI): Pays monthly benefits to people with limited income and resources who are disabled, blind, or aged 65 or older.

Transportation

When engaging CBOs who provide transportation services, it is important to assess the services provided and public opinion on the value of those services, in order to design workflows that can add value. Different types of transportation CBOs and services include the following:

- Public Transportation
  - Paratransit services
  - Public transportation orientations: Some public transportation offices provide educational orientations to alleviate resident concerns
  - Taxi subsidy programs

- Specialized Transportation
  - Medicaid Taxi. This service covers the cost of nonemergency medical transportation for eligible individuals. Coverage for these rides may be different depending on the individual's situation and needs. Some states require pre-approval to qualify for this service.
  - Veterans Transportation Services (VTS). The VTS has established a network of transportation options for veterans through joint efforts with the VA's Office of Rural Health and organizations, such as Veteran Service Organizations (VSOs); community transportation providers; federal, state, and local government transportation agencies; nonprofits; and Veterans Transportation Community Living Initiative (VTCLI) grantees. Transportation services for appointments are available to veterans who are visually impaired, elderly, or immobilized due to disease or disability and particularly those living in remote and rural areas.

Refugee Resettlement

In working with CBOs who aid with refugee resettlement, it will be beneficial to identify the languages spoken and what workflows are currently in place in order to alleviate communication barriers. CBOs and/or CBO services offered include the following:

- *International Rescue Committee.* This Committee responds to the world's worst humanitarian crises and helps affected individuals recover. Programs offered target:
  - Health
  - Safety
  - Education
  - Economic well-being
- *U.S. Committee for Refugees and Immigrants.* This Committee also provides leadership and essential services to help unite families, empower survivors, restore independence, and rebuild likelihoods.
- *State Refugee Services (e.g., Refugee Services of Texas).* These CBOs help refugees and those fleeing persecution. Services offered include the following:
  - Resettlement
  - Survivors of trafficking empowerment program
  - English as a second language

- Refugee youth program
- Legal services
- Economic empowerment

Other Community Stakeholders or Resources

State and Local Health Departments

Health departments have the ability to work with many types of healthcare facilities and, therefore, have a unique opportunity to develop, coordinate, and implement comprehensive local and regional prevention strategies in their state or area. Depending on the region targeted, prevention strategies may also require coordination between states or localities.

Municipalities

The engagement process should focus directly on what is needed; for example, funding, networking, and resources. It is also helpful to highlight how the outcomes/programs align with the various municipality tracks (i.e., public works, public safety, public health, management and administration, quality of life, or civic engagement).

HUD

HUD programs contribute to building and preserving health neighborhoods and communities. Examples include the following:

- Neighborhood Stabilization Programs (NSPs)
- Housing Opportunities for Person with AIDS programs (HOPWA)
- Continuum of Care programs (CoC)
- Housing Trust Fund Organizations (HTF)
- Home Investment Partnership programs (HIP)
- Community Development Block Grants (CDBG)
- HUD Homes

Urban Planners

It may be useful to engage an urban planner when the *CCC* spreads across several community agencies and services because an urban planner can assist in navigating municipal restrictions and networking with other key community members. Examples of Urban Planners include the following:

- *American Planning Association (APA)*. This organization offers opportunities and resources for planners, educators, citizens, students, and professionals. The APA foundation provides philanthropic activities that provide access to educational opportunities and that advance social equity. The APA Ambassador Program is a volunteer activity designed to increase awareness of the power and value that urban planning brings to communities. Particular emphasis is placed on reaching audiences of diverse racial, ethnic, cultural, and economic backgrounds.
- *American Institute of Certified Planners*. This entity organizes volunteer planning teams based on community needs. Communities can apply to have a Community Planning Assistance Team (CPAT) work with them to bolster existing planning initiatives.

Public Libraries

Public libraries can provide a number of knowledge resources as well as initiatives ranging from alleviating homelessness to digital literacy. PCCI recommends engaging the public library early in the ideation process as these entities can provide feedback to increase community buy-in.

- The Public Library Association (PLA) is a division of the American Library Association. It focuses on advancing public library interests and serves 9,000 members across the United States and Canada. PLA initiatives include the following:
  - Digital Literacy
  - Early Literacy
  - Equity, Diversity, and Inclusion
  - Family Engagement
  - Health Literacy
  - Performance Measurement

Advocacy Groups

Advocacy groups are a helpful resource when needing assistance to secure funding and in creating key partnerships in the community and with government groups. These groups have focused agenda; therefore, it is essential

to partner with advocacy groups that align with the program's desired outcomes. Examples of these organizations include the following:

- *National/Domestic Advocacy Groups.* These groups focus on causes
  that directly affect the interests of individuals, groups, or agencies on
  US soil. Examples include Court Appointed Special Advocates (CASA),
  Stand for Children, and America Achieves.
- *International Advocacy Groups.* These groups focus on causes that
  affect individuals or groups outside the United States. Examples include
  Doctors Without Borders, Physicians for Human Rights, and Human
  Trafficking Polaris Project.
- *Non-Governmental Organizations (NGOs).* NGOs are usually nonprofit
  organizations focusing on humanitarian work, education, healthcare,
  public policy, social issues, human rights, and environmental advocacy.
  Examples include Habitat for Humanity, Partners in Health, Wikimedia
  Foundation, and Care International.

Chapter 8

Program Sustainability Track

Introduction to the Program Sustainability Track

Connected Communities of Care (*CCC*) is designed to engage healthcare providers and Community-Based Social Service Organizations *aka* Community-Based Organizations (CBOs) in a combined approach to deliver holistic care that addresses an individual's clinical and social needs. Accomplishing this requires significant capital resources to orchestrate all the technical and workflow changes necessary to achieve a truly functional *CCC*. As the *CCC* grows, the network and set of stakeholders will also continue to expand to include a wider group of CBOs, healthcare providers, and civic and business entities. It is critical to recognize the role that funding and organizational preparedness play in initial *CCC* implementation and ongoing operations. These two functions together represent what we mean by the term "sustainability."

To ensure the *CCC* is sustainable, the Sponsor and Partners and other assigned Track leads must (1) develop a flexible governance structure that provides a well-defined strategic focus and rules and processes for changes to key leadership positions and Partner and Participant engagement in the network; (2) provide a legal and policy framework that incorporates regular review processes to respond to changes in operational and legal requirements; (3) identify future funding and human capital resources after ascertaining needed revenue for expansion; (4) ensure the technology platform can expand with the *CCC*; (5) permit rapid learning and sharing of knowledge in order to facilitate new research; (6) create stakeholder relationships that permit course corrections, encourage expanded community participation, and drive ongoing commitment to the work; and (7) continue to demonstrate and show *CCC* value to the Sponsor, Funders, and the community.

The purpose of this Track is to provide guidance and approaches for ensuring long-term *CCC* success. Consistent stakeholder and Participant support and ongoing revenue generation are two of the most important factors in sustaining *CCC* operations. The *CCC* can garner support through defining and demonstrating its value in providing better services and outcomes and in creating a vehicle for research and innovation benefitting the entire community. To that end, this chapter will examine what it takes to initially set up and run a *CCC* and what is required—both financially and operationally—to maintain and expand operations of the *CCC* as an ongoing concern.

We cannot overemphasize the importance of sustainability in a *CCC* initiative. But as with other complex projects, Sponsors, Partners, and Participants may not focus on this issue until the very last minute before funding runs out or the departure of a major organization or leader, at which time it may be too late. Sustainability is often difficult to fully conceptualize or prioritize, especially following a successful funding and implementation when all eyes are focused on the accomplishments at hand. Because of this, the Parkland Center for Clinical Innovation (PCCI) recommends that during the initial implementation and for several years thereafter, *CCC* leadership should rigorously test the economics of the *CCC* model, refine the structure and guidelines as necessary, and strive to demonstrate value for sustainability.

It is also critically important to keep in mind that what is being asked of CBOs directly impacts these funding/finances. At the same time, these case management activities for high-risk patients are not a regular part of CBO operations, so acknowledging this, while establishing realistic expectations, is critical to success and, in turn, demonstrating value.

Sustainability Key Roles and Responsibilities

Key roles for the Sustainability Track include the following:

- Sponsor
- Governance entity (e.g., Board) and Administrator
- Clinical Advisory Group, Workgroups, and assigned Program Sustainability Track lead
- Accounting, Finance, and Human Resources (HR) subject-matter experts

Requirements to Establish a Model for Sustainability

The requirements to establish a model for sustainability include the following:

1. Seek initial funding
2. Secure ongoing funding to ensure financial sustainability
3. Consider operational sustainability in the initial *CCC* design and implementation
4. Regularly re-examine and refine the elements of the *CCC*, including relationships with Partners, to ensure operational sustainability

Requirement 1: Seek Initial Funding

As a Sponsor or initial governance entity begins to envision the *CCC* that it wants to implement, it is critical for those entities to continually ask, "is this program likely to be successful as designed and, if not, how can changes to the design enhance the probability of success?" As you move from concept to design, you will quickly recognize the amount of funding required to bring about the *CCC* and the potential value a *CCC* can generate, if successful. These initial assessments are critical to determining how much capital is needed to implement the *CCC* and the level of performance required to build the case for sustaining it. Many organizations embarking on implementing a *CCC* actually find securing initial funding less difficult than anticipated, as many philanthropic, governmental, and industry groups may be willing to take a chance on a new project if the program appears sound and the economics make sense. If either of these fundraising basics are missing, then the search for initial funding becomes far more challenging.

Milestone 1: Demonstrate the Value of a CCC

The initial and ongoing demonstration of a *CCC*'s value to stakeholders and the community is at the core of successful and sustainable implementation. Strong outcomes are critical to soliciting future funding sources and participant interest. Despite their best efforts, most health systems lack the expertise and infrastructure to develop a means to connect a community to serve all patients, especially those residents who are most at risk for adverse clinical and social events. The *CCC* serves as that connection point allowing the clinical and CBO Participants to incorporate Social Determinants of Health (SDOH) factors into case management in order to drive down excess health system utilization and to improve the quality of life and the health of the community's residents.

Key Task: Develop and Update the CCC's Value Proposition

The interconnected nature of the *CCC* Participant network permits application of advanced analytics, which in turn should result in various improved outcomes for individuals and the community as a whole (cost savings in the short term, reduction or elimination of social markers like Emergency Department (ED) recidivism and school absenteeism in the long term). It should also result in an environment that permits—and even encourages— research into pressing questions and the creation of innovative solutions to those problems. As the readiness assessment process and initial conversations with Funders will likely show, obtaining funding and key stakeholder (especially Partner) commitment requires that the successful Sponsor or its designated advisor (1) define the values it provides today and will provide in the future (i.e., the value proposition), (2) establish appropriate and valid measures to evaluate the *CCC* and its impact, and (3) publicize prior successes with similar undertakings.

The importance of demonstrating a strong value proposition and impact of Return on Investment (ROI) and Social Return on Investment (SROI) for the *CCC* begins in the Governance Track and remains a priority throughout all Playbook Tracks. As outlined in the Governance Track, the governance entity and designated leads should establish a regular process to measure performance against established goals. This will enable timely interventions or course corrections, if needed. This performance information is critical to ensure continued Participant growth and engagement and to provide ongoing opportunities to secure new funding sources.

Milestone 2: Commit Necessary Resources

While a successful value proposition is a precondition for successful fundraising, it does not in itself guarantee fundraising success. Ideally, to ensure its financial viability, the *CCC* will have dedicated people and resources devoted at a minimum to the following tasks: (1) identifying funding sources that have the interest and ability in funding the *CCC*'s initial implementation, expansion, and future research work; (2) determining the budget needed for each component of the *CCC*'s strategic direction and to support existing activities; and (3) raising the funds necessary to fund each budget component. In determining the budget needed, in addition to using the baseline of the readiness assessment (or current operating budget), the *CCC* Sponsor should consider the cost of (1) bringing new Participants into the existing *CCC* (new Participants often lack resources on their own to join); (2) expanding *CCC* operations either in scope or geographically; and (3) addressing ongoing legal expenses, training, and travel costs. The *CCC* governance entity and the Administrator should consider engaging finance and accounting subject-matter experts (if they do not already exist within the *CCC*) in order to generate realistic budgets.

Fundraising, whether the initial seed money to launch a *CCC* or to sustain it once the initial funding has run out, requires persistence and the patience to commit to a long-term horizon in order for early efforts to bear fruit. However, because fundraising requires special skills and expertise, for *CCCs* that are struggling to secure funding (especially start-up funding linked to a promising program), consider obtaining the help of experienced advisors who are knowledgeable (and highly successful) in this area. While this may be a difficult decision for many governance entities to make, it is one that often pays great dividends if executed successfully.

Milestone 3: Determine Sources of Initial Funding

There are numerous potential funding sources for initial implementation of a *CCC*, but some of these funding sources are more likely than others to be interested in supporting this early work. Start-up funders for programs like *CCC* generally fall into two categories—philanthropic organizations and governmental entities at the state or regional level. Federal government funding may not exist outside of a formal demonstration program that specifies the structure, deliverables, and expected results and is awarded via a highly competitive application process. Philanthropic and governmental entities are distinguished from other early funding sources in that both groups typically sponsor nascent, start-up programs that are intended to improve the health or well-being of communities while also attempting to save money—both key characteristics of a *CCC*.

Key Task: Consider Philanthropic or Private Entities

The Sponsor of a successful *CCC* will need to research the local, regional, and possibly national philanthropic organizations in order to potentially tap into their particular interests, which may generate *CCC* funding. Philanthropic or private entities can be important sources of funding based on their missions. Because these organizations vary in size and scope and missions, determining what areas they typically support is a top priority. It is also important to determine the geographical areas that the philanthropic entity supports as many may prioritize (or limit) funding to their local community or region. It is prudent to examine the amount of funding available, either on an annual basis or by project. While there are a multitude of philanthropic entities, most make relatively small awards, especially to emerging, start-up projects. All of these factors can quickly reduce the pool of philanthropic entities one might approach for funding.

Although their donations further charitable causes, these organizations are keenly interested in the value proposition that a potential awardee brings to the table. Therefore, value propositions to these organizations should emphasize strong financial stewardship and clearly demonstrate how the *CCC* will improve the health and healthcare of the community or specific disease states (e.g., hypertension). Most philanthropic entities are fairly experienced when it comes to finances and accounting; therefore, the applicant should appear clear and credible when presenting financial or operational data to these funders. In many cases, it may be acceptable to include forecasts (as long as they are credible), as philanthropic organizations don't always expect every detail to be fully determined.

Philanthropic and private entities are members of a close-knit community of organizations where relationships matter. This is especially true for private entities that are much less visible to the general public. As you build a relationship with the philanthropic organization and demonstrate the success of the *CCC* in the community, your chances of securing funding extensions measurably increase. In fact, many philanthropic entities work closely with one or more universities, health systems, or other cultural institutions through ongoing grants and other funding vehicles.

Given the importance of relationships, an organization seeking funding from a philanthropic or private entity may benefit from working through a known individual or organization who already has ties with the potential funder. Identify these individuals and organizations common to your business and the funding entity and inquire if they would be willing to make a connection on your behalf.

In summary, the primary advantages of pursuing philanthropic or private entities (versus other entities) to support initial *CCC* funding include the following:

- Key sources of funds
- May not be as competitive as other sources
- May open doors to other funders in the community or region
- Allow for a large degree of flexibility in the design and implementation of the project
- May allow longer and more flexible timelines for demonstrating results than other not-for-profit entities or for-profit businesses
- Strongly advocate for projects with a social mission

Some challenges in pursuing philanthropic or private entity funding include the following:

- May be difficult to engage; correct contacts and messaging will be important.
- May have limited funds or restrict funds to specific uses or geographies.

Key Task: Consider Governmental Entities

Governmental grants or cooperative agreements are likely sources of substantial funding for many *CCC* efforts. The Sponsor should consider both state and local governmental entities charged with caring for the uninsured or those residents experiencing any of a number of material social needs, such as homelessness, lack of food, or personal safety (e.g., Mayor's Council to Combat Homelessness). While local governmental entities may not have the same budgets as state governments, they are often willing to provide some funding and can also make excellent participants based on their experience and connections in the community. Local governments can also influence the community and its businesses and, therefore, broaden support for the *CCC* effort.

The *CCC* Sponsor should determine whether there are grants specifically earmarked for healthcare systems (e.g., Community Benefit Grants). If so, the Sponsor may want to pursue these in partnership with one or more of its clinical Partners. These grants target health systems or other large provider practices that can deliver, for underinsured or uninsured individuals, case management extending beyond typical discharge planning. In addition, the services targeted in these grants often include requirements and program features that a *CCC* would include, such as risk segmentation and stratification and electronic information sharing and referral to community services.

As with philanthropic entities, when constructing a value proposition for a governmental entity, it is important to demonstrate that the *CCC* will improve the health and healthcare of individuals at a local, regional, state, or national level. For programs at the federal level, the population of interest is typically Medicare beneficiaries, followed by those who qualify for both Medicare and Medicaid benefits (dual eligibles), whereas at the state and local levels, greater attention is placed on Medicaid beneficiaries and the uninsured. Unlike philanthropic entities, government grants are frequently driven by the need to demonstrate measurable impact, whether it be reduced hospital admissions or ED visits, or a bending of the cost curve. These requirements place additional demands on the *CCC* to positively impact inappropriate or questionable utilization and healthcare expenditures, often within a defined period of time, with material penalties or sanctions should these outcomes not materialize within the given timeframe.

Because of the high degree of rules and regulations tied to governmental funding, the economics of your *CCC* value proposition and its rationale and supporting documentation must often be more precise than with philanthropic entities. Therefore, they typically require more accurate, precise, and defensible budgets. Also, the reporting and compliance required with government funding is much more demanding, requiring additional resources, expertise, and costs.

In summary, some primary advantages of pursuing government grants to support the *CCC* include the following:

- Government sources provide a strong (high dollar) source of funds, especially at the federal and state levels.
- Successful participation will enhance the visibility and credibility of the *CCC* and attract more industry interest and potential funding resources.
- Grant awardees are in position for ongoing funding for *CCC* implementation and operations via repeat or extended government funding should the *CCC* prove effective in containing or reducing costs.

Some challenges in pursuing governmental funding include the following:

- Funding opportunities, especially at the federal and state levels, are highly competitive.
- Grants may be very specific and targeted in focus; it is usually necessary to show specific improvements per the grants' stipulations.
- Awards may include sanctions and penalties for nonperformance.
- Government contracting requirements are complex and administratively burdensome.
- Funding may be discontinued at the sole discretion of the government should funds not be available (i.e., reduced federal/state budgets).

Requirement 2: Secure Ongoing Funding to Ensure Financial Sustainability

To be successful long term, the Program Sustainability Track lead and other designated leads should establish a process to identify and pursue a number of funding sources and opportunities. This work should begin as early as possible, as the process of identifying and securing funding for continuing *CCC* operations may require multiple attempts and will consume far more time than anticipated. Securing ongoing funding is different than securing initial funding as it often involves different entities and usually is tied directly to generating demonstrable results in the form of ROI-driven outcomes.

While philanthropic organizations and some governmental entities may be willing to fund a promising start-up in the hopes of improving health or reducing inappropriate utilization and costs, long-term funders typically want to see that the *CCC* does what it was intended to do, and that it generates a ROI that makes continued funding justifiable. While accomplishing this may involve some good fortune, the governance entity and *CCC* Administrator can increase chances for success by (1) establishing credible and meaningful (i.e., nationally endorsed) performance measures and (2) closely monitoring the *CCC* performance. Establishing realistic, time-dependent short- and medium-term goals is another way to help keep performance moving in the correct direction. It is also important to capture lessons learned, which will help demonstrate value and justify continued funding. The worst mistake you can make is to wait until you need to seek additional funding to begin to assess your *CCC*'s impact. At that point, it may be difficult (or even impossible) to generate the requisite outcomes sought by a funder, particularly if the project has not been operating as envisioned and it is too late to correct a design flaw or workflow that is negatively impacting your results. Early and frequent assessments of performance, while often burdensome in the short term, can obviate even greater consternation associated with a lack of results or, more importantly, a lack of positive results.

Milestone 1: Secure Ongoing Funding Sources for the CCC

Although sources of long-term funding may be quite different from those approached to secure initial seed capital, the *CCC* leaders should not exclude philanthropic or governmental sources, especially if the *CCC* has performed above expectations as these initial funders may be interested in continuing to stay involved in the work, especially if the work is advancing their goals and mission.

Key Task: Consider Clinical Partners/Participants

The Sponsor and governance entity should consider researching the availability of grants that they could jointly pursue with a Partner or Participant as a means to generate funds for long-term operations. These organizations are logical co-applicants as they are intimately familiar with the *CCC* and understand the social and economic opportunities it provides for their patients. Moreover, many grants are positioned by the funding agency as collaborative and cooperative projects for which multiple, diverse applicants are sought. Partnering with a well-known and respected clinical entity in the community could be especially persuasive in securing funding, especially if the grant is offered by a local funder. This approach also assists in securing the clinical entities' continuing engagement and enthusiastic support of the *CCC.*

Key Task: Consider Hospitals and Health Systems

Hospitals and healthcare systems could be a natural source of funding, especially as an Anchor in the initial stages of the *CCC.* Depending on the local market and the populations served, a safety net hospital or healthcare system may be very interested in providing partial support of a *CCC*, especially if many of the patients they see are indigent and lack insurance coverage, as *CCC* participation may help lower ED utilization and reduce the cost of uncompensated care. Alternatively, participating in a *CCC* may be seen as a competitive advantage by a hospital or healthcare system in a community in which they are one of multiple competing entities. Beyond the ability to positively impact inappropriate utilization and cost, participating in a *CCC* may be seen positively within the community to the extent that the hospital or healthcare system can help address health-related social determinant needs. In many cases, getting one hospital or healthcare system to participate opens the door for other hospitals or healthcare systems to also join the *CCC*, lest they be seen within the community as disinterested in bettering the health and well-being of the populations they serve. If each hospital or healthcare system in a community was to contribute a small but meaningful amount of funding (e.g., 5%–10% of annual uncompensated case expenses), the *CCC's* funding requirements would be met and the total impact across the community could be tremendous.

Hospitals and healthcare systems may also be interested in participating in (and funding a portion of) the *CCC* because new legislation sets forth requirements for nonprofit hospitals to demonstrate the provision of "community benefits" as a condition of their tax-exempt status. For example, Section 9007 of The Affordable Care Act[14] adjusted the Internal Revenue Code existing requirements for 501(c)(3) nonprofit hospitals to conduct Community Health Needs Assessments every 3 years and then create a plan for the provision of community benefits. Many states have similar requirements. For example, in Texas, nonprofit hospitals are required to demonstrate and annually report the community benefits provided to their local community. Through a community benefit program, hospitals allocate resources and funds to meet community needs, particularly needs among the low-income and most vulnerable residents. These programs often engage nonprofit community organizations in collaborative partnerships with healthcare systems to provide necessary care and health education to the community. The *CCC* mission often closely aligns with the mission of community benefit programs and is a fitting vehicle for channeling resources to CBOs in order to meet federal or state community benefit requirements.

In summary, some primary advantages of pursuing hospitals and healthcare systems to support the *CCC* include the following:

- Strong financial capability
- Hospitals and healthcare systems directly benefit from participation
  - Meets community benefits requirements.
  - Improves quality of care.
  - Reduces ED utilization and other costs.
  - Strengthens community reputation through a transformative project to help the health and well-being of residents.

Some challenges of pursuing hospitals and healthcare systems include the following:

- Difficulties in maintaining engagement due to competing priorities
- Requirements to demonstrate dramatic cost benefits and increases in quality of care
- Resistance to new or added technology requirements
- Skepticism of the level of impact of SDOH on health and well-being

Key Task: Consider Ambulatory/Physician Groups/ACOs

Although organized provider groups may not have funds to support the *CCC* initially, they can be useful sources for funding once the proof of concept has been achieved, especially if many of their patients live in the *CCC* catchment area. For example, once a *CCC* is successful and demonstrating meaningful reductions in cost through reductions in the utilization of inappropriate services (or conversely, an increase in beneficial utilization practices, such as increased primary care visits), it may be to a physician group's advantage to participate in (or financially support) the *CCC*. Funding could be structured on a per member per month (PMPM) basis (linking funding to the size of the practice's panel) or on an annual flat-fee basis. Ideally, any funding mechanism selected should be structured fairly to distribute the costs of the information exchange operations to those who benefit from it most.

Another potential *CCC* funding source may be a large group practice that is participating in an Accountable Care Organization (ACO) or other risk-sharing arrangement and whose patients reside in the *CCC*'s catchment area. These types of provider organizations have an economic incentive to optimally manage the care of their members across the entire care continuum, including those social determinants that affect the health and well-being of their members.

PRACTICE POINTER

Going at Risk

Individually or with other provider entities in the community, consider developing your own "at-risk ACO" for your uncompensated care patients. Take a small portion (5%–10%) of your uncompensated care expenses and invest that in a *CCC* model targeting local "at-risk" patients/populations.

Primary advantages of pursuing ambulatory/physician groups to support the *CCC* include the following:

- Participation will help close the gaps in clinical information.
- Providers directly benefit through improved care coordination.

- Providers may have a strong appreciation for the role of SDOH in a patient's health and well-being.
- Providers may have a potential source of scalable revenue (tied to patient population size) to sustain the *CCC*.

Some challenges in pursuing ambulatory/physician groups include the following:

- Lack of strong financial resources
- Requirements to demonstrate dramatic improvements in care coordination, especially if physicians are funding the *CCC* based on a PMPM model
- Resistance to new or added technology requirements
- Need to add resources (e.g., care managers) and new clinical workflows

Key Task: Consider Health Plans and Third-Party Payers

Given the financial risk they bear, health plans and third-party payers often have the most to gain in cost reductions resulting from a *CCC*. Therefore, the governance entity or other designated leads should consider approaching several of the largest health plans or third-party payers in the market. The value proposition should clearly show how the *CCC* will decrease healthcare costs and improve quality of care. Given that most health plans and third-party payers still struggle to engage both members and providers, the value proposition should also highlight how the *CCC* provides the best avenue to achieve active engagement between the two groups. Once the *CCC* can demonstrate measurable success in various health outcomes and cost reductions, health plans and other third-party payers may want to expand the *CCC* services to their own populations or make an investment in further research and innovation through the *CCC* model.

PRACTICE POINTER

Include Payers in Any CCC *Model*

Make the payer (Anchor or Partner) an integral part and active participant in the *CCC*. Deploy *CCC* technology with payer case managers to enable SDOH assessment, screening, and referrals within the *CCC* network for high-risk, high-utilizer patients.

Primary advantages in pursuing payers to support the *CCC* include the following:

- Extremely strong source of funds
- Access to comprehensive, longitudinal patient-level data
- Provide potential opportunities for further research and innovation through *CCC* model

Some challenges of pursuing payer funding include the following:

- Challenges in initial engagement with health plan/third-party payer leaders
- Expectation of dramatic cost benefits that may or may not materialize
- Lengthy decision-making processes, especially if working with organizations that are national in scope
- Complex and burdensome contracting requirements, especially if working with organizations that are national in scope

Key Task: Consider CBOs and Faith-Based Organizations

The *CCC* governance entity and its Administrator should also consider, as potential funding sources, other CBOs or large faith-based organizations that are not currently participating in the *CCC*. While small CBOs will not have the financial resources to invest, these organizations may serve as a conduit to engage local philanthropists to support the initiative. Conversely, larger CBOs and faith-based organizations that provide a crucial source of social information and services for their communities (e.g., food access, housing services) may be interested in participating. This participation could include the provision of in-kind services, such as food distribution, transportation services, or *CCC* initiative sponsorships (e.g., a large food bank sponsoring diabetic screenings for underserved or vulnerable residents).

As the *CCC* generates results, the governance entity and the Administrator may consider targeting additional Anchor or Partner umbrella CBOs, especially those with a regional or national presence (e.g., YMCA), as these entities can offer new ideas, approaches, and important guidance to help grow the *CCC* or replicate the *CCC* in new communities. These larger CBOs can also help "sell" the *CCC* to their own members or to other large CBOs with financial resources. The Supplement to the Community Partners Track provides some information on categories and considerations in working with various CBOs.

Primary advantages of pursuing CBOs and faith-based organizations to support the *CCC* include the following:

- Participation will help close the gaps in fulfilling resident social needs and improved care coordination for the participating community residents.
- CBOs and large faith-based organizations often provide important contacts or serve as direct conduits to engage potential philanthropic funding sources.
- Large CBOs and faith-based organizations can provide financial resources and influence to expand the *CCC*.

Some challenges include the following:

- For some CBOs and faith-based organizations, a lack of strong financial resources
- Wide variety of missions, resources, and strategies, which can make alignment with the *CCC* difficult

Milestone 2: Diversify Revenue Streams to Sustain Operations

Many small, start-up ventures may attempt to improve the health and well-being of a community's populations by relying on continued grant funding following the initial capital infusion. While all of the sources outlined in this chapter are legitimate funders for initial implementation and ongoing operations, these awards are increasingly competitive. A prudent *CCC* governance entity and Administrator should also consider how to generate additional income through diversification.

Diversification means looking for how the knowledge and services the *CCC* provides can be packaged in a way that makes them appealing and of value to other organizations in the community, region, or nation. The Sponsor and governance entity should consider the following type of questions: (1) Can the *CCC*'s clinical Partners provide health screenings and wellness coaching for a local employer, (2) can a CBO that primarily focuses on addressing food insecurity establish a food delivery service to homebound seniors via a contract with a local governmental agency, (3) can the leadership of the *CCC* help other communities or large healthcare systems in designing and deploying *CCC* variants via an advisory services model, and (4) what is it that the *CCC* has that could help others and how could we monetize that offering? While diversifying *CCC*'s revenue stream may not provide all the funding needed to completely sustain ongoing operations, it can nevertheless supplement funding secured through traditional grants or similar awards.

Requirement 3: Consider Operational Sustainability in the Initial CCC Design and Implementation

In addition to a focus on financial sustainability, *CCC* Sponsors and the governance entity should emphasize the operational sustainability of a *CCC*, meaning ensuring the *CCC* can continue to operate in an effective and efficient manner despite unforeseen challenges. This generally includes efforts to anticipate problems before they happen and ensuring that policies and processes are in place to prevent unexpected challenges from disrupting the *CCC* mission and strategic plan. While different than financial sustainability, operational sustainability is no less important and should be viewed as a key element in the *CCC*'s long-term viability plan.

As with financial sustainability, the governance entity and Sponsor should initiate a focus on operational sustainability as part of the *CCC*'s initial design and continuing through every aspect of the work going forward. While it is often easier to deprioritize sustainability due to more "pressing" tasks, this approach is shortsighted and can prove catastrophic. Because sustainability factors should be considered at every stage of initial design and implementation of the *CCC*, PCCI has included sustainability considerations in each separate Playbook Track. For example, as outlined in the Governance Track and Legal/Policy Track, sustainability considerations are important to the selection of the *CCC* Governance model and the process for filling key leadership positions. The Sponsor or Anchors should work with the *CCC*'s initial Funder and key stakeholders to select the form of governance that is most likely to create favorable conditions for the replacement of key governance entity members should the need arise. These stakeholders should consider similar factors when establishing the Clinical Advisory Group or other key committees/ Workgroups. As part of the work of the Governance Track, the *CCC* governance entity will also develop guiding principles for sustainability based on input from the Clinical Advisory Group, Sponsor, Partners, Funder, or other Track leads, as outlined in Chapter 3 Governance Track Requirement 6.

Milestone 1: Follow Sustainability Guidance Provided in each Playbook Track

As sustainability guidance is critical at the beginning (and throughout) *CCC*, the Program Sustainability Track lead should review—and participate in— the following activities and provide sustainability guidance as needed to the other Track leads:

- Consider sustainability in choosing the governance model (Chapter 3 Governance Track Requirement 2).
- Consider creation of Workgroups focused on sustainability (Chapter 3 Governance Track Requirement 3).
- Select measures and a *CCC* evaluation framework that "tells the *CCC* story" (Chapter 3 Governance Track Requirement 4) and provide results that can be shared with potential funders.
- Develop sustainability principles (Chapter 3 Governance Track Requirement 6).
- Create ongoing maintenance and sustainability plans that ensure ongoing legal and business reviews of policies, contracts, and Participant and legal requirements (Chapter 3 Governance Track Requirement 6 and Legal/Policy Track Requirement 5).
- Follow the legal framework guidance (Chapter 4 Legal/Policy Track).
- Ensure the technology platform is sustainable (Chapter 5 Technology Platform Track Requirement 6).

Requirement 4: Regularly Re-Examine and Refine the Elements of the CCC, Including Relationships with Partners to Ensure Operational Sustainability

Once the *CCC* is implemented, the governance entity and other leaders should periodically revisit its infrastructure and other elements to make appropriate adjustments necessary to ensure the *CCC*'s ongoing success. These activities will help position the *CCC* to continue to generate success-ful value propositions for funding sources as part of Requirements 1 and 2. Examples of these elements and questions for the Sponsor or governance entity to consider include the following:

- *CCC* leadership and succession plans
  - Do we have the right leadership model? Are the right leaders in place to adequately represent the community needs? Are leadership succession plans current?
- The *CCC* goals, vision, and mission
  - Do the *CCC* goals, vision, and mission continue to align with the needs of the community and key stakeholders?
- The *CCC* network
  - Do we have the right Partners and are they actively engaged in the work?
  - Are we regularly providing needed support for the Partners and Participants and continuing to strengthen those relationships and attract new network members?
  - Are there large community CBOs (including faith-based organiza-tions) who could become new Anchors or Partners to help provide ongoing *CCC* support?
- The *CCC* metrics and evaluation framework
  - Are the *CCC* goals and the evaluation framework still current? Should the Clinical Advisory Group select new health priorities?
  - Are the measures in place continuing to correctly assess the effec-tiveness of the interventions to the patients/clients and the value of the *CCC* to the community?
- The *CCC* strategic planning processes
  - Does the strategic planning process provide for frequent updates and revisions? Is sustainability included in the strategic plan?

- The programs and interventions
  - Are the programs and interventions still effective? Should we make changes to align these programs with new health priorities and *CCC* goals?
- Written policies and procedures
  - Should we revise policies and procedures based on changing legal requirements or the needs of the community or Participants?
- Accelerating technologies that keep pace with the strategic implementation of the *CCC* vision
  - Is the technology vendor keeping pace with the *CCC* needs? Are updates or other changes to the technology needed? Are these included in the vendor's contract at no charge or must the *CCC* pay for them?
- Training
  - Do revised policies, requirements, goals, etc. require updated training?
  - Is regular training provided for Board members and others responsible for *CCC* governance?
  - Is training provided to new staff members working at Participant sites?
- Marketing for the *CCC*
  - Do the marketing efforts effectively highlight the importance of the *CCC* and the difference *CCC* is making in the community? How current are our results and do they support the value proposition that we espouse?
- Sustainability
  - Do we have a process in place to continually search for new funding opportunities?
  - Do we have a Sustainability Workgroup and is it effective? Does it contain the right individuals?
  - Are we diversifying our revenue? What can be done to enhance these efforts?

Chapter 9

Final Notes

It is imperative to contain healthcare costs. We know that people at risk for poor health outcomes are especially vulnerable because they lack the needed social support, the ability to pay, and insight into their own health problems.

The *Connected Communities of Care (CCC)* addresses these issues through a platform that facilitates exchange of critical case management information at various steps in the process and through a longitudinal perspective of care via referral tracking and increasing access to a broad array of services to improve individual well-being and community health.

The Parkland Center for Clinical Innovation (PCCI) has designed this Playbook based on lessons learned to date through our *CCC* model. We would again congratulate you on your decision to take this vital step in bringing together healthcare and community organizations to enhance the lives, health, and well-being of the residents of your community.

Building and deploying a *CCC* is both a sprint and a marathon. Each organization and market will generate their own leading practices, successes, and Practice Pointers. These things will happen at different rates for different organizations and across different geographies. It is important to recognize that standing up a *CCC* is difficult work, even for experienced Sponsors and their project managers. Expectations must be kept realistic and constantly reassessed. A universal learning is that these undertakings take longer and consume more resources than anticipated and, at least initially, may generate less in the way of outcomes than originally expected. We encourage all organizations already deploying/operating similar initiatives to share their experiences and learnings with others.

If you want to go fast, go alone. If you want to go far, go together.

—African Proverb

Key Documents

Note: The Key Documents provided are sample documents only. They do not constitute the provision of legal advice. Each Connected Communities of Care (CCC) *Participant should obtain its own independent legal analysis, advice, and drafting assistance from attorneys of its choosing and based on the* CCC *program specifics, appropriate federal, state, and local laws, and other legal or programmatic requirements.*

Governance and Legal/Policy Oriented Key Documents

- Sample Memorandum of Understanding for Clinical Participation in a *CCC*
- Sample Letter of Commitment for Community-Based Social Service Organization *aka* Community-Based Organization (CBO)
- Sample *CCC* Board Charter
- Sample Mission Statement/Statement of Purpose
- Sample Clinical Advisory Group (CAG) Guidelines
- Sample Prioritized List of *CCC*-Supported Clinical Programs and Targeted Goals

Sample *CCC* Value Proposition

- Sample Disclosure of Personal Conflicts Forms
- Sample Conflicts "COI" Management Plan
- Sample Considerations for Working with Umbrella Organizations

Technology Platform Oriented Key Documents

- Sample Platform Functionalities and Vendor Specifications
- Sample Criteria for Vendor Evaluation
- Sample Steps for Technology Implementation
- Sample Data Use Agreement Link
- Sample Operational Guidelines for *CCC* Data Sharing
- Sample Project Order for Functionality Change

- Sample Expectations for User Support
- Sample Quality Assurance Processes

Clinical Provider and Community Partner Oriented Key Documents

- Sample List of Participant Clinical Sites and CBOs
- Sample Individual Consent/Authorization Form
- Sample Standard Operating Procedures (SOPs) that Details One *CCC* Workflow
- Sample Training Objectives

Program Sustainability Oriented Key Documents

- Sample Evaluation Measures
- Sample Communication Strategy

Key Document: Sample Memorandum of Understanding for Clinical Participation in a CCC

PRACTICE POINTER

A Memorandum of Understanding (MOU) is a formal agreement between two or more parties. Companies and organizations can use MOUs to establish official partnerships. It is not a legally binding document, but it signals the intention of all parties to move forward with a contract.

Sample Memorandum of Understanding ("MOU")

This MOU establishes the mutual understanding and desires for [*clinical participant*] to participate as a clinical delivery participant in the *CCC* in [*community*] that the [*other party, which is Sponsor, other hosting entity, etc.*] is planning to develop.

We provide [*insert services, such as outpatient, emergency department, and inpatient services*] to [*insert #*] of patients annually, including a significant number living within the geographic target area proposed by [*Sponsor etc.*]. The objects of the *CCC* program are consistent with our mission.

Both parties agree that if [*Sponsor*] is successful in developing the *CCC* program, the parties will enter into a more formal participation agreement.

As a prospective clinical delivery partner in this program, [*clinical participant*] is prepared to commit the time and resources required to work with [*Sponsor etc.*] and other program participants to achieve the objectives of the *CCC* program. More specifically, [*clinical participant*] commits to do the following:

Scale and Scope of Participation

The scope of our participation will be limited to those residents in the geographic target area proposed by the program who have (1) received clinical services in the previous 12 months at the participating sites listed below or (2) utilized the Emergency Department ("ED") two or more times in the previous 12 months at the participating sites listed below.

The participating sites will include (but are not limited to):

[*Insert site/organization names and addresses*]

Role and Responsibilities of Clinical Participant in the *CCC* Program

Either directly or through a third party, we will perform screening and intervention services for health-related social needs using the tool provided by [*insert Sponsor or Funder, etc.*] for all residents living in the target geographic area seeking health care at our participating sites listed above.

As part of our planned protocol, each time a patient seeks care at one of our participating sites, our patient intake staff will ask a series of threshold questions to establish the eligibility of the patient to participate in the *CCC* program and whether or not the patient was previously screened within the previous 12 months at one of the clinical delivery sites. For any eligible beneficiary who has not received the screening within the previous 12 months, our patient intake staff will offer the screening and will provide a tailored community referral summary to those who had at least one unmet social need.

For high-risk beneficiaries with at least one unmet social need who had not received the navigation services within the previous 12 months, our navigation team will provide the navigation services either directly or via the navigation team agreed upon by the parties.

We will report identified and de-identified data for the program patients to [*Sponsor*] as applicable and as agreed upon by the parties, solely for the purposes of model monitoring and evaluation.

We will participate in the *CCC* program Clinical Advisory Group.

[*Clinical participant*] values strong, collaborative partnerships with other nonprofit organizations and medical institutions in our community. Our partnership is vital to our ability to positively impact the lives of our patients. The research conducted by our partners not only aims to improve the lives of those we serve but offers them a voice in matters directly affecting their lives and well-being. We are, therefore, eager to participate in the *CCC* program and look forward to the alignment and action that it will bring.

Key Document: Sample Letter of Commitment for CBO

PRACTICE POINTER

For many CBOs this could be one of their first official engagements with a local or regional health system. This letter of commitment allows both sides to clearly articulate expectations, responsibilities, and timelines. Not only does it ensure that a new relationship gets started on a positive note, it also helps manage disruption as team members cycle in and out of both organizations.

Also, a letter of commitment can be used for an individual or an organization.

Sample Letter of Commitment

Dear [*Insert Name*]:

This letter establishes the intent between [*CBO*] and the [*Sponsor/hosting* CCC *organization*] to work in a collaborative relationship to better serve clients shared by [*Hospital System*] and our organization.

We have learned about the *CCC* and its technology platform and its functionalities from the [*Sponsor or hosting* CCC *organization*] team and we are excited to be a pilot implementation partner. We pledge our support for the *CCC* goal to provide a simple, cost-effective tool that helps organizations better serve their clients. We are prepared to commit the time and resources required to participate in the following activities throughout the pilot implementation phase:

- Participate in joint data analyses conducted by [*Sponsor/hosting* CCC *organization*].
- Adopt and implement the technology supporting *CCC* within 6–9 months.
- Provide ongoing feedback and participate in the *CCC* technology platform enhancements.
- Maintain intention to join the [*Insert City Name*] *CCC* in the next phase.

It is our hope that a successful *CCC* would allow for a two-way flow of information between [*Hospital System*] and social service organizations in the

[*City Name*] community to achieve the goal of better service to our shared populations.

For this collaborative activity, [*Contact's Name*], the [*Insert Contact's Title*] will be our primary contact person and can be reached at [*Address*], [*Phone*], [*email*].

Key Document: Sample CCC Board Charter

> **PRACTICE POINTER**
>
> This outlines the overall purpose and scope of responsibility for the cross-functional *CCC* Board. This is the executive-level governing committee of the *CCC*. Because of the importance of the group, it is important to ensure that the activities of this group are understood and that this group's members have the political gravitas to make things happen. Ideally, the Board consists of ~six to eight committed leaders.

Board Purpose

Sample Purpose. The *CCC* Board was established to bring together leaders responsible for the planning, launch, and expansion of this initiative. The Board will serve as the cross-community governing body and will be tasked with ensuring data sharing, cooperation, and communication happen across the *CCC*.

Scope of Board Responsibility

Sample Scope of Responsibility

- Goal development and prioritization. Make certain that the *CCC* stays focused and doesn't chase activities that are out of scope.
- Obstacle removal. Help remove barriers that could hinder implementation or expansion.
- Cross-collaborative communication. Confirm that all partners are aligned on high priority activities and that Board members have the needed materials to share information with colleagues at their respective organizations.
- Advisory function: Provide thought leadership to solidify continued support from leaders and influencers within a given community.
- Approval of budget expenditures over $100,000 and hiring/firing of dedicated *CCC* management staff.
- Impact tracking. Ensure that the *CCC* is meeting or exceeding impact targets.

Board Member Responsibility

Sample Responsibility

- Will serve a set term [often 2 years].
- Will attend and participate regularly [and may be compensated for their time].
- Will contribute to the data collection and reporting needed to quantify impact.

Meeting Frequency

Sample Meeting Frequency. The Board will meet at least six times in the first year and on a quarterly basis thereafter. The meetings will be a combination of in-person meetings, WebEx, and phone conferences.

Key Document: Sample Mission Statement/Statement of Purpose

Sample Mission Statement

Connected Communities of Care: Dallas, Texas

CCC is a proprietary information exchange platform that focuses on addressing the health and social needs of a community.

Our mission is to connect healthcare providers and community-based organizations (CBOs) to coordinate the communication and care for individuals.

Key Document: Sample Clinical Advisory Group Guidelines

> **PRACTICE POINTER**
>
> There are suggested rules and internal guidelines for CAG members to follow, which are summarized in these Guidelines. Whereas the Board is typically comprised of executive-level leadership, the CAG consists of the frontline clinical teams whose participation is vital to the success of the *CCC*.

Sample Clinical Advisory Group [CAG] Guidelines

1. CAG members may not have Conflicts of Interest (COIs) that jeopardize the [*Grant or* CCC *program*]. A COI is doing anything that: is contrary to the purposes of the [*Grant or* CCC *program*]; puts your own interests or those of a different business, a family member, or a friend ahead of or in conflict with the [*Grant or* CCC *program*]; or failing to disclose in advance of membership on the CAG or before undertaking any activities with the CAG that you have a business or personal relationship that may affect [*Grant or* CCC *program*] business.

2. CAG members are required to be active participants in all meetings or tasks assigned to this group [*this will often be for a set term*]. Because they are often the team closest to the impacted patients, it is their responsibility to bring feedback back to the CAG.

3. CAG members will not accept anything of value from any third party that is or may be doing business with [*insert Administrator or other entity*] or be engaged in any outside activities that would create a COI or the appearance of potential unfairness. If there are extraordinary circumstances that make following this guideline impractical (e.g., an employment relationship with a community partner or being a donor to [insert Administrator or other entity]), [Administrator or other entity] will work with you to document the relationship/outside activity so that you can maintain membership on the CAG if appropriate.

4. As a CAG member, you may learn confidential information about the [*Grant or* CCC *program*], [*Administrator or other entity*], community partners, and healthcare providers participating in the [*Grant or* CCC *program*]. We don't expect you do receive any patient-specific data. CAG members will treat information that is labeled "confidential," including but not limited to [*technology vendor*] tools, user interface, and work flows as confidential and not use or disclose it to any third parties, except if required by law to do so.

Key Document: Sample Prioritized List of CCC-Supported Clinical Programs

PRACTICE POINTER

Sometimes knowing where to start with a *CCC* is the hardest part. This Key Document provides a few starting points that target specific populations that immediately benefit from community-wide care coordination.

Sample Program: Nutrition and Diabetes

Program to implement intervention strategies to improve the diet and nutrition of food-insecure patients who have been diagnosed with diabetes and/or hypertension. Targeted goals: Reduce ED utilization among high utilizers.

Sample Program: Senior Transportation Assistance

Program in which a clinical care team for seniors offers special care, which includes help with transportation problems and connection to support services in the community. Care teams could include a doctor, nurse, social worker, registered dietitian, foot care nurse, and pharmacist. Targeted goals: increase the percentage of seniors that can age in place.

Sample Program: Senior Home Visits

Program that provides primary medical care to homebound elderly patients. Care is provided in the patient's home where staff can best work with family members and community resources, like home healthcare, as needed. The program provides medical care and social work assessment, referrals to CBOs, and nutrition support. Care team includes doctors, a nurse practitioner, social worker, nurse, and chaplain. Help from a clinical pharmacist, dietitian, and financial counselor can also be arranged. Targeted goals: increase the percentage of seniors that can age in place.

Key Document: Sample CCC Value Proposition

> **PRACTICE POINTER**
>
> A value proposition describes how what you are doing solves or improves problems, it introduces what your users [customers and partners] can expect and why what you are offering is better or different from services that individuals currently have access to. This is a necessary step in creating a *CCC* to ensure that all parties agree on the value that is possible and how it will be delivered.

Sample Value Proposition

Sponsor [*or other Entity Creating Value Proposition*]

The [*insert your community*] *CCC*

Program Details [*insert applicable program language*]

The [*insert community*] *CCC* is designed to address patients' nonclinical needs (e.g., housing, food, transportation) along with their medical needs in order to significantly improve the patients' health outcomes. The novel strategy for achieving this goal is the implementation of a real-time health information sharing platform to connect clinical delivery sites with CBOs. Once established, this connection between the clinical and community providers will enable patients to receive assistance for their socioeconomic needs (identified at the time of a clinical encounter) in concert with their clinical needs, thus creating a holistic method for the care of patient's health and wellness, reducing the utilization of unnecessary medical services, and reducing the cost of care for the community's Medicare and Medicaid beneficiaries.

Benefits of Participating [*insert benefits specific to the program, grant, community, etc.*]

- By participating in the *CCC*, you may significantly increase your ability to address the needs of your vulnerable populations through access to a well-coordinated referral network.
- Access to the [*existing software platform*] technology platform that is already linking over [*insert number*] of community service providers in real time, across [*insert community*].

- Access to a unified, accurate, dynamic community resource inventory to be used by all community participants in this effort.

Impact [actual and/or projected] [Include any successes and/or ROI—these can be economic, quality, and/or patient impact-oriented]

- During the first 6 months, we have reduced ED visits by 20% and hospital readmissions by 28%.

Key Document: Sample Disclosure of Personal Conflicts Forms

PRACTICE POINTER

Disclosures of personal conflicts are standard practice for the Board executives and the frontline staff who are part of the Clinical Advisory Group. If conflicts exist [which is common], there are mitigation strategies that *CCC*'s can employ [see next key document].

Statement of Outside Interests Review

1. During the past twelve (12) months, did YOU, a FAMILY MEMBER, or any other member of your household hold any OWNERSHIP INTERESTS that are related to any ENTITY or receive any COMPENSATION, THING OF VALUE, ENTERTAINMENT, GIFTS, SPONSORED TRAVEL ARRANGEMENTS, MEALS, ENTERTAINMENT, or royalties from: conducts business with *CCC* ENTITY, or seeks (or may seek) to conduct business with XXX, or competes or may compete with XXX?

   OWNERSHIP INTERESTS in mutual funds or retirement accounts that are managed by an independent third party do not need to be disclosed here. Honoraria do not need to be disclosed here.

2. During the past twelve (12) months, did YOU receive an HONORARIUM from any ENTITY in recognition of your voluntary participation and contributions? In responding to this question, do not report salary, sales commission, revenue, wages, fee stipends, or royalties received.

3. During the past twelve (12) months, did YOU, a FAMILY MEMBER, or any other member of your household serve in a capacity to exercise influence or make decisions regarding the affairs of any ENTITY that: conducts business with, or Seeks (or may seek) to conduct business with, or competes or may compete?

4. During the past twelve (12) months, did YOU participate in any OUTSIDE ACTIVITY in a capacity that relied on professional competencies used to carry out your *CCC* ENTITY responsibilities? Examples of such activities include but are not limited to advisory or governance boards, advocacy or community services, Industry groups, Professional organizations, and Safety or data monitoring committees.

5. During the past twelve (12) months, did YOU participate in any OUTSIDE ACTIVITY or hold any OTHER INTERESTS (not previously disclosed herein) that could be perceived to influence your *CCC* ENTITY responsibilities or decision-making activities?

6. In the next twelve (12) months, do YOU anticipate participating in an OUTSIDE ACTIVITY that could be perceived to influence your *CCC* ENTITY responsibilities or decision-making?

7. Is any FAMILY MEMBER or any other member of your household employed or contracted by *CCC* ENTITY? For purposes of this question, a FAMILY MEMBER also refers to a(n) aunt, uncle, cousin, niece, or nephew.

8. OTHER (CUSTOMIZE FOR FUNDING SOURCE, ETC.)

Key Document: Sample Conflicts of Interest (COI) Management Plan

PRACTICE POINTER

Conflict management plans are necessary due to the diversity and tenure of executives who are part of a *CCC*.

This provides ground rules for what is acceptable and ensures that all *CCC* leaders operate via a common set of guidelines.

1. With respect to Financial Interest(s) including you or a family member receiving any compensation or other thing of value from or serving as an officer or director of a person, business, or entity that conducts business, may seek to conduct business, or competes with *CCC* ENTITY, either currently or within the last 3 years. NAME will:
   - Not share any *CCC* ENTITY Confidential Information with any third party.
   - Refrain from exerting any influence or participating in any decision-making activities on behalf of *CCC* ENTITY regarding business with ORGANIZATION.
   - Will review *CCC* ENTITY's COI Policy with any affected family member so that they are aware of the restrictions on NAME.

       *Thing of value means money, gifts, gift cards, meals, vacations, travel, accommodations, entertainment, goods or services with a value of more than $___ within the last 12-month period.

       *A thing of value not offered in exchange for promoting, recommending, purchasing, or leasing goods or services does not include the following:
     - Gifts of perishable or consumable goods normally given as tokens of appreciation that are shared among members of NAME's department.
     - Travel reimbursement from a professional society or similar group (not a vendor) and small honoraria (<$___) for professional speaking or similar engagements that recognize NAME's professional standing, so long as the reimbursement and honoraria are disclosed, and NAME is not sharing a podium with or promoting a vendor's products or services, absent Board approval.

- Infrequent business meals of modest value—use good judgment—when NAME is conducting business with a vendor or similar entity, the host is present, the meal is provided in conjunction with a business discussion or presentation, and the setting is conducive to a discussion of business. When conducting business with a vendor during mealtimes on a frequent or repeated basis, each party should pay for their own meal.
- Entertainment of modest value at a near-by, non-extravagant venue where the host is present with NAME during the event, the invitation does not include NAME's family members, and occurs no more than once per year, so long as the entertainment is disclosed.
- Participation in a vendor-sponsored charity event that is consistent with *CCC* ENTITY's mission, vision, and values and does not advance any particular political or religious agenda (note: any gifts, awards, or winnings during the event are subject to the limits set forth above).

2. With respect to service to a community board, professional society, etc. (with speaking role) that is related to NAME's *CCC* ENTITY responsibilities but performed in an independent capacity, NAME will:
   - Notify his/her manager (or if the CEO, *CCC*'s Board), in writing, prior to engaging in this outside activity.
   - Carry out this activity in an independent capacity, acting on his/her own time, without using any *CCC* ENTITY resources and in a manner as to not interfere with his/her *CCC* ENTITY responsibilities, as discussed with and agreed to by his/her manager [Board].
   - Inform audiences that opinions expressed are his/her own and state that he/she does not speak on behalf of and does not represent his/her *CCC* ENTITY.
   - Not share any *CCC* ENTITY Confidential Information.

3. With respect to service to a board, professional society, etc. that is related to individual's *CCC* ENTITY responsibilities and is performed in a *CCC* ENTITY capacity, NAME will:
   - Seek prior approval of this activity in advance by his/her manager or if CEO, the Board.
   - NAME is to not share any *CCC* ENTITY Confidential Information.

4. With respect to Family Members in the workplace (not in NAME's direct line of report), NAME will:

Regarding NAME's disclosure that a family member is employed by XXX:

– Not participate in *CCC* ENTITY decisions regarding the evaluation of the Family Member's performance.
– Not exert any influence regarding the family member's pay, work assignment, schedule, transfer, promotion, demotion, or any other consideration related to the Family Member's work responsibilities.
– Follow all *CCC* ENTITY policies and procedures related to appropriate workplace conduct.

Key Document: Sample Considerations for Working with Umbrella Organizations

---

PRACTICE POINTER

Often CBO's will organize into larger umbrella organizations to magnify community impact and possibly gain operational efficiencies. Working with an individual CBO is different from working with an umbrella. This Key Document outlines some of the considerations to be mindful of when initiating such discussions.

If your community has "umbrella" organizations to which many/most of the CBO's working on a specific challenge belong (e.g., City Homeless Alliance; Region Food Bank), it may be possible to work with the umbrella organizations to obtain their agreements on behalf of their member organizations for participation generally or for more specific purposes such as a software sales and service agreement. Relevant considerations include:

- Do the bylaws of each umbrella organization permit it to bind its members to contracts?
- Do the bylaws of the member organizations allow the umbrella organization to bind them to an agreement for all members?
- Do the vendors the *CCC* retains permit one organization to bind all its members? This is likely to be a particular concern for the technology vendor because their software will be deployed at different sites controlled by different legal entities, and thus, they may require individual contracts.
- If an umbrella contract would be helpful, but is not specifically addressed in the applicable bylaws, confer with the umbrella organizations to determine if they might be willing to approach their members to obtain such an agreement related to *CCC* technology, participation, etc. (and offer to draft a one-page MOU between the umbrella and its members to memorialize the agreement).

- Be sensitive to the role the individual members play in the community and the degree to which seeking an overarching agreement will be viewed as wise simplification versus overbearing action in which the members did not have an adequate voice.
- Consider whether the time and effort in drafting an MOU between the umbrella and each of its members might be better spent in drafting an MOU between each entity and the relevant *CCC* organization.

Key Document: Sample Platform Functionalities and Vendor Specifications

PRACTICE POINTER

While technology needs will vary by each community and by the specific goals of the *CCC*, there are several foundational attributes the new *CCC*s should look for as they select a technology vendor.

This Key Document provides a short list of both technical considerations and vendor requirements that may be important for selecting the right technology partner.

Sample Platform Functionalities

- Envisioned to be a person-centered platform and built to be as seamless as possible for the person it is built to serve.
- Consists of a robust statewide resource database with a call center, as well as a referral platform for providers, social workers, care coordinators, and others to connect directly to resources in their communities and track connections and outcomes.
- Fosters resource connections, linking health and social services in communities, and generated high-quality data outputs regarding the nonclinical factors impacting health outcomes and costs.
- Open to all providers, payers, "CBOs", agencies, and residents across the county, with integrated workflows.
- Supports flexible architecture to facilitate scaled adoption and allow for interfaces and integration to native technology systems.
- Easily accessible to all users. This would include a user-friendly website and call center. The resource directory should also have resources listed at a fifth-grade literacy level and translated in the top five languages in the county/state.
- Able to tailor resource entries in the database to eligibility. Many resources have specific funding requirements and regulations and, therefore, very specific eligibility criteria (e.g., a homeless shelter that is only eligible to women or teens). All eligibility criteria should be built into the tool to ensure that the people being referred to a specific resource are able to access it.

- Generate referrals to community resources for which a person is eligible and provide feedback loop functionality—where a provider or organization can make a direct referral to a CBO, such as a local food bank, and the CBO can respond back to the initial referring provider or organization with the resource provided (e.g., taxonomy code, dosing information, service-related notes, Current Procedural Terminology [CPT] code), and the outcome of the referral.

Sample Vendor Specifications

- Should have a timeline and goals for phased rollout, including reaching a specified total of CBOs with county/statewide reach within the first 2 years of the start of the contract.
- Should already have an established robust statewide resource database and/or directory within the county/state and knowledge of [*insert specific*] county/state communities and CBOs—or have the ability to build one within the first year of the contract.
- Should have a plan for keeping the database up to date through data coordinators, work with CBOs, and ideally, the ability to integrate with other local and statewide resource databases, such as specific county/state 2-1-1, and national databases. Integration includes pulling resources from these databases and sending updates or flags, so users can report missing, broken, or changed information.
- Should have the ability to vet quality and accessibility resources within the resource directory.
- Should be able to report on all referral metrics in real time and report on referral outcomes monthly in the first year of the platform and quarterly thereafter.
- Should support application programming interfaces (APIs) and integration allowing users to access the platform's capabilities from another tool. The Platform should be integrated into a provider's Electronic Health Record (EHR)—meeting all/any Health Insurance Portability and Accountability Act (HIPAA) requirements and into the CBOs' technology (e.g., Salesforce), if they have one. The platform should be able to integrate into care management platforms and other resource platforms that may be present in communities.
- Should provide substantial technical and business capability assistance and training to providers and CBOs to implement the platform and ensure understanding of all features, how the platform integrates

with their workflow, and how it adds value for their organization and constituencies.

- Should create a portal or dashboard that reports data in real time. In addition to creating a dashboard that reports data in real time or near real time, the vendor must report on referral outcomes and their progress in meeting implementation goals. These reports will be monthly in the first 2 years and quarterly thereafter. This data will be used to understand the needed resources in the community; the outcomes of the people using it; the barriers to care; and other information necessary to improving the health, safety, and well-being of the beneficiaries.
- Must comply with all laws, ordinances, codes, rules, regulations, and licensing requirements that are applicable to the conduct of its business, including those of federal and state local agencies having jurisdiction and/or authority.

Key Document: Sample Criteria for Vendor Evaluation

PRACTICE POINTER

There will likely be several vendors who could provide a technology platform that meets the needs of your *CCC*. The previous Key Document provided some guidelines functionality and vendor specifications. This Key Document provides some additional parameters to consider.

Evaluation Questions

Functionality and Technical Specifications

- How well does their proposed solution align with your needs?
- Have they addressed core issues such as data security and HIPAA compliance?
- Is the value for money clearly explained?
- Is the timeline and resource plan for implementation reasonable?

Demonstrated Success

- What value has the solution been proven to deliver?
- How many sites are pilot sites versus fully implemented?
- Are they in your market or geography?
- How pleased are the company's current clients with the offering and the service model?
- What makes the company unique (good or bad)?

About the Company

- How is the company describing what they can do relative to the scope of problem? Is it clear, differentiated, and do you believe?
- Is the company led by high caliber management?
- How mature are they and how are they financed?
- Is the company stable?
- Can you work with their team?
- Can they support their current customer base as well as future growth?

Key Document: Sample Steps for Technology Implementation

> **PRACTICE POINTER**
>
> While specifics for technology will differ by vendor, some core elements will be common across vendors. This Key Document provides a view into what to look for in an implementation plan.

Implementation Steps

Step 1: Gather and Analyze Requirements

- Organization—End users and assigned roles
- Programs—Descriptions, policies, qualifications, documentation required, tracking practices
- Services provided
- Internal and external reporting practices.

Step 2: Design

- Design configurations across the *CCC*.

Step 3: Configure and Convert

- Tailor to fit specific CBO needs.
- Convert existing data.

Step 4: Test and Train

- Test configuration and data conversion.
- Make any necessary corrections.
- Train end users.

Step 5: Deploy

- Rollout to all end users.

Step 6: Monitor and Review

- Monitor and review performance of through support calls and feedback meetings.

<u>*Key Document: Sample Data Use Agreement Links*</u>

PRACTICE POINTER

Data use agreements, especially ones with state agencies, are proscriptive and leave little room for negotiation.

The attached links provide examples of what is likely to be included in data use agreements your *CCC* will encounter.

- Notre Dame Research Sample Data Use Agreement
  - https://research.nd.edu/assets/204294/sample_data_use_agreement. docx
- Harvard Catalyst Data Usage Agreement
  - https://catalyst.harvard.edu/docs/regulatory_support/Harvard_ Catalyst_Template_LDS_DUA.docx
- Johns Hopkins/Mayo Clinic Data User Agreement
  - www.hopkinsmedicine.org/research/resources/offices-policies/ora/_ documents/agreements/MayoDataUseAreement.docx
- Yale University HIPPA Data User Agreement
  - https://hipaa.yale.edu/sites/default/files/files/5039-FR-Data-Use-Agreement.pdf
- CDC Sample Data Use Agreement
  - www.cdc.gov/nchs/data/nhamcs/Sample_DUA_NHAMCS.pdf
- Texas Digital Library Sample Data Usage Agreement
  - www.tdl.org/dataverse/sample-dua/

Key Document: Sample Operational Guidelines for CCC Data Sharing

> **PRACTICE POINTER**
>
> Data sharing is critical for the success of a *CCC* and requires that trusted relationships get built across the *CCC* participants. Clear operational guidelines for data sharing are a core requirement for initially building trust and maintaining it over time.

Data

- Only certain data elements allowed for exchange
- De-identified data not to be reidentified
- Role-based access controls
- Restrictions on functionalities (e.g., social service participants cannot alter medical information and cannot alter data in Epic)

Systems

- Minimum system requirements (e.g., authentication) to be able to sign in once to local system

Consent

- Each participant must obtain affirmative consent at each encounter (using standard, electronic authorization form and patient education materials, including checklist of understanding) to load data to and retrieve data.
- Participants must record "yes" consent given or "no" consent not given.
- Consent expires at next encounter (must be renewed) and after 1 year of inactivity.
- No access allowed without consent (even in an emergency, except, of course, for court orders).

Records

- Court orders for information will be directed to the *CCC*; *CCC* will direct participants how to respond if necessary.
- Records retained for at least 6 years (compliance with existing laws).
- Breach response protocol (and managing the media).
- Participants acknowledge that they may be subject to providing records through Public Information Acts.
- *CCC* will maintain and review audit trails.

Provisions

- Agree to have provision for individual complaint process.

Training

- Adhere to uniform training standards (with option to supplement with organization-specific training).
- Adhere to uniform auditing guidelines.

Key Document: Sample Project Order for Functionality Change

> **PRACTICE POINTER**
>
> Working with a *CCC* technology vendor is a long-term relationship. As a *CCC* grows, specific needs will change and new requirements will arise. Having a clear process for articulating functionality changes and/or to request the addition of new features is a vital part of a successful vendor relationship. This Key Document describes some of the common elements found in project orders.

Name of Organizations Involved in the Request [list all entities involved in the project order]

Project Order Number [the unique identifier for the request]

Project Name [the specific project name]

Project Description [provide an overview narrative of the project itself]

Description of Project Order:

The work described in this Project Order includes the following components as set forth below: [outline the specific project order]

Project Order Value:

The total value for this Project Order is not to exceed [a specific dollar value].

Payment terms: [provide details of payment]

Appendices [if needed]

Change Management Process [if appropriate]

Acceptance and Authorization [relevant signatures, and date]

Key Document: Sample Expectations for User Support

User Support Considerations

A *Knowledgeable Support Team.* Look for user support teams that fully understand internal processes and how they apply to your needs. This level of understanding should be present across the entire technical and escalation team.[15]

Responsiveness. Ask about response times. After the initial response to the request, expect the support team to stay in contact until the problem is resolved to your level of satisfaction, without exception.

Vibrant User Groups. Leading vendors want to "walk in the customers' shoes" and should take the time to listen to feedback. Vendor user community is a good source of "how to" information that include client forums, product best practices, and ongoing education sessions.

Being an Extension of the Team. Good user support should be another layer of resource to ensure that teams don't waste time, repeat work, and/or underutilize essential functionalities of the technology platform. Good customer service isn't just listening; it's also offering suggestions and expertise.

Help during Emergencies. Being there in times of extreme need separates the good from great. Knowing that someone is going to record the information about the problem, be able to troubleshoot, and fix what happened as quickly as possible, offers reassurance and enhances trust.

Acting as a Thought Partner. Knowing that a vendor is available to help with design considerations is very important, especially for new *CCC* projects being led by newly formed *CCC* teams. The vendor's implementation and project team should understand the full scope of the project in advance, including what's previously worked. Vendors should evaluate processes in advance, then they brainstorm with our team how the new system will work alongside our current system.

Key Document: Sample Quality Assurance Processes

PRACTICE POINTER

To obtain effective and intended outcomes, Quality Assurance (QA) is an important feature that must be applied in all steps and stages of *CCC* implementation. Quality checks must be placed at different checkpoints to evaluate the functioning and integrity of Clinical Workflows, Community Workflows, Technology, and respective training components.

Quality Assurance Processes					
CCC Requirement	Clinical Providers	Community Partners	Technology Platform	Training Programs	Mitigation Strategies
Technology platform selection	Check that the technology supports the workflow requirements for clinical programs and functions; implement and evaluate the technology with use cases for responsiveness, validity, and reliability.	Check the technology supports the workflow requirements for community programs and services; implement and evaluate using use cases, response time, reliability, and user friendliness.	Check technology requirements for the CCC program against vendor specifications and other client experiences.	Check and evaluate the need for training after adequate technical testing with proper use cases to reflect CCC program requirements; make sure training materials are developed at the correct reading level.	Make sure all "bugs" are addressed and software functions perform all requirements as specified; ensure vendor provides technical manual to project lead before technical sign-off complete.
Community partner selection	Will the Clinical Provider and Community Partner work well together and bring scope and scale to the project; do the two workflows integrate well together without major modifications.	Check that the organization's turnover, volume of individuals served, and financial viability are in-line with CCC requirements; assess entities reputation in community and track record of success.	Check level of technology preparedness (hardware, software) to support CCC requirements along with level of comfort of staff using technology platform.	Check and evaluate the training requirements and processes at Community site; what provisions exist for repeat trainings and getting in touch with vendor if problems develop.	Implement prioritized, data-driven approach to problem identification and work with vendor to address any shortcomings.

(Continued)

Quality Assurance Processes					
CCC Requirement	**Clinical Providers**	**Community Partners**	**Technology Platform**	**Training Programs**	**Mitigation Strategies**
Clinical provider selection	Check that the organization's turnover, volume and type of patients served, and financial viability are in-line with CCC requirements; Assess entities reputation in community and any outstanding malpractice suits.	Will the Clinical Provider and Community Partner work well together and bring scope and scale to the project; do the two workflows integrate well together without major modifications.	Check to assess level of preparedness of clinical provider to implement CCC, i.e., hardware, software, and staff expertise/ comfort level with new technology.	Verify and evaluate the training requirements and processes at the clinical site and evaluate staffs' competency post-training.	Implement prioritized, data-driven approach to problem identification and work with vendor to address any shortcomings.
CCC performance	Check the clinical program requirement: Do the programs complement CCC clinical needs? Do the clinical programs evolve to keep pace with changing clinical needs? Do clinical programs deliver good clinical outcomes?	Check the community program requirements and objectives; do the programs complement CCC community needs. Do community programs evolve to keep pace with changing community needs? Do community programs improve health and well-being?	Does the technology make the programs more effective and efficient; Can individuals use technology to access programs or deliver better self-care?	Is new training required every time programs change or are updated? Can training on new programs be automated and self-paced? Are processes in place to evaluate the effectiveness of training?	Are processes in place to avoid duplication of programs? If programs are not performing as expected, are mechanisms in place to address shortcomings and introduce change?

Key Document: Sample List of Participant Clinical Sites and CBOs

> **PRACTICE POINTER**
>
> Mapping out a strategy to engage the clinical and nonclinical communities is a key part of building a *CCC*. The first step towards completing this task is to first better understand the mix of relevant services that are currently being provided and how they align with community need.

Sample List of Participant CBOs

Community Service Provider Partners	Social Needs Addressed	Clients Served
X Food Bank and its [insert#] partner agencies	[insert needs addressed; e.g., food insecurity, education]	[insert #] meals served
X [Homeless Service] and its [insert#] programs	[insert needs addressed; e.g., homelessness; food insecurity, financial assistance]	[insert #] residents supported
X [Eldercare] and its [insert#] programs	[insert needs addressed; e.g., transportation, home visits]	[insert #] residents supported

Sample List of Participant Clinical Sites and Total Patients Served

Clinical Entity	Participating Site [List Number]	Relevant Service Offerings	Number of Patients Served Annually
Health system A	Hospital [3 hospitals]	• Inpatient services • Inpatient psych services	*XXX*
Health system A	Primary care clinics [10 sites]	• Routine primary care • Nurse practitioner leads after-hours clinics	*XXX*
Hospital B	Hospital [1 hospital]	• Inpatient services • High-volume ED	*XXX*

(Continued)

Clinical Entity	Participating Site [List Number]	Relevant Service Offerings	Number of Patients Served Annually
Hospital B	Outpatient clinics [2 BH clinics]	• Behavioral health provider	*XXX*
Long-term care facility A	Nursing home and assisted living [4 sites]	• Long-term care • Rehabilitation services • Dementia care	*XXX*

Key Document: Sample Individual Consent/ Authorization Form

> **PRACTICE POINTER**
>
> Securing patient consent is a foundational aspect of an effective *CCC*. Through our experience, we've crafted individual consent forms that are clear, speak to concerns or potential objections, and outline how a navigator team can provide support.
>
> Remember to always seek guidance from your attorney before using any consent form.

Part 1: Written Consent

Sample Consent and Authorization to Share
Personal Information for *CCC* Program

[*Insert entity*] administers a program [*insert with funding from X if applicable*] to assist people with their medical care by providing them with the help they need in their daily lives from their community. This is not a welfare program. [*Insert technology vendor*] provides the software used to help us gather patient information. We are asking patients like you to participate in the program by providing [*insert entity*] and the participating "CBO" (e.g., food pantries, shelters, organizations that provide help with utilities, clothing, transportation) with information so we can study it and create better programs to help community members like you. You may also be asked to participate in the "Patient Navigator" program, which just means that we'll give you some help connecting with resources in the community. If you do not sign this consent, it will not affect your medical treatment, but you will not be able to participate in this *CCC* program.

CONSENT. I authorize and consent for [*insert hospital, Administrating Entity, technology vendor*], CBOs, and other healthcare providers that I obtain services from, to share information with each other about me, such as my name (including nicknames), addresses, phone numbers, email addresses, date of birth, sex, race, ethnicity, marital status, name of spouse, age, and sex of my spouse(s)/partner(s) and children, a description of when and what services I obtain from [*insert hospital*] and the CBOs, and whether I attend any appointments at the CBOs. I understand that the information shared may contain medical information, and I have signed a separate

HIPAA Authorization regarding that information [contact internal Counsel for your organization's HIPAA authorization form].

USE OF INFORMATION. I understand the information I have agreed may be shared by [*insert hospital, administrating entity*], the CBOs, and other healthcare providers may also be shared with their business partners and other researchers who are studying healthcare and community services and how they relate to each other, but that the information will only be shared for purposes related to the *CCC* program and determining how to help people with their medical care.

REVOKING CONSENT. I understand that I may revoke this consent at any time by writing to the following address: [*insert address and contact*]

My revocation will not apply to, nor have any effect on, information disclosed before the receipt of the revocation.

Part 2: Sample Verbal Consent Script

Based on your recent visit to [*insert hospital*], you have been identified as eligible to participate in a *CCC* program to determine the best way to help people with their medical care by providing them with the help they need in their daily lives from their community. This program is not a welfare program.

We are asking patients like you to participate in the new program by providing information about yourself to [*insert entity*] and the participating CBO such as food pantries, shelters, and organizations that provide help with utilities, clothing, and transportation. A company named [*insert technology vendor*] provides the software to help us gather your information.

We would like to collect your information from the CBO and [*insert hospital*] and study it to help create better programs to assist community members like you. You may also be asked to participate in the "Patient Navigator" program, which just means that we'll give you some help connecting with resources in the community if you agree. If you do not agree to this, it will not affect your medical treatment, but you will not be able to participate in this *CCC* program.

Do you agree that [*insert hospital*], the [*insert administering entity and technology vendor*], and the CBO may share information with each other about you, such as your name (including nicknames), addresses, phone numbers, email addresses, date of birth, sex, race, ethnicity, marital status, name of spouse, age and sex of your spouse(s)/partner(s) and children, a description of when and what services you obtain from [*insert hospital*] and the CBO, and whether you are able to keep your appointments.

Do you understand the information you have agreed may be shared by [*hospital, technology vendor, and administrating entity*] and the CBO may also be shared with their business partners and other researchers who are studying healthcare and community services and how they relate to each other but that the information will only be shared for purposes related to the program and related research and determining how to help people with their medical care?

Do you also agree that you may participate in the Patient Navigator program and be given some help connecting with community resources?

If you want to stop participating in the *CCC* program or to revoke your consent, just call [*insert hospital name and contact information*] and let us know.

Key Document: Sample SOPs That Details One CCC Workflow

There will be SOPs for multiple topics as part of clinical workflows, including [but not limited to] technology, staff hiring and training, quality assurance activities.

While their purpose is to ensure consistency in approach, they are also revisited on a regular basis to ensure that they are optimized, and if needed, systematic changes are made.

CCC Screening Referral Process

For example: "This SOP outlines the processes, timeframes, and quality assurance activities to ensure that eligible patients are identified and screened for Social Determinants of Health (SDOH) and are referred to appropriate community-based social service organizations (CBOs) for services."

Intended Audience or Participants for the SOP: (List roles at specific clinical sites, which include both *CCC* frontline staff and functional leaders as well as others who will be involved in the referral process).

Prerequisites (Include References to These Materials or SOPs)

- Determination of sites where screening and referrals will take place (e.g., ED, outpatient clinics)
- Determination of differences in SOPs based on site location/type.
- Determination of patient eligibility criteria (e.g., Medicaid, lack of insurance)
- Determination of questions to ask when approaching patients to consent to participate
- Determination of patient consent/authorization process

- Determination of screening questions/tool to use in making appropriate CBO referrals (e.g., approximate address, social needs (e.g., food))
- Determination of entry of patient encounter information in the *CCC* technology platform (may be covered in Technology or Data SOPs)
- Determination of timing/steps for how long a patient will receive referrals (i.e., when will closeout of *CCC* services occur)

The Screening SOP consists of an eight-step process [which is included as part of this key document]. For each step, the [1] responsible party, [2] potential challenges and mitigating solutions, and [3] frequency and timing will need to be specified.

Detailed SOP for the *CCC* Screening Workflow		
Step	**Action**	**Details**
1	Apply prerequisite eligibility criteria to each patient at designated site	
2	For eligible patients, approach with interview questions to determine patient interest in *CCC* participation	• If patient declines to participate, record that information
3	Approach patient to determine interest in participating in *CCC*	• Use interview questions created in the prerequisites
4	Obtain patient consent to participate in *CCC*	• Obtain signed consent forms • Document consent in and/or upload the patient consent form to the *CCC* technology platform
5	Conduct initial screening if patient agrees to participate	• Deliver screening tool/questions to patient to determine social needs (see prerequisites above) • Enter patient screening/interview information in the *CCC* technology platform based on prerequisite process

(Continued)

Detailed SOP for the *CCC* Screening Workflow		
Step	**Action**	**Details**

6	Determine appropriate CBOs and prepare referrals	• Based on screening needs and patient location, identify potential CBOs from the technology platform referral directory
		• Print off and review the CBO referral information
		  • Review each CBO and social need it can help address as part of the patient's referral/action plan
		  • Provide the patient a copy of the referral/action plan
		  • Schedule a follow-up appointment with the patient for X timeframe
		• Document the referral in the technology platform via established process

7	Patient follow-up	• Reach out to patient based on follow-up appointment plan
		• Assess the progress based on the referrals/action plan
		• Update the goals/progress on each need in the referral/action plan in the technology platform
		• Document the reasons for any unresolved issue in the technology process via prerequisite data entry established processes
		• Discuss with the patient any barriers encountered in the referral process
		  • Determine if new CBO referrals could resolve issues; if so, issue new referral plan
		  • Document all barriers in the technology platform per established processes
		  • Schedule follow-up with the patient for X timeframe

8	Close out the patient encounter	• Schedule a closeout interview or encounter with the patient • Inform the patient that the *CCC* program is complete • Document the information in the technology platform (per established process)

Key Document: Sample Training Objectives

> **PRACTICE POINTER**
>
> Consistency in approach within sites and across sites is vital for the success of a *CCC*. Knowing that staff turnover will be a perpetual challenge, it is essential that *CCCs* develop and maintain a robust training program. Step 1 in this process is a clear articulation of training goals and objectives.

CCC *Navigator Training Objectives*

1. Understand the *CCC* model.
2. Understand the importance of the *CCC* purpose.
3. Understand the workflow process for screening and referral at clinical sites.
4. Understand the workflow process for receipt of referrals and individual follow through at CBO sites:
   - Eligibility requirements
   - Individual engagement skills/motivational skills
   - Knowledge of screening questionnaire or tool; how best to review with individuals and develop action plans
   - Timeframes for screening, referral, and follow-ups
   - Backup processes
5. Understand the process (and importance) of using the *CCC* technology tool as specified:
   - Credentialing and login requirements
   - Authorizations
   - Knowledge and ability to use the referral directories and other functionalities
   - Knowledge of system reporting capabilities
   - Documentation
   - Specific processes for enrollment and referral
6. Understand individual responsibilities for *CCC* role requirements.
7. Train-the-trainer responsibilities.

Training Methods and Timeframes for 1–7 above (e.g., initial training in person lasting a total of X hours). Subsequent and refresher training to be provided at [list intervals] via [list methods, such as webinar, etc.]; additional training on ad hoc basis as needed.

Key Document: Sample Evaluation Measures

Seek guidance for *CCC*s that have already begun measurement tracking to learn what has been most instructive in evaluating the impact of the *CCC*.

Characteristics	Examples	Rationale
Characteristics of patients and specific vulnerable populations [study population]	• Demographics • Severity of illness comorbidities • Mental health • Justice involved • Types of insurance coverage	Understanding characteristics of specific markets is essential for any successful pilot. For vulnerable populations, additional factors, beyond traditional demographic and clinical measures, are also important to consider.
Characteristics of the intervention [process measures]	• Conversion from screening to navigation • Navigation duration • Quality of navigation • Tangible link of navigation services to supporting healthcare treatment plan • Availability, quality, and commitment of community services in the network • Ability of technology and analytics to enable, empower, and improve efficiencies of referrals and services	There are many measures that can be evaluated that speak to the overall effectiveness of a CCC.

(Continued)

Characteristics	Examples	Rationale
Clinical and operational improvements [outcome measures]	• Clinical improvement • ED utilization • Primary care and chronic care follow-up • Cost of care\value • Claims paid $ • Resource utilization • Social services utilization • Return on Investment (ROI)\ Social Return on Investment (SROI)	Several different improvement measures can be tracked as part of a pilot. Understanding pilot length, sample size, and specific goals are required for ultimately deciding on the right outcome measures.

Key Document: Sample Communication Strategy

PRACTICE POINTER

Establishing a robust communication approach with partner organizations and their participating sites is essential for program sustainability. This key document addresses three parallel communication pathways.

1. *Engagement and Sustainability Communication.* For matters concerning partnership accountabilities, level of commitment and addressing identified gaps in community care through the *CCC*, executive leadership team engages the executive leadership of the partner organizations directly. This engagement can be carried out either as direct communications or within the forum of the *CCC* Board.

2. *Programmatic Execution Communication.* Each of our partner sites has a designated "Champion" or "Lead." This individual serves as the point of contact for all programmatic and operational communications. The timing of the model, progress towards milestones, QA concerns, and similar topics are discussed with these individuals. Communication is bidirectional between the site "Champion" and the *CCC* Project Director or members of the *CCC* implementation and QA team. Engagement at this level is done on either an ad hoc basis through phone, email, or in person, as well as through the *CCC* Newsletters and broad consortium-wide emails, as appropriate.

3. *Workflow and Operations Communication.* In addition to a *CCC* site "Champion," each of our sites has designated frontline staff that will carry out the workflows. Enabling transparent and effective communication with the frontline staff is critical for timely and accurate execution of *CCC* workflows. The *CCC* QA supervisor and implementation lead should stay in contact with the frontline staff at the partner site to facilitate knowledge sharing and collective problem-solving.

References

1. Coe, E. H., Cordina, J., Parmar, S. *Insights from McKinsey Consumer Social Determinants Health Survey*, McKinsey & Co, New York, 2019.
2. "Parkland by the Numbers." Parkland by the Numbers | Parkland Health & Hospital System. Accessed October 1, 2019. www.parklandhospital.com/parklands-statistics.
3. "Financial Summary." Financial Summary | Parkland Health & Hospital System. Accessed October 1, 2019. www.parklandhospital.com/financial-summary.
4. Katz, A., Chateau, D., Enns, J. E., et al. Association of the Social Determinants of Health with Quality of Primary Care. *Annals of Family Medicine*. 2018; 16(3):217–224.
5. Grembowski, D., Marcus-Smith, M. The 10 Conditions That Increased Vermont's Readiness to Implement Statewide Health System Transformation. *Population Health Management*. 2018; 21(3):180–187.
6. DFWHC, September 27, 2019. https://dfwhc.org/.
7. "RACI Chart." RACI Charts. Accessed October 1, 2019. www.racichart.org/.
8. "Fundamentals of the Legal Health Record and Designated Record Set." Fundamentals of the Legal Health Record and Designated Record Set / AHIMA, American Health Information Management Association. Accessed October 1, 2019. http://library.ahima.org/doc?oid=104008#.WnEBP03fOM8.
9. Rogers, M. Solving the Opt-in/Opt-out Debate, Inc.com.
10. Davidai, S., Gilovich, T., Ross, L. The Meaning of Default Options for Potential Organ Donors. *Proceedings of the National Academy of Science*. 2012; 109(38):15201–15205.
11. www.data.cms.gov, October 2, 2019.
12. "Welcome to the Taxonomy Web Site." Welcome to the Taxonomy Web Site. Accessed October 1, 2019. https://211taxonomy.org/.
13. "RACI Chart." RACI Charts. Accessed October 1, 2019. www.racichart.org/.
14. "Read the Affordable Care Act, Health Care Law." HealthCare.gov. Accessed October 1, 2019. www.healthcare.gov/where-can-i-read-the-affordable-care-act/.
15. "6 Must-Haves for Effective Customer Support in Health IT." Healthcare IT News, May 3, 2012. www.healthcareitnews.com/news/6-must-haves-effective-customer-support-health-it.

Index